Velvet Jihad

UNIVERSITY PRESS OF FLORIDA
Florida A&M University, Tallahassee
Florida Atlantic University, Boca Raton
Florida Gulf Coast University, Ft. Myers
Florida International University, Miami
Florida State University, Tallahassee
New College of Florida, Sarasota
University of Central Florida, Orlando
University of Florida, Gainesville
University of North Florida, Jacksonville
University of South Florida, Tampa
University of West Florida, Pensacola

UNIVERSITY PRESS
OF FLORIDA

Gainesville · Tallahassee · Tampa
Boca Raton · Pensacola · Orlando · Miami
Jacksonville · Ft. Myers · Sarasota

Faegheh Shirazi

Velvet Jihad

MUSLIM WOMEN'S
QUIET RESISTANCE
TO ISLAMIC
FUNDAMENTALISM

Copyright 2009 by Faegheh Shirazi

Printed in the United States of America

This book is printed on Glatfelter Natures Book, a paper certified under
the standards of the Forestry Stewardship Council (FSC). It is a recycled
stock that contains 30 percent post-consumer waste and is acid-free.

14 13 12 11 10 09   6 5 4 3 2 1

Library of Congress Cataloging-in-Publication Data
Shirazi, Faegheh, 1952–
Velvet jihad : Muslim women's quiet resistance to Islamic
fundamentalism / Faegheh Shirazi.
p. cm.
Includes bibliographical references and index.
ISBN 978-0-8130-3354-9 (alk. paper)
1. Muslim women. 2. Islamic fundamentalism. 3. Feminism—Religious
aspects—Islam. 4. Women's rights—Religious aspects—Islam. I. Title.
HQ1170.S48 2009
305.48′697—dc22
2009011120

The University Press of Florida is the scholarly publishing agency for the
State University System of Florida, comprising Florida A&M University,
Florida Atlantic University, Florida Gulf Coast University, Florida
International University, Florida State University, New College of Florida,
University of Central Florida, University of Florida, University of North
Florida, University of South Florida, and University of West Florida.

UNIVERSITY PRESS OF FLORIDA
15 Northwest 15th Street
Gainesville, FL 32611-2079
www.upf.com

I dedicate this book to
the memory of my parents,
Dr. Mahmood Shirazi and Mrs. Aghdas Simafar (Shirazi),
and to
my children,
Geeti Shirazi-Mahajan and Ramin Shirazi-Mahajan,
and to
all velvet jihadists of the past, present, and future

CONTENTS

ILLUSTRATIONS

Illustrations

Illustrations

ACKNOWLEDGMENTS

A University Cooperative Society Subvention Grant was awarded by the University of Texas at Austin toward the publication of this manuscript.

I wish to express my genuine gratitude to those individuals who contributed to the completion of this book. Over the past three years, many friends and colleagues have assisted me on this remarkable journey. To create a comprehensive list of all these generous souls would be impossible in this limited space.

However, I must thank Amy Gorelick, senior acquisitions editor at the University Press of Florida, for her initial interest in and ongoing support of this book project. Also, sincerest appreciation to Shahla Haeri, Lamia Rustum Shehadeh, and the anonymous reviewers for their time and effort in commenting on this book.

I am particularly indebted to my dear friend Laila Belhaj, who hosted me and served as translator and guide during several research trips to Morocco. I also wish to thank Sepideh Khaksar in Tehran for her persistence in accessing key information and for providing outstanding photographs, often at great risk to her own personal security. Words cannot express the depth of my appreciation to her. I want to acknowledge my brother, Kamel Shirazi, and his family for their gracious hospitality during my numerous research trips to Iran. Kamel's ongoing support and willingness to access invaluable resources for me ensured the quality of this book.

Gratitude also to my editor and wonderful friend, Anya Grossman, for her keen insight, unmistakable intelligence, advice and constructive suggestions in shaping and improving this manuscript. Thanks equally to my friend and dear husband, Ken Barnett, whose encouragement and optimism fueled this project. He assisted with photography, provided invaluable input, and allowed me the luxury of a peaceful work environment.

Thanks especially to my loving children, Geeti and Ramin, for their interest in and support of this project. I owe them both more than I can express.

I am indeed fortunate to be surrounded by *baraka*. Wherever I turn, there are wise, loving people to support me.

Alhamdulillah.

Velvet Jihad

Introduction

The title of this book makes reference to 1989's "velvet revolution," the peaceful triumph of Czechs and Slovaks over communism. While this book was in progress, the connection between a bloodless democratic revolution and the peaceful efforts of Muslim activists to subvert Islamic radicalism became apparent. Further research led me to Professor Martin Matustik's article "From 'Velvet Revolution' to 'Velvet Jihad'?" He also had noticed the parallels in these two nonviolent movements, describing the Czech "velvet revolution" as a "regime change without a democratic political deficit. It was indeed a pure embodiment of the ideal of democratic revolution, even if it never intended to seek economic democracy."[1]

Matustik explores the meaning of the Arabic word *jihad*, explaining that its original intent was to signify an internal spiritual struggle, a grappling with one's own demons. Unfortunately, the meaning of *jihad* has been twisted and exploited to serve a fundamentalist mission, to convert and forcefully impose a particular brand of Islam by invoking the name of God. Matustik insightfully proposes that the concept of a "velvet revolution"—a model uniting democratic and existential values—may be used effectively to replace conservative, proselytizing regimes with a "public *for* change but *against* violence." Indeed, as demonstrated in Czechoslovakia, mass public support may be singularly successful in replacing conservative fundamentalist ideologies without violence. The subtitle of this book, "Muslim Women's Quiet Resistance to Islamic Fundamentalism," refers to those individuals working steadfastly to effect positive change for Muslim women throughout the world.

While I primarily emphasize the courageous efforts of Muslim women to resist the oppressive rule of Islamic fundamentalism, clearly their male counterparts are to be strongly acknowledged as well for lending critical support in making this quiet revolution possible. One outstanding velvet jihadist is Tariq Ramadan, professor of Islamic studies at Oxford University and at Erasmus University in the Netherlands. His efforts to reform Islam through the advocacy of studying and reinterpreting Islamic texts sets him apart as a champion for progressive thought.[2] Muslim activists, both male and female, recognize the need to leave a hopeful legacy for their daughters. Change is slow, but inevitable.

Likewise, I certainly acknowledge that other organized religions are also grappling with their own internal fundamentalist movements and with issues of gender inequality. In fact, Ziba Mir-Hosseini points out that "gender inequality in the old world was assumed and that perceptions of women in Christian and Jewish texts are not that different from those of Islamic texts. The early Western feminists too found it necessary to confront and challenge these perceptions, and they did so not by rejecting the Bible or their faith but by appealing to its higher values and principles.[3]

While this book is necessarily limited to issues relevant to Muslim women and their respective communities, I would like to point out that my conversations with non-Muslim women have suggested the following: As Steve Gushee points out, "Jewish and Christian traditions may not be as harsh [as Islamic traditions] but still severely limit women. They are . . . taught that God calls them to be obedient to men. Each religion that springs from the Bible—Judaism, Christianity, and Islam—has used the faith to denigrate women."[4] The core of fundamentalism, according to Dilip Hiro, is "the effort to define the fundamentals of a religious system and adhere to them."[5] The term *fundamentalism* covers a wide spectrum, from religious revivalism to extremist political movements. In this book, I use "fundamentalism" in the sense of a political ideology rooted historically in specific social and cultural environments of a religious community. In Sharia-based nations—nations based on Islamic law, in the Middle East and in other Muslim communities as well—Islamic authorities continue to embrace extremist policies and endorse political agendas that deny women their basic rights. This type of fundamentalism represents a radical shift away from moderate (or traditional) Islam, based on arbitrary and rigid interpretations of the Qur'an. Thus the terms *fundamentalism* and *radical Islam* are interchangeable.[6]

According to Minoo Moallem, fundamentalism exists within every religion and "is not peculiar to an Islamic context." She places "fundamentalism as a modern discursive formation (no less modern than 'progress' or 'development') with a genealogy and history of representation." She further states that although application of the term *fundamentalism* may seem to be a problematic term running the risk of demonizing Islam, using the term is useful for "an understanding of both religion and secularism."[7]

What forces have been driving the velvet jihad? Muslim women today are far more educated and more aware than previous generations of women—not only of the world beyond their narrow communities but also of their basic human rights. This includes those rights granted to them by the Qur'an. The velvet jihad is partly a response to the resurgence of fundamentalist Islamism,[8] such as occurred in the Islamic Republic of Iran in 1979. As the younger generation of Muslim women have learned the value of relying on their own knowledge, understanding, and humanistic interpretation of Qur'anic scripture, they are resisting and questioning patriarchal dictates. Compared to their mothers, young Muslim women have more choices available to them and are taking full advantage of those opportunities.

Muslim women have also benefited tremendously from the technological revolution; satellites now connect even the most remote villages to the wider world. Increasingly, repressive governments are less able to censor and selectively monitor information reaching their citizens on the Internet. In fact, no other medium offers women as open a window onto the world as does the Internet. For example, one can use any search engine to access YouTube, a free video-sharing Web site founded in 2005. This Web site includes amateur video content, some of which is captured by cell phones. One can use the search mode on YouTube's home page to view Muslim women across the globe, whether they are engaged in daily activities or passionately making a political statement. For example, I found a video of a young Iranian woman responding to the harassment of a chador-clad policewoman. In this video, recorded on a cell phone from the top floor of a Tehran apartment building, one sees the young woman refusing to be intimidated by the "chastity police," who find her style of veiling inappropriate. She refuses to be victimized, aggressively resists arrests, escapes, and drives away. Spectators on the sidewalk just watch, afraid to intervene, yet obviously pleased with the outcome.

This unparalleled access to information is responsible, in part, for driving the velvet jihad. The Internet is a new global community, where invaluable information is shared across national, cultural, linguistic, and political boundaries.

Introduction

Emerging technologies are benefiting millions of women in developing countries. A good example of this is the introduction of cable and satellite television to rural India. A study published in 2007 explored the positive effects of this new technology on gender attitudes toward women. This three-year study found "significant increases in reported [women's] autonomy, decreases in the reported acceptability of beating, and decreases in reported son preference. We also found increases in female school enrollment and decreases in fertility (primarily via increased birth spacing). . . . These results have important policy implications, as India and other countries attempt to decrease bias against women.[9] Sharia-based governments, in particular, fear Internet and satellite television technologies that not only allow the streaming of global news but also support the widespread practice of blogging—a perfect venue for exposing and criticizing restrictive regimes.

Who are the women behind the jihad movement? Muslim women from all walks of life and from all socioeconomic backgrounds have joined with men sympathetic to progressive issues—particularly those related to human rights. I would like to acknowledge that non-Muslims, men and women alike, also contribute to the jihad's momentum by sharing resources, offering moral support, and providing pro bono professional services and advice. This coalition of like-minded individuals, eschewing political labels, continues exposing the injustices carried out by forces of fundamentalism. Many of these peaceful warriors go unnoticed, without acclaim or award, while achieving remarkable outcomes against unimaginable odds.

There can be no doubt that the velvet jihad is a contemporary manifestation of what began in nineteenth-century Egypt as the Islamic reform movement. As such, the "warriors" of this modern jihad are giving voice to the basic tenets of reform: "It is the main task of a reformer to recognize the core teachings of a religion and distinguish those core teachings from the accretions of various social traditions, which lead to distortion of core teachings of religion."[10] Extremist movements (such as the Islamic Republic of Iran or the Taliban in Afghanistan) have, in fact, distorted the core teachings of Islam. Miriam Cooke observes that these "newly pious men have arrogated to themselves the right to monitor women's appearance and behavior." However, harsh treatment of and brutal policies toward women have not translated to a docile female population in every Islamic society. On the contrary, whenever possible, velvet jihadists have responded to extremist policies by engaging in activism at the grassroots and global levels and "articulat[ing] their criticism and opposition to the various institutions that oppress them."[11]

If, in fact, the velvet jihad is a natural extension, or evolution, of earlier reformist movements, then Lila Abu-Lughod has correctly observed, "Urban women today, of a variety of classes, veiled and unveiled . . . are the inheritors of the early twentieth-century Egyptian feminists."[12]

One might also maintain that, although the twenty-first-century velvet jihad encompasses a wide spectrum of Muslim women, the core group is necessarily composed of Islamic feminists. For the purpose of this book, I am using Miriam Cooke's definition of Islamic feminism: "Islamic feminists are not Muslims only, although by religious practice or cultural belonging they do qualify as Muslims. 'Islamic' describes the speech, action, writing, or way of life engaged with questioning Islamic epistemology as an *expansion* of their faith position and not a *rejection* of it. These religiously engaged public intellectuals are struggling with and on behalf of all Muslim women and their right to enjoy full participation with men in a just community." These women are not necessarily interested in identifying with or imitating Western feminists. Rather, as Dr. Cooke points out, "They are highlighting women's roles and status within their religious communities while declaring common cause with Muslim women elsewhere who share the same objectives."[13]

Cooke describes the Islamic feminist of today as one who asserts "that yes, Islam is the ideal just society, but that social justice entails equality, dignity, and respect for all, including women." In a particularly prescient article published in the year *before* September 11, 2001, Cooke discussed the inevitable need for Muslim women to establish transnational coalitions, united in strategies of "resistance, engagement, and steadfastness." She added: "In a world divided no longer by ideologies but rather by vague notions of civilizations in collision, conspiracy, and connections, it may be necessary to situate oneself transnationally in order to affirm oneself, to function effectively, and to reach out to others."[14]

Although countless women across the globe have contributed to promoting basic human rights and gender equality—within religious and secular contexts—the limited scope of this book precludes my ability to mention all of them.

Sources and Methodology

In writing this book, I have employed a wide variety of methodological practices, with a primary focus on archival and library research. I have examined an array of cultural and historical documents, including books, scholarly journals, daily newspapers, popular slogans, autobiographies, and policy-oriented literature. Several documentary films, some of them made by and about Muslim women, also served as source material. The documentary videos proved particularly helpful.[15]

I have made extensive use of the Internet to attend to issues and debates relevant to my topic. Unlike other sources, the Internet provided immediate information about current events as they unfolded and facilitated access to global information as much as a half day earlier than I would have been informed by local media. This kept my research on the cutting edge, allowing me to follow up on global developments hour by hour.

I purposefully traced the fatwas of online mullahs and was reassured to find a corresponding network of Web sites and informative links that unify, educate, and connect Muslim women across the globe. To my knowledge, no other scholarly volume (addressing the issues of gender discourse, Islamic feminism, and the clash and cross-breeding of Islamic and Western values) has incorporated Internet research in exactly the same way. I developed a sequential strategy: following breaking news stories as well as their updates, analyzing the consequences of those events, comparing discourses that such events generate globally, and relating them not only to scholarly materials and theories but also to the reality of women's lives.

My numerous trips to the Middle East, as well as my personal connection with friends and family in that region, have provided a wealth of information (including access to rare documents and personal testimonials) that otherwise would not have been possible. I have spoken with women in Iran, Jordan, Morocco, and Israel about the phenomenon of religious fundamentalism, be it Islamic, Jewish, or Christian. These conversations took place in widely diverse locales, such as gender-segregated beaches (Israel), private and public spaces in Iran where fanatical mullahs delivered sermons, small villages such as Ben Zoli in Morocco, and professional conferences across the world. Some of my information was garnered in direct dialogue with fundamentalist Iranian women, and with numerous Muslim emigrés residing in the United States.

My fluency in Persian and knowledge of Arabic enhanced the research process. I was able to converse freely and read source texts in their original languages. Thus I did not have to rely entirely on the translations and interpretations of others.

For the past eight years, I have volunteered with SAHELI, a nonprofit organization based in Austin, Texas. SAHELI assists families dealing with domestic violence, abuse, and other oppressive behaviors. Since 2001, I have written multiple affidavits requesting religious asylum for Central Texas refugees, mostly women from Iran and Afghanistan who would be executed by hanging or jailed indefinitely if extradited to their native, Sharia-based Islamic communities. In my role as language interpreter and cultural liaison, I have learned from personal stories what one cannot necessarily learn from books or seminars.

Furthermore, my record of publications with various refereed academic journals has made me aware of the process of reliable research in the field. Although I have accumulated and analyzed an enormous amount of data, and I am confident that my observations hold true, there is still room for further research to define the trends and patterns of the fundamentalist phenomenon as regards Muslim women.

Finally, in teaching and preparing lectures and materials for graduate seminars and undergraduate courses, I have realized the growing need for presenting the reality rather than the myth of today's Muslim woman. However, what many in the West are unaware of (and have no way of knowing) is that Islamic women are remarkably resourceful and accomplish unimaginable good when united in common purpose. This applies to the illiterate, impoverished rural villager as much as to the highly educated urban Islamic woman. These are the velvet jihad warriors; some have limited or no capacity for making their voices heard. It is my fervent wish to provide a forum for those voices.

On the Frontlines: The Internet

My Internet research led to a new understanding of the current role and potential impact of information technology on the velvet jihad. Many progressive organizations and movements rely heavily on online technologies to deliver their messages. One such movement is the White Ribbon Campaign, initiated in Canada (1991). The White Ribbon Campaign, in partnership with many women's organizations, is a global movement involving individuals from fifty-five countries. Its main objective is "to engage men and boys in the struggle to end men's violence against women."[16]

Few would argue that the Internet is proving to be a "revolution in information gathering," one that holds the potential to subvert the power base of traditional clerics. According to Amear Ali, "Inquisitive Muslim minds do not have to wait for a cleric to arrive for consultations on theological issues. With the help of the Internet any verse or chapter of the Koran and any sayings of the Prophet can be accessed from multiple sources and the reader has the luxury of choosing from among a variety of interpretations, meanings, and elaborations."[17]

While proving to be an invaluable tool in the quiet opposition to radical Islam, one must also concede that the Internet offers unprecedented opportunity for the dissemination of hate and the promotion of medieval viewpoints. Radical Islamic Web sites contain veiled warnings to all Muslim women. Leila Hessini notes that the Hamas Web site states that women's roles are

> looking after the family, rearing the children, and imbuing them with moral values and thoughts derived from Islam. The Muslim Brotherhood [of Egypt] requires women to cover every part of their bodies, except for the face and hands; otherwise they are considered "naked." Algerian Islamists attacked and killed women who held positions—such as hairdressers or writers—that were considered "un-Islamic," and women were given two choices: Wear the hijab (veil) or face the gun.[18]

Many self-appointed "imams" (claiming to be religious experts) prowl the Internet with the sole intention of snaring impressionable young minds. Peddling their vituperous interpretations of Islam, they sow the seeds of rigid patriarchy by offering advice, answering questions, and randomly issuing fatwas (religious decrees). Fatwas are no small religious matter; they require authority of the highest religious Muslim leaders, authority earned through years of Islamic scholarship and accrued knowledge. However, on many unofficial Islamic Web sites, one finds that issuing fatwas has become a casual practice. As a result, the concept of fatwa is quickly losing religious respect, authority, and power.

Young Muslims living in the West frequently visit Islamic Web sites, form their own chat rooms, and create ongoing forums for discussion. In this way, the Internet plays a critical role in providing networks that foment fundamentalist ideologies. According to Canadian journalist Omar El-Akkad, in Canada, "where Islam plays a significantly smaller societal role . . . the [Muslim] teens turn largely to the Internet, where some find a nearly endless supply of interpretations of Islam that justify everything from killing civilians to toppling democratic rule." El-Akkad calls attention to the fact that few of these teens are fluent in Arabic, the language of the Qur'an. Therefore, they are totally reliant on skewed interpretations of the holy text: "Without being fluent in the language, most of the teens must depend on translations and interpretations of the Koran and the life of the Prophet. And for those, they turn to the Internet, putting their questions to on-line imams, downloading audio and text interpretations, and quoting at length from articles on other Islamic websites, many of which have since been taken off-line."[19]

Unfortunately, the Internet is a perfect venue for radical Islamists to prey on young minds and to purvey their venomous brand of Islam—including propaganda against women. In response, women are establishing unprecedented networks of solidarity via the Web and, as bloggers, subverting censorship by their respective governments and countering the ongoing efforts by radical Islamists to use the Internet as one more weapon in their arsenal of oppression. Margo Badran holds a particularly sanguine viewpoint: "If early secular feminist thought circulated with the advent of the press and the rise of print journalism in Muslim societies, Islamic feminism is spreading infinitely faster and globally via the Internet and the satellite. It has a vibrant presence in cyberspace reverberating in what Fatima Mernissi colourfully calls the 'digital Islamic galaxy.'"[20]

Islamic feminists, for example, now have the opportunity to participate in online communities, mailing lists, and meet-ups such as Muslims for Progressive Values, a virtual assembly of people who "self-identify as progressive Muslims, or just consider themselves progressives who happen to be Muslims, or vice versa."[21] The Internet's role in relationship to velvet jihad will be further addressed throughout the book.

The Role of Women in Early Islam

Muslims and non-Muslims alike assume that the only important source of Islamic teachings other than the Qur'an are those sunna and ahadith attributed to the Prophet.[22] This is an accurate assumption. However, the belief that the Prophet is the only model for piety disregards the important role that women played in early Islam.

Tazim R. Kassam accurately notes that both Muslim and non-Muslim views of Islamic cultures and history are by and large androcentric. This centuries-old patriarchal perspective has always created a dilemma for Muslim women. Kassam emphasizes that

> in the context of Islamic cultures, the androcentric trope of history-making is centrally tied to the figure of Muhammad as the exemplary model to be emulated by all Muslims. While the example of Muhammad as Prophet is both crucial and inspiring as bringer of the Qur'an—a divine revelation that dignified and empowered women in an unprecedented manner—the studied and detailed imitation of the Prophet (taqlid) and the establishment and routinization of his sunna transformed and froze Muhammad's life (so dynamic, creative, and responsive to its context) into an entity that exacted conformity and set up a dilemma for Muslim women. That is, Muslim women would have a male body to aspire to as the exemplar of Muslim piety.[23]

Perhaps some may object to, or question the propriety of, viewing the Prophet as a model for women during his lifetime. It is therefore understandable that many Muslim feminists have turned to the early women in Islam instead, especially the wives and daughters of the Prophet, as role models for piety as well as progressive thought.

The first convert to Islam was a woman—Khadija, who converted after becoming the Prophet's wife. Believing in and trusting Mohammad's prophetic vision, Khadija aligned herself with this extraordinary man. The Prophet remained in a monogamous relationship with Khadija until her death. In her own way, Khadija helped shaped the status of women in early Islam, as did A'isha—another beloved wife of Mohammad, who was especially well versed in the Qur'an and was held in high esteem for her knowledgeable interpretation of scripture. It is widely believed that A'isha left behind numerous ahadith that speak to women's issues.

Unfortunately, for reasons still unknown, a large portion of her ahadith has been omitted from the two prominent collections (or *Sahihain*) of al-Bukhari and al-Muslim. Each hadith included in these collections has been judged to be authentic by religious authority, representing a true and clear account of an event or episode of the prophet Muhammad's life. These ahadith are used to evaluate, interpret, justify, or draft a judgment based on recorded example. Fatima Mernissi posits that the omission of a great number of A'isha's ahadith was no accident but rather a deliberate, well-calculated act. Mernissi provides the following evidence to substantiate her claim:

> One can read among al-Bukari's "authentic" Hadith the following one: "Three things bring bad luck: house, woman, and horse." Al-Bukhari did not include other versions of this Hadith, although the rule was to give one or more contradictory versions in order to show readers conflicting points of view, and thus to permit them to be sufficiently well informed to decide for themselves about practices that were the subject of dispute. However, there is no trace in al-Bukhari of A'isha's refutation of this Hadith.[24]

Mernissi also makes reference to Imam Zarkashi, an Egyptian religious fourteenth-century scholar who spent his entire life in search of knowledge. A significant number of his works have been lost. However, one of his few surviving materials appearing in book form emphasizes A'isha's contribution to Islam:

> A'isha is the Mother of the Believers. . . . She is the lover of the Messenger of God. . . . She lived with him for eight years and five months; she was 18 years old at the time of the death of the Prophet. . . . She lived to be 65 years old. . . . We are indebted to her for 1,210 Hadith. . . . This book is devoted to her particular contribution in this field [collection of authentic ahadith], especially the points on which she disagreed with others, the points to which she supplied added information, the points on which she was in complete disagreement with the religious scholars of her time. . . . I have entitled this book *Collection of A'isha's Corrections to Statements of the Companions (Al-'irada fi ma istadrakathu A'isha 'ala al-sahaba).*[25]

This book remained in manuscript form until 1939 and was discovered in the Al-Dahiriya Library of Damascus.

Education: The Shield of the Quiet Revolution

Fundamentalism is expanding and stalking the globe, but Islam is not its synonym.[26] Although the social and religious constructs of radical Islam claim control over women's bodies and minds and therefore their basic free-doms, Muslim women are patiently resisting these forces of fundamental-ism in a variety of innovative ways.

Not surprisingly, education and activism are their weapons of choice. For example, two female Moroccan lawyers, Zineb Miadi and Farida Bennani, have published a directory on gender equality and women's rights in Islam.[27] At present, the Organization of Egyptian Women and Memory Forum is collecting oral histories to document women's voices of both past and pres-ent in an effort to educate the public.

In her 2006 book *Women Shaping Islam,* Pieternella van Doorn-Harder discusses new women's groups in Indonesia, explaining that these women "did not set out to be activists or feminists but [simply] wanted . . . to fulfill the status originally given to them by Islam: equal human beings in front of God."[28] Recently in Indonesia Sharia has been imposed in certain re-gions. This change in law has created a new challenge for activist Indonesian women who view such radical trends as incompatible with Indonesian cul-ture. In their argument, they claim that such legislation stems from "unde-sirable influences from the Middle East."[29]

Similarly, in Iran, attendees at a March 2007 rally in Tehran protested the imprisonment of women activists whose only crime was to author the One Million Signatures Campaign, a petition strategy that gained the majority of its signatures via the Internet. The objective of this velvet jihadist campaign was to educate women and to inform the world community about discrimi-natory laws against Iranian women:

> Opposed to Islam as an ideology, as a set of canonical laws, as a critical
> component of identity, and as a set of myths, Iranian reformist women
> look at Islam as a source of spirituality and mysticism that has nothing to
> do with political authority.[30]

Mahboubeh Hossein Zadeh and Nahid Keshavarz, the primary architects of this reform campaign, were released on bail from the notorious Evin prison on April 15, 2007. I will be referring to this important campaign later in the book.

Scholarly studies and papers written by women, as well as the dissemi-nation of written materials by nonprofit organizations, also impact public awareness regarding issues critical to Muslim women's welfare. The Moroc-can Association of Democratic Women and the Centre FAMA publish easy-to-read books on such subjects as sexual harassment in schools and universities, legal discrimination, and women's testimonies of violence. FAMA also provides legal aid and counseling to women.[31]

In December 2004, while visiting Morocco, I had the honor of meeting an outstanding champion for women's education, Halima Oulami. At that time, she was serving as president of Women's Development in Marrakech. Assisted by an interpreter, I listened attentively while Halima explained in French the objectives of her organization: to educate women from traditional Moroccan environments and to empower them to attain economic self-sufficiency. In Halima's opinion, education is the key to releasing young women from the shackles of patriarchal domination.

Another unsung Moroccan hero with whom I visited was Majida (last name withheld), director of the Association of Women for Development and Solitary (AFDES). We met in the small Moroccan town of Beni Zoli, where one medical clinic, one physician, one nurse, and one midwife served a population of almost 5,000 residents. Working alongside her brother (a good example of a male velvet jihadist) and with a grant from the Red Cross (as well as a matching grant from the Moroccan government), Majida's goal was to educate girls from the villages surrounding Beni Zoli. The specific mission of her project was to offer young girls a free education and an alternative to arranged marriages and subsequent pregnancy (at the tender ages of twelve or thirteen). Majida explained that uneducated girls marginalized by their own traditional culture have no option but to follow the same desperate paths of early marriage and childbearing as their mothers and grandmothers did before them. At the time of my visit, students ranging in age from eleven to thirteen were living at Majida's institute, all receiving free housing, meals, and a quality education. The girls were also learning how to cook, take care of themselves, and become independent. Majida's hope was that all the girls would attain a high school diploma. With a solid education, these girls would have choices: to work toward economic independence, to attend college, or to marry. If they chose to marry, at least they would be well informed about birth control. It is women like Majida and Halima whose dedication and devotion to the younger generation place them at the forefront of the quiet revolution.

Also in the vanguard of change is Iran's Shirin Ebadi, the first Muslim woman to receive the Nobel Peace Prize (2003). After the 1979 Islamic Revolution in Iran, Ebadi was demoted from her position as a judge and assigned to a lower office. Conservative clerics insisted that, according to Islamic law, a woman could not hold the position of judge. After numerous protests, Ebadi and other female judges were assigned to a slightly higher position, that of "law expert." Ebadi requested early retirement and repeatedly filed petitions to continue working as a lawyer. During the waiting period, she used her time to write a number of articles and books, including a memoir entitled *Iran Awakening*. This book has been translated into sixteen languages and has topped best-seller lists in Germany and Canada. Although her book is banned in Iran, Ebadi remains a dynamic spokesperson on behalf of victims of injustice and discrimination. Her publications serve as exemplary fortifications in the struggle for human rights, educating and enlightening the public as to the plight of oppressed women and children.

Qur'anic Interpretation:
The Shield of Fundamentalism

The Qur'an is a living text, and every mother is a child's best teacher. We must educate our children from a very young age how to use Qur'anic stories and ahadith in meaningful, peaceful ways to find solutions to daily problems and challenges. Children need to be taught the relevance of the verses, the specific situation for which the verse was revealed, and how the ancient texts can be used to shed light on contemporary issues. Perhaps only then will our children retain the essence and depth of the verses and be able to apply the teachings wisely in their daily lives.

Ehsan Masood calls attention to the fact that the Qur'an is often taught with little reference to the context of its revelation or to the unique circumstances facing the very first community of Muslims.[32] Unless the Qur'an is interpreted within a historical context, how can one understand the depth, logic, or relevance of its teachings?

For centuries, Islamic law had been controlled by male scholarship; however, women are gradually advancing to the front lines. Among the activists and scholars reading and interpreting Qur'anic text from a feminist perspective are Amina Wadud, Lynn Wilcox, Asma Barlas, Barbara Freyer Stowasser, and Nimat Hafez Barazangi. Their understanding of the holy text differs significantly from the conservative and patriarchal interpretations.[33] Their scholarly efforts reflect one of the most important questions facing modern Islam: how is the Qur'an to be interpreted?

An excellent example of how Qur'anic interpretations may vary is the controversial subject of *hijab* (veiling). In my own study, *The Veil Unveiled: Hijab in Modern Culture*, I demonstrated the semantic versatility of hijab— not only in various Muslim cultures but also within the same culture at the same time. Clearly, conservative interpretations related to veiling have been—and continue to be—made on an arbitrary basis in order to support existing social and political systems.

The two sets of Qur'anic passages most frequently quoted regarding veiling (33:59–60 and 24:30–31) are used by both groups—those in favor of and those opposed to the practice of veiling. Conservatives usually do not read "behind the Qur'an," since they prefer not to contextualize the teachings. "Nor, for that matter, do they read in front of the Qur'an in the sense of recontextualizing its teachings in light of the present historical needs of Muslims themselves," states Asma Barlas. She further asserts that "by refusing to *contextualize* the Qur'an, they also render the process of its *recontextualization* problematic since 'one cannot proceed *to* the abidingness of the Qur'an, in word and meaning, unless one intelligently proceeds *from* its historical ground and circumstance.'"[34]

In contemporary societies, whether veiling is imposed by force to "save a woman's soul" or denied to women in the name of emancipation and progress, patriarchal paradigms are rarely impacted or challenged. The forces of modernization and Westernization have "merely divided patriarchy into hegemonic and subordinated semiotic regimes positioned to compete for control of women's bodies and minds."[35]

Yesim Arat defends the right of women to wear the veil in Turkish society. She writes about the challenges that many devout Muslim students and teachers experience by wearing their headscarves as a sign of religious piety.[36] For example, on May 31, 2000, one such Turkish woman was accused of "obstructing the education of others" by the Istanbul Faith Primary Court.

In Turkey, discriminatory laws pertaining to appearance and clothing are set for both men and women. Arat stresses that such bans are incompatible with the International Covenant on Civil and Political Rights (ICCPR).[37] Arat points to Article 13 (1)(c) of ICESCR, which states, "Higher education shall be made equally accessible to all, on the basis of capacity, by every appropriate means. . . . These provisions require that access to higher education should be based upon a student's ability to study at an advanced level, and not their religious orientation."[38]

Introduction

Yesim Arat asserted that "wearing of the headscarf by students or elected representatives has not presented a threat to public order, health, or morality, and it is difficult to imagine circumstances in which it might."[39] Arat's argument against the ban on headscarves and beards forces one to acknowledge that legal pronouncements of this type may be just as offensive as those in the Islamic Republic of Iran, where the veil is mandatory and a beard is highly encouraged.[40]

Yesim Arat's research also calls attention to the fact that women have been manipulated in the Turkish political system, since Ataturk's policies mandated their equal participation.[41] In fact, the gender power structure remained the same when women first entered the Turkish parliament, because their entry into politics was only possible through male backing and approbation, not on the strength of their own merit. Strict criteria were set forth for women in parliament: they had to disassociate from women's organizations altogether and play nicely by the political rules set forth by men.

Arat's most recent work, however, paints a different and more hopeful picture. In the 1990s, Turkish women made great progress in strengthening their political autonomy. Surprisingly, they did so while developing progressive agendas *and* embracing principles of Islam within the Islamist Refah (Welfare) Party.[42] They demonstrated that religion can be used to inform political perspective without necessarily acquiescing to fundamentalist doctrine: "Just as a comprehensive Islam did not define the lives of these women, an exclusive liberalism did not hold its sway either."[43]

This atypical cross-fertilization between liberal values and Islam was aborted by the secular Turkish court system in 1998. However, Arat insists that the "stories of Refah women tell us why the development of liberalism in a Muslim context is not only possible but also necessary."[44]

No matter the region, culture, or language, innumerable Muslim women deal with patriarchal domination in their daily lives. According to Valentine Moghadam, even in nomadic cultures where women are not veiled or secluded, they are still controlled by men. "Thus [the] social structure and stage of economic development is a crucial factor in the persistence of patriarchy." Moghadam also examines the strength of patriarchal power in relationship to "the state, political system, and ruling elites." In patriarchal cultures, issues around gender and discourse about women are commonly used to achieve political goals. Thus women's issues serve as an effective weapon; in such systems, morality, piety, and religion take central positions, diverting "attention from economic problems or political corruption."[45]

In addition, Moghadam asserts that during periods of social upheaval women naturally become cultural and political symbols. Depicted as the mothers or nurturers of the nation, women therefore "belong" to the state, and their behavior must be controlled accordingly.

The same fact has been demonstrated by my own work. Not surprisingly, in the Islamic Republic of Iran, "the criminalization of offending public chastity by not veiling properly coincided with Iran's mobilization in 1980 for war against Iraq . . . policing the hijab diverted attention from the horror of the fronts; it drew the nation's attention to a situation that, unlike the war, was more controllable and thus gave the nation a unifying boost."[46]

Nayereh Tohidi's research on women in Azerbaijan also addresses the exploitation of women's images during wartime. Tohidi focuses on the Soviet occupation of Azerbaijan and the subsequent post-Soviet era. Citing contrasting images of a "glamorous blonde smiling [like a] Turkish beauty queen" and "a demure young girl veiled in a white scarf, timidly looking down at a set of prayer beads," Tohidi describes how both images served widely divergent political agendas. As Azerbaijani women were increasingly portrayed as "guardians of the Nation, their new image embodied qualities of . . . modesty, morality, Islamic values, and Muslim identity."[47]

It may seem contradictory that certain Islamic regimes would force veiling and other behavioral restrictions on women while at the same time portraying women as the standard bearers of religious and social virtues. Like Moghadam and Shirazi, Pinar Ilkkaracan posits that the oppression of women in Muslim societies is not an Islamic or religious issue but relates instead to socioeconomic and political agendas. In fact, Afaf Lutfi Al-Sayyid Marsot, in his historical survey of the eighteenth through the twentieth centuries, "concluded that the principles of Islam do not so much determine the position of women as do social practices and political structures."[48] Ilkkaracan also considers women's sexuality and the control of women's bodies to be one of the most effective ways that patriarchy maintains power.[49]

A practicing psychotherapist, Ilkkaracan is founder and coordinator of Women for Women's Human Rights. This nonprofit organization campaigned along with more than 120 other women's organizations in Turkey to successfully reform the Turkish civil code, making violence against women a crime. Ilkkaracan argues that sexual oppression of Muslim women is hardly representative of the Islamic vision of sexuality; rather, such oppression results from a combination of political, social, and economic considerations. Denigrating women in the name of religion not only violates human rights but also violates core religious precepts.

Economic resources translate to independence. Both Suad Joseph and Moghadam stress the fact that historically, the division of labor in all societies and cultures has favored men and placed women at a distinct disadvantage. Joseph states, "Social welfare legislation has given citizens benefits often on the basis of participation in the labor market, making women who are not employed dependent on working men."[50] In this respect, both Moghadam and Joseph stress women's unequal and disadvantaged status. This sociopolitical dynamic fosters gender inequality since it "usually places women in a subordinate position and men in a dominant position, whether in household, the labor market, the polity, or some other social institution."[51] However, Moghadam notes that this dynamic may be shifting in the Muslim world:

> The male breadwinner role is no longer guaranteed, unemployment has grown, wages have deteriorated, per capita incomes have fallen, inflation has soared, poverty has worsened, female-headed households are increasing, and more and more women are seeking jobs out of economic need.[52]

In her recent anthology, *From Patriarchy to Empowerment*, Moghadam explores in detail these changing economic conditions in "the patriarchal belt" of the Middle East, North Africa, and South Asia.[53]

Margot Badran describes gender equality as a notion "that the Qur'anic revelation introduced into seventh-century (CE) patriarchal Arabia." According to Badran, this notion was nothing less than radical and "did not sit well with the patriarchal cultures into which Islam was first introduced and spread. As recently as the early 1990s, a new Islamic feminist paradigm began to emerge in Iran, South Africa, and the diaspora Islamic communities of Europe and North America. With the intention of exposing and eradicating patriarchal ideas and practices passed off as "Islamic," this feminist movement "derives its understanding and mandate from the Qur'an" and explains the concept of gender equality as "part and parcel of the Qur'anic notion of equality of all *insan* (human beings)."[54]

Jane Idleman Smith, professor of Islamic studies at Hartford Seminary, notes that "the history of women in Islam reveals a clear pattern of male domination." Despite this pattern, Muslim women still remain devout followers of Islam and are increasingly questioning patriarchal interpretation of the Qur'an. I cannot make the language strong enough in insisting that one can be a devout Muslim *and* practice gender equality. One can cherish the precepts of Islam *and* allow a woman the right to decide her own destiny and to act independently. Badran observes that Islamic feminism is not a secular movement. In fact, it is "the creation of women and men for whom religion is important in their daily lives and who are troubled by inequalities and injustices perpetrated in the name of religion. . . . The theoretical core of Islamic feminism continues to be grounded in Qur'anic interpretation or *tafsir*."[55]

The scripturalist interpretation of religious texts has not only prevented Muslim women from achieving equal status with men but has also prevented them from fully participating in their respective societies.[56] Muslim nations such as Indonesia, Bangladesh, Pakistan, and Turkey serve as reminders that society may successfully implement sexual equality without compromising Islamic principles. In these nations, women have already been elected presidents or prime ministers. Asra Q. Nomani, a Muslim feminist, reporter for the *Wall Street Journal,* and author of *Standing Alone in Mecca,* became the first woman in her mosque in West Virginia to refuse to leave the main area of the hall reserved exclusively for men to pray. Two years later, she organized the first public woman-led prayer of a mixed-gender congregation, stating, "We are standing up for our rights as women in Islam. We will no longer accept the back door or the shadows; at the end of the day, we'll be leaders in the Muslim world. We are ushering Islam into the *21st century,* reclaiming the voice that the Prophet gave us 1,400 years ago."[57]

At the first International Congress of Islamic Feminism (held in Barcelona in 2005), a young Muslim man stood up and made the comment, "In Islam, there is no place for feminism." From the middle of the audience, Amina Wadud, an Islamic studies professor at Virginia Commonwealth University, stood up and replied, "You are out of order. What you are doing is exactly the kind of thing that we are here to be able to stop." The audience broke into cheers.

Activists such as Dr. Wadud are drawing a line in the sand of discrimination and exclusion. In her 2006 publication, *Inside the Gender Jihad:*

Women's Reform in Islam, she emphasizes that "the major canon of Islamic public discourse and ethical articulation makes the male experience and articulation the norm and the standard measurement for what it means to be human in the public arena. That which is explicit to being woman has been prohibited from public space and discourse."[58] Not only are women like Dr. Wadud stepping forward to challenge segregation in the mosques. They are also building mosques of their own, assuming leadership positions within those structures, and even conducting prayer among mixed-gender congregations.

On March 19, 2005, the *Daily News* reported, "Woman Leads Muslims in Prayers." Amina Wadud led both men and women in a prayer service on March 18, 2005, in Manhattan. Another woman, Suehyla El-Attar from Atlanta, gave the *adhan*, or call to prayer. Traditionally, adhan is only recited by men, since a woman's voice is considered to be sexually alluring and to cause sexual temptation, a kind of *fitna* (chaos). Not surprisingly, critics accused these women of being publicity seekers, pointing out that "the service was heavily scrutinized by Arab media and on Internet discussion boards." Members of the Progressive Muslim Union and Dr. Amina Wadud, all of whom had organized the event, received abusive telephone calls and e-mails. Protesters outside the prayer hall brandished signs saying, "Mixed-gender prayer today, hellfire tomorrow." Amina Wadud had overthrown a thousand-year tradition in Islam. Perhaps most worrisome for fundamentalists is the possibility of a ripple effect—not just in the United States but throughout the Muslim world. Their fear is that all those "women who are learned and frustrated that they cannot be the imam are going to see that someone had the guts to break ranks and do it."[59]

On September 29, 2005, the BBC News reported on Salma Qureshi's "Quest to Become 'UK's First Female Imam.'" This report was aired on the BBC World Service series *"I Challenge,"* a program highlighting individuals around the world who have challenged authority, traditions, and beliefs in the face of enormous odds." Qureshi, an imam, acknowledged her revolutionary role: "I'm quite religious but at the same time I'm quite a liberal person. . . . What I'm doing at the moment is something new." Qureshi learned the Qur'an from her father. By age seven, she had read the entire text. As a young woman, Qureshi saw little difference between "what was religion and what was culture," and she was sensitive to the reality that Islam imposed too many restrictions on women. Consequently she began training as an imam, learning how to run a mosque, engage effectively in public speaking, and contact appropriate government offices and agencies. At the end of the BBC interview, Qureshi modestly recalled, "I had a lot of parents coming up to me saying, 'We're really proud of what you're doing. . . . You are an inspiration to our daughters.'" Young women like Salma Qureshi, serving as role models for the next generation, deserve recognition. Their remarkable efforts to promote egalitarian principles in religious and social spheres are advancing the cause of Muslim women everywhere. The quiet revolution led by Islamic feminists is tapping into the roots of moderate Islam, in alignment with Islamic teachings of the seventh century, dating from the time of the prophet Muhammad.

Of course, the notion of nonsegregated mosques and women-led prayer does not sit well with prominent religious authorities, even those living in Western societies. On July 1, 2006, an article in the *Arab American News,* entitled "Gender Apartheid or Respectable Interaction?" written by Sayyid Muhammad Rizvi, the *imam* of the Ja'ffari Islamic Centre in Toronto, challenged Asra Nomani:

> Asra Nomani suggests that the separation between men and women in mosques was established much later in Muslim history than during the days of the Prophet. She has also tried to link that with the Wahhabi influence on the Muslim world. Those views are either sheer ignorance on her part or plain intellectual dishonesty. The separation of genders is found in mosques run by all sects of Islam, from Sunni to Shiʻa, and from Wahhabi to Sufi, based on the explicit example left by the last Prophet [Muhammad]. Separation is just a facilitator towards modesty, used according to circumstances, for maintaining respectable interaction as opposed to free mixing of genders in public spaces.

Rizvi further elaborates on Qurʼanic verses, declaring, "One of the core Islamic values is modesty in interaction between genders." He concludes that it is un-Islamic for men and women to pray together in the same space. Although a secularly educated man, Imam Rizvi joins the ranks of rigid, patriarchal-based ideologues who, like a Madressah-trained student, memorizes Qurʼanic verse without striving to understand its underlying historical relevance. Individuals like Rizvi are missing the point. Islam is necessarily evolving to accommodate the shifting, changing perceptions of its believers. This is a gradual development, a process of growth that is flow-ing freely into all corners of Islamic experience—even into spaces as sacred as the mosque.[60]

Formidable Foes and Allies

Taking a courageous stand against traditional Islamic patriarchy is not for the fainthearted. Margot Badran recognizes that Islamic feminism has created enemies both "within and without the Muslim community: 1) from within—men who fear the loss of patriarchal privilege and women who fear the loss of patriarchal protection, and 2) from without—those whose pleasure and politics are found in denigrating Islam as irredeemably anti-women."[61]

Fear has always contributed to every form of religious intolerance and will likely continue to do so. Many Muslim women have been brainwashed by patriarchal propaganda to fear the West and to accept outmoded, increasingly irrelevant interpretations of Islam. These women do as they are told. Forbidden from trusting their own judgment and intelligence, their only option is to accept a life of submission and ignorance. Indeed, the fundamentalist woman often proves to be the most merciless aggressor, perhaps sensing that she stands on shifting sands. What level of societal pressure produces this type of woman?

From an early age, women living in Sharia-based societies receive subtle and overt messages regarding their limited value, messages that constantly batter self-esteem. While women are "protected" in patriarchal systems, the irony is that they are constantly at risk of losing self-respect. Without the opportunity to explore their own personal talents, without the choice to pursue their own desires and dreams, they are held back from realizing their full potential as equal human beings. In these narrow and powerless environments, they grow from young girls into single dimensional adults, fearful and mistrusting of all that lies beyond the narrow confines of their immediate households and communities. It comes as no surprise, then, that even when given the chance to exercise their basic right to vote, they often decline.

Muslim women who are entirely dependent on male authority figures have little choice other than to accept radical, or scriptural, interpretations of the Qur'an. In short, it is easy to understand how they become mouthpieces of their male counterparts and often prove to be the most formidable opponents of progressive Muslim women. Prime examples of this are the *chomaghdaran* (female police) of Iran.

On June 12, 2006, Iranian women and male supporters protested against imposition of medieval *Islamic* laws. With signs and posters held high, they chanted, "We are women, we are human beings, but we have no rights!" According to reporter Mahmood Ketabchi, "Thousands of women and male supporters came together on June 12, 2006, in Haft Tir Square in Tehran, Iran, to protest against anti-women Islamic laws and gender apartheid. A similar rally was held last year on June 12, where participants declared their determination to follow up their just struggle for equality and women's liberation." The protest became the target of brutal suppression when Islamic security forces, including the *chomaghdaran* (literally, "those carrying batons"), appeared on the scene. The female police were draped in dark veils from head to toe. Along with other security forces and plain-clothed *Islamic* guards, the chomaghdaran attacked and savagely beat the women protesters. They "verbally abused women and insulted them with filthy sexist slurs. They also called the protesters 'agents of foreigners and imperialism.' Many protesters were injured."[62]

According to religious precepts, no rules exist to prevent women from touching, pushing, and shoving other women—while men, especially men outside the family circle, are forbidden to participate in such behavior. Social and religious etiquette forbids men from using filthy language around women, while no such boundary exists to prevent women from unleashing obscenities on other women. Increasingly, the shrewd men at the helm of Iran's Islamic government are strategically positioning female police to verbally and physically abuse women protestors.

In the struggle against abusive policies of Islamist governments, not all males are oppressors. Many male Muslim—progressive, educated, and open-minded—stand at the barricades as allies, joining hands with women. One such ally is Ismail Serageldin, the Muslim intellectual in charge of Alexandria's library in Egypt. Serageldin's efforts to promote open debate about Islam are to be applauded. It should be noted that the free flow of discussion around Islamic issues is possible in this library "partly because it is protected by having as its chair Suzanne Mubarak, wife of President Hosni Mubarak."[63] Men who support Islamic reform populate all parts of the globe, in Western societies as well as inside Muslim nations. Tariq Ramadan (Swiss-Egyptian), Abdolkarim Soroush (Iranian born in exile), and the evangelist Hamza

Yusuf Hanson (American born) are all stellar examples of men striving for positive transformation regarding how Islam is used and taught.[64]

Velvet Jihad: A Brief Overview

In writing this book, I have looked at patriarchal patterns and emerging resistance to those patterns. I have explored and examined relationships between historical influences and contemporary practices. Chapter 1, "Honor and Virginity," deals with cultural beliefs and behaviors related to the Islamic honor and shame complex. In this chapter, emphasis is placed on the following issues: social construction of women's bodies, women as property, honor killings, and the importance of virginity. In chapter 2, "Sterility, Childbirth, Taboos, and Popular Religious Practices," I examine traditional practices that dominate Muslim women's reproductive life in patriarchal-based environments. These practices represent a mélange of religious doctrines, cultural taboos, and a belief in the supernatural. The dominance of male power structures over women's bodies, including the use of medical technologies to support gender selection, is also discussed. Chapter 3, "Even Dolls Must Wear Hijab," relies heavily on the religious "etiquette" manuals and moral guidebooks written for women by religious male authorities. In particular, I analyze the writings of Allameh Mohammad Baqer Majlesi, a well-known seventeenth-century Iranian Shi'i scholar, and Mulana Ashraf Ali al-Thanvi, a Sunni scholar in early twentieth-century India.

Chapter 4, "Arts and Athletics: Stepping over Boundaries," deals with the challenges Muslim women face as they participate in public venues, whether on the athletic field or in the visual and performing arts. Religious clerics believe, based on conservative Qur'anic interpretation, that women should not compete or perform publicly. When such religious restrictions become unbearable, women respond in remarkably creative ways. In fact, the more repressive the patriarchal policy, the more passionate the artistic expression and dynamic the athletic achievements. In chapter 5, "Gender Preference: An Islamic View," the reader discovers that attitudes toward homosexual behavior vary significantly among contemporary Islamic societies. The Qur'an makes no reference to same-sex love among women; however, one would never suspect this based on the number of online "fatwas" against this behavior. Lesbianism, in particular, has become an Internet obsession for self-appointed mullahs who issue fatwas without religious authority. The theme for chapter 6, "Bodies Confined, Spirits Cleansed," is the phenomenon of spatial segregation. Over the past fourteen centuries, Muslim women have been subjected to spatial limitation and, in some instances, complete segregation. Their mobility and participation in the wider world have been monitored relentlessly by the patriarchal establishment.

Under the veil of invisibility, women have had to adopt strategies to survive emotionally and psychologically. Indeed, in many instances women have learned how to thrive, working within the male-dominated system without offending it. Such adept maneuvering has resulted in women-only healing rituals, practices, and gatherings that enrich their lives. In these private spaces, women have rare opportunity to speak, act, and think as they wish, to support each other, and to transcend age-old restrictions.

A parallel may be drawn here with Pandora's box: once opened, it can never be closed again. I submit that the box in question is Islamic reform and that the velvet jihad plays a central role in opening new opportunities for women in every Muslim environment. As Mehran Kamrava, professor and chair of political science at California State University, insists, "Islamic reformation may not be upon us yet. But all indications are that it cannot be too far in coming."[65]

ONE

Honor and
Virginity

The cultural beliefs and practices related to the honor and shame complex that originated in the Mediterranean region are still pervasive in many cultures today. The focus of this chapter is on the ways that the honor-shame complex affects women, particularly Muslims. Ideas that are central to honor-shame will be discussed, such as the social construction of women's bodies, women as property, honor killings, and the importance of virginity.

The Social Construction
of the Female Body

The female body has long been a source of dread and fascination. There is a vast literature of sociological, political, anthropological, medical, and religious studies about how women's bodies are socially constructed and how such constructions are used and misused to gain control over women's lives. In addition, much study has been devoted to how some women resist such forces or offset the negative effects.

The social construction of women's bodies develops through battles between groups with competing political interests and with different access to power and resources. For example, some claim that "premenstrual syndrome," or PMS, was created by physicians, whose "ability to convince the public to accept these ideas has depended both on their economic and social power and on the support they have received from women who believe they have PMS and want validation for and treatment of their symptoms."[1] This social construction of women's bodies may be used, for example, by employers who decide not to hire or promote women on the grounds that women's menstrual cycles make them physically and emotionally unreliable. The association of menstruation with "female weakness" is not unique to one culture; it shows up in various religions and cultural taboos. Foucault described as "docile bodies" those who willingly surrender their own social control.[2] But not all women are passive; some choose to resist cultural taboos and religious fundamentalism based on their biological makeup or other characteristics.

From a historical perspective, women's bodies have always played an important role in the relationship between men and women. Laws have typically defined women's bodies as the property of men. Sometimes this notion is extended to the state or governing power. For example, in the Islamic Republic of Iran where Sharia (religious law) is constitutional law, the state indirectly claims women's bodies by prohibiting the use of female images in advertising for consumer goods. Political propaganda, however, is replete with the "Islamic" image of women in order to promote various government causes.[3]

Women as Property

At some point in history, women's legal status as property was based on the belief that they were inherently different from men—and not benignly different but defective and dangerous. Aristotle theorized that only embryos having sufficient heat could develop into full—that is, male—humans, while insufficiently heated embryos would be born as females. Thus a woman was only a "misbegotten man" and a "monstrosity" that was not fully developed.[4] Others validated this wildly inaccurate theory. For example, the Greek physician Galen declared that there is no difference between the reproductive organs of men and women except that the female organs are placed inside the body in order to produce sufficient heat to be able to create the fully human form. Women's lack of heat resulted in such deficiencies as smaller body frame, smaller muscles, lack of strength, and a smaller brain, which limited her intelligence.

During the eighteenth century, English laws regarding non–slave women's legal status essentially defined women as property. Upon marriage a woman experienced "'civil death,' losing any rights as a citizen, including the right to own or bestow property, make contracts or sue for legal redress, hold custody of minor children, or keep any wages she earned. . . . The husband had a legal right to beat his wife . . . as well as a right to her sexual services."[5] The notion of women as property is so ancient that it is embedded in language and culture, such as the popular Urdu phrase *"zan, zar, aur zameen"* (woman, gold, and land).

When law or custom makes women's bodies the property of men, then rape or sexual violence against women doubles as a weapon against the men who "own" those women. This connection between rape and the notion of women as property goes back to ancient civilization. Babylonian law treated rape as a form of property damage, requiring the rapist to pay a fine to the woman's husband or father.

Rape has always been a tool of war. The recent "ethnic cleansing" wars in the Balkans provided horrific examples of the explicit use of rape by an army not only to conquer but also to humiliate their opponents. Serb soldiers raped Bosnian Muslim women to impregnate them with "Chetniks" to claim ownership of the bodies of other men's women and, by desecrating them, reinforce their victory over their male enemies.[6] Rape, torture, and egregious humiliation were also used viciously and deliberately in the civil war in East Timor, especially after Indonesia invaded that region in 1975. The crimes committed by the Indonesian military and the local militias it commanded—opponents of independence—included not only massacres, widespread destruction, and mass deportations but also rape and sexual slavery on a wide and possibly systematic scale.[7] Hundreds of years ago, when England invaded Ireland, virgins had to submit to the English lords of the village before they were allowed to marry. This legally sanctioned rape was symbolic of the power of the invader over the conquered, and although armed rebellion by their men often proved futile, many Irish women committed suicide in resistance to this brutality.

There are countless other examples of the institutionalized use of rape in power struggles. Pakistani women have been raped so that their male relatives would be too ashamed to appear in the public arena, thus preventing them from running for political office. Muslim Bengali women have been raped by Pakistani solders to "cleanse" them of their alleged tendencies to uphold their Hindu traditions. Indian Hindus have raped Indian Muslim women to shame and render them impure, causing their own families to murder them in order to remove the "dirt."[8]

In Pakistan, media activism has stirred public sympathy around a critical issue pertaining to women and rape. In 1979 General Zia ul-Haq, a Pakistani military dictator, introduced the Hudood Ordinances as part of an active campaign to Islamicize Pakistan.[9] *Hudood* is the Arabic and Urdu word for "limitations" or "boundaries." The Hudood Ordinance is a law that enforces punishments mentioned in the Qur'an and sunna for such crimes as extramarital sex, false accusation of adultery, theft, and drinking alcohol. If a woman claims that she was raped, she must have four pious male witnesses to testify that she was not committing adultery. But only Muslim men can testify in cases involving Muslim women. Non-Muslim rape victims require four non-Muslim male witnesses. If a woman cannot provide four witnesses but rape is proved by other means (e.g., medical evidence), then the jury can punish the accused according to the Pakistani penal court. For married couples, the punishment for adultery is death by stoning, but this has never been carried out. Unmarried people receive one hundred lashes. This ordinance has sometimes been misused against rape victims if they are not able to provide four male witnesses. However, the extent to which this occurs is disputed. In certain situations, the alleged rapist accuses the raped woman of confessing to consensual intercourse.

The subsequent Pakistani governments of Benazir Bhutto and Nawaz Sharif were unable to repeal these laws, which hard-line Islamic groups insisted were rooted in the Qur'an. As a result, thousands of women have been imprisoned, including many who attempted to defy arranged marriages. In 2006, GEO TV produced a groundbreaking television series, *Zara Sochieye* (Please think), which provided a forum for debate on the Hudood issue. Vital public opposition has ensued because, according to the religious scholar Mohammad Farooq Khan, the Hudood "does not [even] distinguish between fornication and rape. . . . The overall verdict of this unprecedented public debate—that the laws are *not* rooted in the Koran—[gave] President Musharraf the cover needed to consider changes."[10]

Death in the Name of "Honor"

When women are considered property and rape is used as a weapon, honor killings are a common practice. A man kills his female relative for dishonoring the family reputation through actual, perceived, or suspected sexual transgressions and, by doing so, restores the family's honor in the community.[11] Honor killing "centers around the interdependent concepts, honor and shame, and around related practices governing family integrity and the virginity of young girls."[12]

The Arabic *namus*,[13] religious law or honor, from the Greek *nomos*, meaning customary and religious law,[14] is related to *namasa*, meaning to conceal. Thus it is not surprising that the sexuality of women is related to the *namasa*, or the thing one should protect and conceal from the public. It is very common in Iran for a man to say, "*be namusam ghasam*" ("I swear to my namus"), meaning he is swearing to his honor—the female folks in his household, including his mother, wife, sisters, and daughters. The Persian *shekaste shodan-e-namus* (breaking one's namus) is a metaphor for revealing a secret, such as when a private affair becomes public knowledge. In Iran, the Arabic word *auwrat* (genitals) was traditionally used as a substitute for "woman," and *setr-e-auwrat* (coverage of genitals) can be interpreted as "veiling the woman." The Arabic *aib* (shame) also substituted for "genitals." When I was growing up in Iran, I recall girls being told, "*be aibet dast na zan*" (do not touch your shame).

The focus of common interest among the men of a family or lineage is its women. A woman's status defines the status of all the men who are related to her in determinate ways. In this respect, these men all share the consequences of what happens to her, and therefore they share the commitment to protect her chastity and virtue, since she belongs to their patrimony.[15] Sexual violence committed against women and girls, especially virgins, is a social stigma. It brings shame not only on the girl's immediate family but on the larger clan as well. Honor killing of rape victims by Afghan men is common. Wali documents the rage and frustration of Afghan refugee men who had witnessed atrocities committed against Afghan women during the war and in refugee camps in Pakistan but who could not prevent them. Wali also reports that young virgin Afghan girls are sold to Arab countries or forced into prostitution in Pakistani brothels. Afghan men burned the women's refugee camp in Pakistan, apparently out of frustration over not being able to protect their honor by protecting their women.[16]

Because an Arab represents his kin group, his behavior must be honorable so that the group is not dishonored or disgraced: "a man can bring honour both to his kin and to himself by showing generosity or courage, or by having many sons." There are some subtle differences in the ideas of honor finely differentiated by two words: *sharaf* and *ird. Sharaf* means honor in a general sense, while *ird* is directly linked with sexual conduct. Thus a man's honor in the "sense of *ird* is so important that he will swear by it like the name of God; a man might swear by the ird of his sisters, for example." Sharaf can be built up by personal effort and can be inherited by a person by belonging to an honorable or respectable family. The morality of Iraqi women is dependent upon the behavior of their mothers, as the Iraqi proverb states, "*al-bint tala ala-umha,*" meaning "The daughter takes after her mother morally." The loss of ird is irreparable when a woman's sexual misconduct becomes public knowledge, since this sexual honor is the greatest of all the honors reflected in male circles.[17]

However, if a woman tries to defend her own honor, she can also be condemned to death. "In Iran, if a woman is raped, she is considered an adulteress and faces death by stoning. But if a woman fights off a sexual predator and kills him, she can then be tried for murder and face death by hanging."[18] Afsaneh Nowrouzi was sentenced to death for the "unjustified murder" of the local chief of police intelligence, who she says tried to rape her in 1997. At first, the sentence was upheld by Iran's Supreme Court following an appeal.[19] But after widespread protests by the Iranian press, female members of parliament, and international human rights organizations, it was suspended and she was released on furlough.[20]

The concept of "crime of passion" is directly or indirectly incorporated into the penal codes of many Western countries and is very similar to honor killing. Buddell says that "countries which incorporate the crime of passion directly have a much more lenient approach to their treatment of the offence, sometimes not even classing it as an offence, than those countries which incorporate it indirectly as part of the provocation defence." Moreover, Buddell asserts, "France is not the only jurisdiction to have embraced the crime of passion as a separate issue in its past. The penal codes of Belgium (1867, article 413), Romania (1937, article 155), Italy (1930, article 587), and Spain (1944, article 428) allowed absolution for the husband who killed his wife *in flagrant délict* whilst article 428 of the Spanish penal code (1944) and article 587 of the Italian penal code (1930) allowed a father or a brother to benefit from the same absolution."[21]

Similarly, Katz notes that Article 340 of the penal code of Jordan once contained an exemption from penalty for a man who killed his wife or female relative after finding her committing adultery with another man.[22] Article 543 of the penal code of Syria also provides an exemption from penalty if a man kills or injures his wife or female relative after finding her committing adultery or other "illegitimate sexual acts with another." Ironically, honor killing is reported in the Western media as unmitigated savagery and cultural backwardness, but many crimes of passion likewise involve a woman's sexuality and her death—and yet are enshrined in modern Western penal codes.

The importance of honor is seen not only in laws but also in numerous proverbs across the Muslim world. A Moroccan proverb says, "If the wife is unfaithful, even though she has a child, divorce her, don't love her." Notice that the proverb advocates divorce, not murder. In many Arab cultures, a cuckolded husband is duty-bound to kill the wife's lover, who violated his right to sexual exclusivity, while the adulteress is killed by her own father or brother because she dishonored her family, whose sullied reputation must be restored by blood relatives.[23] A common Arabic saying is, "An unchaste woman is sometimes worse than a murderer, since she is affecting not just one victim but also her family and her tribe." A few years ago, when the daughter of a prominent and highly respected family in Jordan ran away with a man, the family was disgraced and held in contempt, even by relatives, who urged them to restore their honor by killing the young woman. Her 10-year-old brother pulled the trigger.[24] This brutal cultural tradition now occurs in Germany, England, and France. European Muslims, even those who oppose such crimes, frequently remain silent in the face of such barbarity, for fear of fueling Islamophobia in the larger community.

There have been reports that some suicide bombings in Palestine are actually honor killings of women who are not volunteering to be *shahida* (female martyrs) but are restoring their family's honor through this blood sacrifice; however, there is little confirmation of this.[25]

In cultures that adhere to an honor-shame complex, girls and boys are taught proper codes of honor at a very young age, and female chastity is seen in the Arab world as an indelible line. A young Egyptian journalist remembered his high school biology class during which his teacher sketched the female reproductive system and pointed out the entrance to the vagina, saying, "This is where the family honor lies!" However, many Arabs don't agree with honor killing as a remedy for regaining one's reputation. A tribal leader in Jordan mocked the idea of honor killing by saying, "If you spit, does it come back clean?" He added, "A guy who kills might think that dishonor goes away, but when he walks past, people will say, 'There goes the guy who killed his daughter.'"[26]

In Iran what is considered acceptable and morally appropriate for women varies according to social class. Women from the lower socioeconomic classes bear a heavier burden with regard to the constructs of sexuality that communicate moral standing and regulate women's conduct. Religious stories recited among the rural working classes frequently focus on the concept of *khejalat* (propriety or shame) and the *aberou* of Fatima al Zahra, the beloved daughter of the Prophet of Islam.[27] A woman's own judgment about appropriate behavior is less important than what others expect of her or the impression she makes on her kin. Women are responsible for the care and use of their bodies through purity rituals and for preserving their honor. To avoid gossip, women carefully control any bodily gesture that might be interpreted as sexually provocative. Many Iranian women consider their personal feelings about honor to be very different from what is expected of them socially. In private conversations, they are much more open and vocal about their own feelings. Abu-Lughod says that women's "admitting the existence of an attitude toward others and a range of sentiments which lie outside the confines of those recognized by the system of honor may demonstrate the voluntary nature of an individual's conformity to the code in everyday actions."[28] Women in honor-shame societies learn to manipulate their behavior to fit expectations in the interest of self-preservation.

Unwritten codes say that the unchaste woman has no place in her family or outside of her home, and the sanctions for a woman's sexual disobedience can be dire. Her family will be ostracized, her sisters will be deemed unfit for marriage, her brothers will be taunted in the street, and their marriage proposals may be labeled unacceptable by other families. Men will question the manhood of her father and brothers, and until the issue is resolved, the family members will have to walk in public with their eyes lowered in shame. It is not unusual for the victims of honor killings to be buried in unmarked graves and all records of their existence wiped out. Most honor killings occur in countries where the concept of women as the bearer of the family reputation predominates, but this practice of violence against women cuts across cultures, religions, and social classes. Reports to the United Nations Commission on Human Rights indicate that honor killings have occurred in Bangladesh, Great Britain, Brazil, Ecuador, Egypt, India, Israel, Italy, Jordan, Pakistan, Morocco, Sweden, Turkey, and Uganda. The practice was also condoned by the Taliban in Afghanistan and has been reported in Iraq and Iran. Like crimes of passion, dowry deaths in India bear a resemblance to honor killings because they are often committed with impunity or not even reported.[29]

So strong is the honor-shame imperative that women are often complicit in honor killings of their female relatives, which only strengthens the notion of women as property and the perception that such violence is a family matter rather than a judicial issue. In Pakistan in 1999, Samia Imran sought legal help to divorce her abusive husband, and while in the office of her lawyers (two sisters involved in human rights struggles), Samia's mother (a doctor), uncle, and a hired gunman entered, and the gunman shot Samia dead at close range. Samia's father, the president of the Peshawar Chamber of Commerce, issued death threats against the lawyers.[30] It is not surprising that female family members frequently support honor killings. Because honor-shame is based on a community and cultural mentality, all women in a family or community can suffer if one is alleged to have transgressed. And although honor killings are more often found in cultures that adhere to a tribal system with a tradition of self-administered justice, even well-to-do and well-connected people like Samia's family condone them.

Although many people associate honor killings with Islam, the Qur'an does not permit or sanction honor killings. The honor-shame complex existed in tribal cultures before the arrival of Islam, and in those cultures, women were considered the property of the men in their family regardless of class, ethnicity, or religion. Chapter 24 in the Qur'an states that a woman can only be convicted of adultery if four male witnesses actively saw her having intercourse. However, men who accuse their spouses without any witnesses will have their testimony accepted if they swear to Allah four times that they are telling the truth. The penalty for adultery is death unless the participants are unmarried, in which case the Qur'an states, "You should whip each of them one hundred lashes," a clear indication that killing is not permitted by the Qur'an for the honor of anyone. The leading Muslim clerics in Jerusalem and Jordan have denounced such killings. The Turkish penal code does not appear to condone honor killings, but traditional society encourages it. The Balkan region also suffers the scourge of honor killings. In parts of former Yugoslavia, tribal codes withstood the socialist regime's attempts to implement legislation that would have introduced and preserved the legal equality of women. Balkan women's support centers have seen a rise in incidents of violence against women following the collapse of the socialist state. The increase in violence against women included mass rapes as part of the ethnic cleansing policy.[31]

> Amnesty International has reported on one case in which a husband murdered his wife based on a dream that she had betrayed him. In Turkey, a young woman's throat was slit in the town square because a love ballad had been dedicated to her over the radio.[32]

Victims of rape are vulnerable to honor killing as well. Amnesty International reported that in 1999, a sixteen-year-old mentally retarded girl was raped in the northwest frontier province of Pakistan. The crime was reported to the police, and the perpetrator was arrested, but the Pathan tribesmen decided that she had brought shame to her tribe. She was turned over to her tribe's judicial council and killed in front of a tribal gathering.[33]

In contrast to this tragic outcome, a later incident pertaining to another Pakistani woman named Mukhtar Mai (also known as Mukhtaran) had a happier ending. Mai, an illiterate young woman, was gang-raped in 2002. The rape was carried out in retribution for her twelve-year-old brother's sins, on the orders of a village council in the southern Punjab village of Meerwala. The influential Mastoi tribe had convened the council to seek punishment for Mai's brother, Shakoor, who was accused of being seen in the company of a Mastoi woman. This event brought shame on the Mastoi clan. Mai fought for her rights and eventually was awarded damages by the Pakistan government. She used the award money to build two schools in her village. Mai received other humanitarian donations, $5,000 of which she earmarked for female victims of Pakistan's massive 2006 earthquake. She is using other monies to set up a hotline and shelter for those Pakistani women victimized by domestic violence or recovering from the trauma of rape.[34]

As a result of Pakistani national news and global international coverage, Mai has become a powerful symbol for women's empowerment. She has written a memoir and traveled extensively, speaking on behalf of Pakistani women and addressing the plight of Muslim women trapped in patriarchal cultures. According to Wikipedia,

> On 2 May 2006, Mukhtaran spoke at the United Nations headquarters in New York. In an interview with United Nations TV, Mai said that "she wanted to get the message across to the world that one should fight for

their rights and for the rights of the next generation." She was welcomed by UN Under-Secretary General Shashi Tharoor, who said, "I think it is fair to say that anyone who has the moral courage and internal strength to turn such a brutal attack into a weapon to defend others in a similar position, is a hero indeed, and is worthy of our deepest respect and admiration."

Mai's emphasis on education, as well as her concern for the humane, digni-fied, and equal treatment of all women, places her at the forefront of the velvet jihad. In her own words:

I hope to make education more readily available to girls, to teach them that no woman should ever go through what happened to me, and I eventually hope to open more school branches in this area of Pakistan. I need your support to kill illiteracy and to help make tomorrow's women stronger. This is my goal in life.

Actually, the women of my area are unaware of their rights. Yes, some women are afraid to empathize with me. They are afraid of men, con-servative social values, and the male-dominated society. In our school, we teach girls the regular syllabus as well as special chapters on women's rights, human rights, and women's empowerment.[35]

Mukhtar Mai transformed her tragic experience into an opportunity to edu-cate others. Unfortunately, her "happy ending" is the exception in Pakistan's Punjab region, where over 1,700 honor killings were reported in a five-year period (1997–2003).[36] Tribal tradition remains very strong and, in practice, frequently supersedes civil or religious law.

A 2002 documentary film portrayed the strength of such traditions. In the documentary, a woman in India's Punjab named Hurmati wanted a divorce, and after running away from her husband's village and being re-turned by her family several times, she sought out a lawyer. The response of the judge was:

I can give you the legal papers and declare that you are divorced, but you know better that in reality you are not divorced, you belong to the people of your village, your tribe, your husband's family, and the culture of Punjab. This legal divorce paper will not serve your purpose unless you can fight the entire culture of Punjab and your tribal heritage.[37]

The Virginity Imperative

Hymenaeus was the Greek god of weddings, and he is associated with the wedding song.[38] The biological function of the hymen is uncertain—some scientists hypothesize that it protects the vagina from infection in infants—but its social function is crucial in many cultures. Upon initial intercourse, a woman's hymen ruptures and bleeds, ostensibly providing proof of virginity. However, some sporting activities, the use of tampons, and the elasticity of some hymens are among the reasons that bleeding with first sexual intercourse is not inevitable. In some cultures, what makes a woman a desirable bride is not her exceptional talents, good looks, intelligence, family connections, or pleasant personality; instead, it is an intact hymen. A woman's marriage prospects, her family's reputation, and sometimes her very life depend on this membrane.[39]

Mernissi reflects on the "Mediterranean man's most treasured commodities: the virgin, with hymen intact, sealing a vagina which no man has touched." She notes that virginity is considered "a matter between men, in which women merely play the role of silent intermediaries." She also argues that virginity as an institution is to prevent women from seeking pleasure and desire. Similarly, Catholic dogma for centuries taught that sexual pleasure was shameful and sinful if it didn't involve procreation. A very different religious and cultural tradition from Africa has elevated the status of virginity to the detriment of women. Female genital mutilation, sometimes referred to by the wildly inaccurate and innocuous term of female circumcision, is still practiced in Christian, Muslim, and animist cultures in Africa as well as in parts of the Middle East, Asia, and immigrant communities originating from those cultures. Clitoridectomies and infibulation (sewing up the labia) literally imprison women's sexuality and often cause ghastly complications and diseases. The horror doesn't always end with marriage. A woman might be resewn after each childbirth in order to be presented to her husband as a virgin again.[40]

Virginity has also long been a focus in analyses of Muslim women's sexuality. In the Islamic Republic of Iran, even allowing women to ride horses or bicycles is frowned upon because those activities require the spreading of legs. People vigorously debate whether *hadith* (sayings and actions of the prophet Muhammad) provide the basis for moral guidance on the matter. Ayatollah Ali Khamenei of Iran, following religious orthodoxy, proclaimed, "Women must avoid anything that attracts strangers, so riding bicycles or motorcycles by women in public places involves corruption and is forbidden."[41]

The Muslim Women's League, a nonprofit American Muslim organization working to promote the values of Islam and to reclaim the free and equal status of women, addresses the psychological impact of the virginity imperative on young Muslim girls:

> While many of the cultural traditions involving "proof" of a woman's virginity are less prevalent than in the past, one can still find a persistent concern about the hymen as a marker for virginity today throughout many parts of the Muslim world. . . . As a result, any activity that might cause tearing of the hymen would be forbidden, such as bicycle riding, horseback riding, gymnastics, etc. Unfortunately, the prohibitions against these activities are rarely accompanied by an explanation (most likely due to shyness on the part of the parents); thus the young girl learns that because she is a girl she cannot participate in activities enjoyed by other children. Again, such an attitude promotes a negative self-image. These attitudes are culturally entrenched and not based on Islam. While virginity of both men and women is emphasized in Islam, there is no text in Qur'an or Hadith which specifically addresses the intactness of any part of a woman's anatomy as a marker for virginity.[42]

Although preserving premarital virginity is often associated with Islam and with areas where Muslims live, virginity was important to those cultures prior to their conversion to Islam. The origins of the fixation on virginity have to do not just with religion but also with landownership and inheritance laws of agricultural societies and the customs of patriarchy. A "pure" woman is responsible for continuing the link to the next generation, and virginity guarantees the purity of bloodline and establishes the family lineage (at least for the first child). An unmarried woman who is not a virgin is considered "damaged goods," and like a commodity, she would not be a consumer's first choice unless he were looking for a bargain. Even today, virginity is sold as a commodity; as reported in a British tabloid, a woman placed an ad to sell her virginity to the highest bidder (starting at £5,000)—doctor's proof on request.[43]

As mentioned earlier, women are often considered the property of men, and the value of such property depends on several factors, including virginity status. Virgins command a high price and are in great demand as brides, while nonvirgins who receive marriage offers are considered exceptionally lucky. Nonvirgins usually have to marry much older men, become burdened with a household of children from his previous marriages, and take responsibility for a large portion of household chores with co-wives. Even if she were the only wife, such a woman would be expected to be grateful for having food, shelter, and the social status of being married. Since "beggars can't be choosers," she has to accept this lot in life.

In a world where men own women's bodies, the consequences of not bleeding on the wedding night or of being a nonvirgin bride can be severe. In many Mediterranean and African cultures, the husband's family may take revenge through violent punishments and banishment of the bride because she shamed them. Among the Yungar people of Australia, girls without an intact hymen before marriage are starved, tortured, or even killed. In Arab countries, their brothers, uncles, or fathers may kill them, often without fear of prosecution. The image of a bloody sheet on the wedding night is highly celebrated and proudly displayed in many cultures because it represents the purity of the bride and the virility of the groom. In China, the bride's virginity determines the amount of betrothal gifts and guarantees that the lineage of prestigious families is not "contaminated."[44]

Gonzalez-Lopez argues that Catholic sexual morality is only one of several variables influencing ideas of virginity among Mexicans and Mexican immigrants. She suggests that virginity is valued as a form of capital, ensuring happiness and financial security through marriage. It is especially important in a patriarchal and sexist society for women with little access to higher education and opportunities for financial independence, and so mothers pass on the lesson of its value to their daughters. As in many other cultures around the world, marriage is a fundamental social institution for economic survival. Gonzalez-Lopez also notes that many mothers emphasize premarital virginity of their daughters as protection against gender oppression. Mothers believe that if daughters are virgins before marriage, they will have higher self-esteem and their husbands will respect them. Several women in this study said that their first sexual experience was rape, but "even though their loss of virginity was forced, not voluntary after marriage, these women's husbands reproached them at some point in their marital lives for not being virgins." These kinds of attitudes remain prevalent throughout Latin America.[45]

An opinion writer in Thailand says that overvaluing virginity leads to gender oppression. It makes women believe that sex is dirty and makes men prone to domestic violence because they believe they own their wives after having taken their precious commodity of virginity. The dangers of premarital sex for the young—pregnancy, diseases, abortion, psychological enslavement—could be better avoided through education rather than the burden of virginity to be borne only by women.[46]

Reconstituted Virgins

Some brides are "artificial virgins." Hymenoplasty (also known as hymenorraphy) is the surgical reconstruction of the hymen and often includes the suturing in of a gelatin capsule with a substance that mimics blood that will burst during intercourse and simulate loss of virginity.[47] Women seek it for their social status, happiness, and even preservation of life. With this surgery, women can overcome social taboos and the obsession with female virginity. It makes them marriageable and allows them to avoid shame, dishonor, and gossip. In some cases, it prevents them from being murdered. In Egypt, hymen reconstructive surgery has drastically reduced the number of murders committed when a bride was found not to be a virgin on the wedding night. However, some doctors refuse to do the procedure because it violates their beliefs. Others, such as the physicians with Doctors Without Borders whom I interviewed in the summer of 1997, said that they often perform hymen repair surgery to save women's lives and that their patients come from a variety of backgrounds—Jewish, Muslim, Christian, and Druze.

A student of mine from Greece told me of a case in which a doctor performed the procedure. She said that a friend of hers was madly in love with a classmate and, after courting for a while they began to have sexual intimacy. After three years, the boyfriend abruptly left her to marry a virgin "good" girl. The girlfriend was disconsolate because not only had she been betrayed but she was now considered damaged goods. Her friends collectively arranged for a hymen repair operation, which changed her life for the better. Within three years, she married a nice man. At the wedding, she suddenly turned white and appeared on the verge of fainting because she saw that her surgeon was among the friends of her husband. She knew that her life would be ruined if the groom or his family knew of her surgery. Fortunately, the doctor abided by the strictures of patient confidentiality.

The Internet is filled with providers of hymen repairs of various forms and prices. One may also find religious guidance in cyberspace concerning the issue of hymenoplasty. Hamid Tavakoli, manager of a blog focusing on the issues of temporary marriage, regular marriage, divorce, and virginity, provided feedback from "expert" clerics. A young woman contacted Tavakoli concerning temporary marriage, particularly in relation to the virginity issue. What follows is my translation of the correspondence between Tavakoli and the Iranian cleric Grand Ayatollah Al Rohani:

Hamid Tavakoli. Manager of Web-Blog on the issue of Temporary Marriage javab_hamid@yahoo.com

Subject: Hymenoplasty

November 2004

In the name of God.

There is a young lady who feels the necessity of getting married in a temporary marriage; if she does not, then she believes she is committing a sin. However, her family opposes this temporary marriage so she is considering doing so secretly. She is aware that if she loses her virginity through this temporary marriage and later on enters a regular marriage, her [new] husband and his family will discover that she is not a virgin and shun her or consider her a prostitute.

[Mr. Tavakoli's questions]

1. Is it religiously sanctioned for this girl to undergo hymenoplasty so no one will discover she was involved in a temporary marriage?
2. If her [new] husband stipulates virginity as a prerequisite for marriage, will this girl be able to present herself as a virgin, even though she is a fake virgin?

Thank you

[Grand Ayatollah Al Rohani's answers to Mr. Tavakoli]

Glorified Be His [Allah's] Attributes.

1. A girl who loses her virginity can regain her virginity through surgery; there is no [religious] problem concerning this issue.

2. If virginity is one of the conditions of the marriage contract, the girl who has regained her virginity [through hymenoplasty] still qualifies as a virgin. There is no difference between a real or fake virgin in this case. The marriage will be considered authentic, and there should be no problem.

Signed: al Rohani
(Seal reads: Mohammad Sadegh al Hossani al Rohani)[48]

One particularly comprehensive Internet site is the Allan Centre for Women, which offers laser vaginal rejuvenation, labia reduction, vaginoplasty, cosmetic gynecology, hymen restoration, BOTOX treatments, collagen injections, laser hair removal, microdermabrasion, and sclerotherapy for spider veins. A woman who came to the Laser Vaginal Rejuvenation Institute of San Antonio said: "After two children, I had serious incontinence problems. My vagina had that 'flippy-floppy' feeling. I could barely feel anything. Sex was just not the same." She claimed that her surgical transformation was "a miracle."[49]

In "Please Make Me a Virgin Again," an article published in the August 2000 issue of *Marie-Claire*, Silvana Paternostro investigates hymenoplasty in the United States, where she is surprised to find women who feel compelled to get this surgery secretly in order to get a husband. She says that many Latin American men, even those who live in the United States, insist that the women they marry must be virgins, preferably demure. One clinic in New York that boasts of doing a variety of Fifth Avenue–style plastic and cosmetic procedures, but at much lower prices, advises getting the surgery six weeks before the wedding day. To make its clientele feel comfortable and relaxed, "Above the beds where women rest after surgery, an open-armed Jesus blesses their recovery."

Some Latinas who can afford it fly to the United States for hymenoplasty—like the daughter of a politician who could not risk having the surgery done in her country for fear it would be discovered and used as a subject for blackmail. Many Asian women also get the procedure. In some families, Korean women have to provide a certificate of virginity to the groom's family. A Los Angeles doctor, whose clinic receives e-mail inquiries from all over the world, often performs hymen reconstruction (which cost around $3,500 in 2000) on women of Arab descent. He bragged, "I can fool any man. . . . My benchmark is not to fool the husband-to-be but to fool another gynecologist whom the groom's family chooses."[50]

The cost of hymenoplasty is quite high, especially for those in developing countries, adding to the mental agony of women who need the procedure in order to save their lives. In Morocco in the mid-1990s, the cost of hymen repair was estimated between 500 and 1,000 DH ($1=10 DH) at a time when the average annual expenditure of a family of agricultural workers was about 65 DH, although that is a significant decrease from the 2,000 DH it cost in 1968.[51]

Dr. Laila Al-Marayati, a respected gynecologist and past president of the Muslim Women's League (based in Los Angeles), believes women seek out hymen repair surgeries to cope with cultural pressures and not to comply with Islamic law—which does not stipulate a need to check a woman's virginity. Dr. Al-Marayati told Sandy Kobrin of Women eNews:

> While Islam requires that both men and women be chaste before marriage, it doesn't require women to prove it. The need for surgery is because of the culture in some countries. Those same cultures do not require a man to prove his chasteness.

Kobrin spoke with a number of physicians in the United States, all of whom agree that requests for hymen repair surgeries are on the increase. According to Dr. Leroy Young of Los Angeles:

> The patients are most often women of Middle Eastern descent, some with origins from countries such as Iran and Saudi Arabia. They frequently give false names and pay in cash. They arrive alone, faces hidden, under elaborate hats, wigs, scarves and sunglasses, and afraid. . . . It's not just women with Middle Eastern backgrounds seeking the surgeries. There has also been an increase in the number of women requesting hymen repair from both the Orthodox Jewish and Christian fundamentalist communities, as well as from women of all nationalities who want the surgery as a sexual enhancement.

Another Los Angeles gynecologist, Dr. David Matlock, claims to have performed hymenoplasties on hundreds of women—mostly from the Middle East—over the past twenty-one years. Dr. Matlock and his office employees have received death threats and gruesome letters:

> They called my office numerous times and sent letters to my office with pictures of dead and bloodied people," he said. "It was unnerving to say the least. I can now better understand when these women come in and say to me: "I must do this. I'm going back to Iran and I could be killed."

Honor and Virginity

In Atlanta, Dr. John Miklos has been performing hymenoplasties on women ranging in age from 19 to 30. He told Kobrin, "I have had many Middle Eastern women beg me to come in at night and then ask me to destroy the records. They say they could fall into the hands of family members and both of our lives could be in danger."[52]

All the physicians interviewed spoke with grave concern about their own safety and that of their patients. One suggested that the situation was reminiscent of the rabid outbreak of Christian fundamentalist threats to abortion clinics. As a result, most of these physicians no longer advertise in local newspapers or via Web sites. They rely, instead, on personal referrals. The testimonies of these physicians emphasize the tragic plight of Muslim women across the globe, ensnared in a vicious trap of patriarchal and cultural traditions.

Fake Virgins and Home Remedies

However, lack of monetary resources for plastic surgery does not stop a woman from seeking other avenues to pretend or appear to be a virgin on her wedding night. For centuries, women have practiced home remedies. *Harper's* magazine published an English translation of the instruction manual for the "Jade Lady Membrane Man-Made Hymen," a Chinese hymen repair kit.[53] In many places, using chicken blood (or pigeon's blood in Iran) as ersatz virginity-loss blood has been a common practice. Soaking a homemade tampon in blood and inserting it in the vagina or presenting a previously blood-soaked white handkerchief is a common way to provide evidence to save a woman's honor and perhaps her life. In 2002, a woman in her late fifties recounted to me the horrible episode of her wedding night. She was not a virgin; she had carried on an intimate love affair with her neighbor's son, with whom she was madly in love, for over two years without being caught. But then she was forced into an arranged marriage. She told me:

> I hated the fact that I had to offer my body to someone whom I did not love. I hated the fact that my society and elders in my family chose my marital life destiny. More than that, I hated that being a "bleeding" virgin was expected of me. I couldn't seek help because I had kept my affair so secret. My love affair was known only by *khoda* ("God" in Farsi), my man, and I. Yet I did not want to bring shame to my parents and create a scan-

dal. That would have been a big price to pay compared to what I decided to do. I made sure to have a brand-new sharp razor blade close to my side of the wedding bed. I had practiced in my own mind how I will cut a part of my body enough to bleed so the sheet would be smeared with that blood, and I was sure that due to dim lighting in the bedroom, I would not be caught. When the time arrived, I just closed my eyes and cut the tip of my own finger. I was in pain but did not care. I was concentrating on my mission to be accomplished.

Often when a woman must resort to such tactics, a trustworthy confidante will be involved. Usually, this woman is not an immediate family member, since dishonoring the family is not easily forgiven. It is not uncommon to find this role played by an elderly woman who is sympathetic to the bride, such as a wet nurse, a live-in nanny, or a cousin. This woman's participation in preparation of the show is crucial. Every detail of the plan is discussed and reviewed ahead of time. The confidante not only has a big role in arranging the details but also plays a crucial psychological role by comforting and supporting the bride, who faces such a heavy burden on the night that will shape her life destiny. The value of such a confidante is shown by the degree that she will be showered for the rest of her life with favors from the bride.

A topical cream called Virgin Me promises to make you "feel like a virgin, touched for the very first time"; you will "feel pain and offer proof" in the form of fake blood. The product targets women from cultures that view virginity as a symbol of a woman's purity and innocence, but the Food and Drug Administration has never heard of it, and doctors say it is most assuredly a scam.[54] A man who seems to be the victim of another scam sent this inquiry to Robert McDowell's Herbal Treatments:

> My future wife would like to become a virgin again. We have heard that a herb called "comfrey" has the healing power to repair the hymen, thus restore virginity. As such can you provide us with more information? Is it true? If so what will the cost be and will it be administered?

McDowell wisely answered,

> It is not true that comfrey will repair a damaged hymen, nor will any other herbal medicines. You must know that Virginity is a state of mind and not a state of body and seeking to physically restore the membrane is a quest not worthy of making.

Another savvy advice columnist on the California-based Salam Worldwide Web site replied to "Mohammad," who, after living in the United States for twenty-five years, was planning to go to Iran to seek a bride and was disturbed by rumors that Iranian women were engaging in premarital sex and then having restorative surgery:

> Dude! What's with the whole virgin bride obsession? I personally have never understood the appeal of a sexually ignorant woman. . . . Are [you] so lacking in confidence in your sexual prowess that you don't want to suffer any comparison? Whatever your hang-ups may be, it just ain't cool to put your potential life partner under such unfair scrutiny (especially if you have had your share of sexual partners).[55]

The columnist briefly describes hymen repair surgery and notes that it is almost undetectable after healing, and then concludes with another admonition against the obsession.

Virginity and the Law

Is virginity codified and enforced by religious or secular law? Islamic law is ambiguous on the issue of fornication and adultery. The Qur'an speaks of *zina,* or sexual intercourse between a man and a woman not married to each other. It therefore applies to adultery (which implies that one or both of the parties are married to a person or persons other than the ones concerned) and to fornication (which implies that both parties are unmarried). Punishment for an act of zina may vary depending on the school of Islamic law practiced or the cultural setting. One Islamic society may assign one hundred lashes as just punishment while another may say stoning is just punishment. The following verses from two chapters of the Qur'an address the issue. In chapter 24, *al Nour* (The Light), the believer is warned and guided by the following verses:

> The woman and the man
> Guilty of adultery or fornication
> Flog each of them
> With a hundred stripes:
> Let not compassion move you
> In their case, in a matter
> Prescribed by God, if ye believe

In God and the Last Day:
And let a party
Of the Believers
Witness their punishment.
Let no man guilty of
Adultery or fornication marry
Any but a woman
Similarly guilty, or an Unbeliever:
Nor let any but such a man
Or an Unbeliever
Marry such a woman:
To the Believers such a thing is forbidden.
(Qur'an 24: 2–10)

Verses 4–10 of the same chapter speak of the charge against unchaste women and the requirement of four witnesses to support the allegations; if a witness is proven guilty of a lie, he will be flogged with eighty stripes because he is a wicked transgressor. The verses also speak of those who cannot provide four witnesses. They should bear witness four times with an oath by God that they are solemnly telling the truth; the fifth oath should be that they solemnly invoke the curse of God upon themselves if they tell a lie. Unfortunately, in some incidents, only the oath of a man is counted as solid evidence in the accusation of a woman for adultery—and it is justified based on the Qur'an while the woman is not given the same justification granted to her in the Qur'an. Another brief reference to adultery is cited in chapter 17, *Bani Israel* (Children of Israel):

Nor come nigh to adultery:
For it is a shameful [deed]
And an evil, opening the road
[To other evils]. (Qur'an 17: 32)

I have yet to find any Qur'anic verses on the need for virginity testing or murdering women to save anyone's honor. But there are many writings on virginity and secular law, especially by human rights groups and agencies advocating women's rights. Recently, there has been a struggle in Turkey between the law and culture regarding the legality of virginity tests. According to Cindoglu, there are two modern medical practices regarding virginity in Turkey: the virginity test and virginity surgery. Through in-depth interviews with physicians, Cindoglu concludes that some physicians are against hymen repair because, informed by their own religiosity, they consider it *haram* (forbidden by Islam). Other physicians said they would not perform such operations but don't care if other physicians do. Still others would not hesitate to perform the surgery, knowing that if they didn't, the patient would find another willing physician. The physicians said that, not surprisingly, most of the unmarried women who come for hymen repair claim that the loss of their virginity was an accident.[56] Since hymen repair is illegal in Turkey, it cannot be performed in government hospitals. Therefore, most hymenoplasties in Turkey take place in the privacy of the physician's clinic, and patients pay in cash. No paperwork is done, in order to protect both the physician and the patient.

In 1998, Isilay Saygin, the Turkish minister of women's and family affairs, caused a firestorm of controversy when she defended the right of the government to enforce virginity tests in state orphanages and when she belittled the five girls who subsequently attempted suicide.[57] In 1999, Justice Minister Hasan Denizkurdu officially banned forced virginity tests except with permission from a judge when required for criminal evidence.[58] Part of the rationale for the ban was Turkey's attempt to improve its human rights record in order to be accepted into the European Union. Even before virginity testing was banned, women were entitled to refuse the test, but many doctors who performed it didn't know that, showing that a law to protect human rights is only as good as its enforcement. Virginity testing was used not only to screen applicants for government or nursing jobs but also to abuse arrested political activists, women in jail, and women simply accused of being immoral.[59]

Governments in other countries have also codified virginity tests. The founder of Women's Rights Watch Nigeria condemned the forcible and humiliating testing of girls for virginity and boys for venereal diseases without parental consent, saying that this is not the responsibility of secondary schools.[60] Uganda has received international praise for the success of its abstinence program in reducing the rates of HIV/AIDS. The health minister of Uganda's largest internal kingdom proclaimed strict adherence to the traditional custom of virgin brides, in which a paternal aunt takes up vigilance outside the bridal chamber and produces the bloody sheet to confirm virginity. But focusing on promoting virgin brides—by offering them electrical kitchen appliances, for example—sets a double standard, say critics, who argue that boys also bear responsibility for preventing the spread of AIDS.[61] The double standard is so thoroughly integrated into so many cultures that it is reflected in language. In the Merriam-Webster online dictionary, the first three definitions of the noun *virgin* refer to females; only the fourth is generic: "a person who has not had sexual intercourse," while the fifth is again gender-specific: "a female animal that has never copulated."

Another example of this kind of double standard is in Swaziland, where the government instituted a five-year ban on sexual relations for young women—but not for young men. Girard says this is another example of when a "public health argument—the urgent need to reduce the rates of HIV infection—is invoked to curtail the sexual activity of young women." Not only is the decree highly discriminatory and unlikely to stop the spread of the disease, but it also puts young women in danger by requiring virgins to wear yellow tassels, which makes them vulnerable to being preyed upon by those who believe in the "virgin cure" myth—that having sex with a virgin will prevent or cure diseases like AIDS. Although the virgin cure myth has roots in sixteenth-century Europe, today it is especially prevalent in Africa, which has some of the world's highest rates of HIV infection—as well as increasing rates of child and even infant rape, which some scientists suggest is due to the virgin cure myth.[62] A more equitable AIDS prevention policy, and one more likely to succeed, would involve sex education and condom use by men.

The double standard seems to be at work in South Africa, too, as politicians there "urged young women to observe the old Zulu culture of preserving their virginity and self-discipline, saying this would help to curb the spread of the killer HIV/AIDS virus."[63] However, in at least one township, boys are being tested as well ("a hard foreskin is considered a sign of purity"), although critics contend that there is no way to scientifically prove virginity for boys or girls. But the fear is that both boys and girls identified as virgins will become targets of sexual predators and believers of the virgin cure myth.[64] Zimbabwe is yet another African country where traditional virginity tests are being revived to fight the spread of AIDS. Again, critics say that the effort is misguided because men spread AIDS more than women due to cultural acceptance of male, but not female, promiscuity. And, as in other African countries, Betty Makoni, director of the Zimbabwean Girl Child Network, says, "We would like to confirm to you that girls are under siege from men who think sleeping with virgins cures the deadly HIV/ AIDS virus. In this context, virginity testing becomes a harmful cultural practice."[65]

The Chinese government is also conducting virginity tests on Tibetan women applying for jobs, to determine their "fitness" for employment. Those who pass must sign contracts stating they will not have sex or marry for three years. It is reported that men and boys must likewise sign such contracts, but apparently they do not have to submit to the humiliation of having an examiner insert a finger inside their bodies as a condition of employment.[66]

Morris cites a Human Rights Watch report showing that since the fall of the Taliban in Afghanistan in 2001, women still suffer systematic human rights abuse, including forced virginity tests, and their behavior and appearance are monitored by men and gangs of schoolboys—who presumably don't have to submit to such tests. And another type of double standard operates there, too: part of the international community's justification for the war against the Taliban was the liberation of Afghan women, yet it supports warlords and commanders who abuse women's rights.[67]

Voluntary Virginity and Revirginization

While laws and customs attempt to enforce virginity in some places, elsewhere a few women are choosing to be chaste "brides of Christ." The Catholic Rite of Consecration to a Life of Virginity, an ancient rite that arose in the early church before the establishment of religious orders, is being revived by women, usually older, who are called neither to marriage nor to a vocation with a religious community (like nuns). These "consecrated virgins" give up sex and devote themselves to church and prayer. Now that women are educated and do not have to be dependent on men, they say, they can opt to both support themselves economically and dedicate their lives to service through the church, though few are called to the extra step of taking a vow of chastity and having a ceremony to solemnify it.[68] Although the choice of this ministry is voluntary, its focus on chastity reflects the Church's pre–Vatican II fixation on nonprocreative sex as sinful, a notion that has incarcerated millions of minds and bodies over the centuries.

In Pakistan, half a world away from Vatican City, women are living out their lives as virgins under circumstances that stretch the imagination. For the majority of Pakistani women, their narrow world is structured around strict religious, family, and tribal customs—such as the rituals of Karo-Kari, Vani or Soowa, Watta Satta, and "arranged" marriages with the Qur'an. Karo-Kari is honor killing when a woman is accused of being an adulterer. Vani (or Soowa) is a tribal custom whereby the wife or daughter of a murderer is given to the family of the victim, in order to make peace between the families. Watta-Satta is the Urdu tribal custom of exchanging brides between two families. In order for you to marry off your son, you must also have a daughter to marry off in return. If there is no sister to trade in return for a son's spouse, then a cousin or other female relative can be bartered instead.

The marriage of young women to the Holy Qur'an has become a common phenomenon among tribal families, especially in situations where property is inherited from one's father. This un-Islamic marriage, known as Haq Bakhswana and/or Haq Bakshish (giving up what is rightfully yours), requires a young woman to swear on the Qur'an that she will never marry anyone and that she will remain a virgin forever.

Greed and economic interest sit at the foundation of this practice. Since no marital consummation takes place in Haq Bakhswana, the woman's share of her father's land will remain with the father or brother instead of going to a husband. Thus the family avoids losing ancestral land. Frequently male family members use this type of "marriage" to maintain control over their sisters and daughters. The practice of marrying Pakistani women to trees or to young boys or very old men has also been reported as a strategy to protect property. Because families tend to keep these rituals secret, it is impossible to determine precise details or to know the exact number of young women who have succumbed to this practice.

In some areas of Punjab and Sindh provinces, daughters are kept unmarried till the age of menopause when they take up the Qur'an and Tasbih [prayer beads] "voluntarily." Women are usually forced to accept such marital decisions made by their fathers. "This cruel tradition runs usually in families of agrarian landed aristocracy to avoid the transfer of land property out of family hands at the marriage of their daughter or sister. The male members of the family force the girls to wed the 'holy book' and withdraw from the right to marry," said Aftab Hassan Khan, a human and

Honor and Virginity

women's rights activist. Although no religious sanctions exist to favor this kind of marriage, in customary law it is acceptable.[69]

The reader should note that Haq Bakhswana goes against the Islamic institution of marriage. Islam opposes denying women the right of inheritance or denying women the right to choose a marital partner. In fact, many would argue that Haq Bakhswana defiles the Holy Qur'an. According to Rana Riaz Saeed, a Pakistani development advocate and lobbyist, women's rights groups and human rights activists made legal attempts in 2006 to end such tribal customs, pointing out their inhumanity and arguing that these customs are nothing more than a *bid'ah* (fabrication or innovation) against Islam. They insisted that this feudal tradition should be forbidden.[70]

As of June 2007, the legislative bill in question was still pending in the Ministry of Religious Affairs. If the Ministry of Law and Justice approves this legislation, then the bill will be brought before Pakistan's parliament. Meanwhile, as the bill is shuffled through the bureaucratic process, a multitude of young women's lives are being sacrificed—all in the name of landownership and economic gain. Even if this bill becomes law, there is no guarantee that the existing government will enforce it, given the entrenched feudal culture in Pakistan.

Although there is no such legislation pending in the U.S. Congress, one can only imagine that the issue of voluntary virginization remains in the hearts and on the lips of virtually every neoconservative politician. Since the early 1980s, the neoconservative movement in the United States has unleashed a backlash against progressive movements of the 1960s and 1970s—civil rights, feminism and reproductive rights, the sexual revolution, recreational drugs, free speech, and human rights for ethnic, religious, and sexual preference minorities. Part of the backlash has been an attempt to encourage or enforce sexual abstinence in teenagers, and an enormous increase in state and federal funding for such programs has fed the trend. Organizations like Abstinence Clearinghouse have conventions in hotbeds of vice like Las Vegas and Miami Beach and take the abstinence message into schools—again, with government funding pushed by conservatives who insist that drops in teenage birth rates are due to their abstinence efforts, not to sex education and the availability of birth control. They dole out misinformation about the ostensible failure of condoms and cheerfully recount tales of revirginization in which people mentally regain their lost virginity.[71] A quick review of their Web site offers a virtual bazaar of abstinence products, including posters, bookmarks, tattoos, magnets, key chains, bumper sticks, and jewelry.[72]

Just what does it mean to be a virgin? It depends on whom you ask. For example, in a survey of University of Arizona students, some believed that only intercourse ended one's virginity, while others believed that anything past kissing eliminated one's "purity." Other opinions expressed about oral and anal sex, including that between homosexual couples, indicated that the concept of virginity isn't monolithic. Some students commit to abstinence until marriage after losing their virginity, a mental state called secondary virginity, but other students believe that you can "regain" virginity only if it has been "stolen" from you, such as through rape. The director of the Arizona state-funded Abstinence First says that abstinence is becoming more mainstream, and while the program prefers that students use abstinence to avoid pregnancy and sexually transmitted diseases, it does include contraceptives, "but in a kind of sneaky way," to avoid sending students mixed messages.[73]

A lesbian undergraduate student (and nonpracticing Catholic) writing for the University of Oklahoma daily newspaper says that because the Church doesn't recognize the gay, lesbian, bisexual, and transgender community, they must come up with their own standards for what constitutes loss of virginity. She notes that heterosexuals seem to put more emphasis on losing virginity as a rite of passage, whereas homosexuals, at least lesbians, put more emphasis on the whole experience of a relationship. She argues, "We feel that in a feminist culture, sex is about gaining a new sense of one's self versus losing one's self to the whims of the patriarchy."[74] A quick perusal of the Internet indicates that she probably receives hate mail frequently.

A Tragic Legacy

Enforced virginity, honor killings, sexual subjugation, and violence take an enormous toll on the women and families living under such inhumane conditions. Although families or clans claim that they will suffer if an honor killing is not committed to cleanse a besmirched reputation, the killing, too, must have a traumatic effect on them. So does pretending that such a killing never occurred or that the victim never existed. The young boys who are coached to participate in murdering their own sisters or other female relatives carry a psychological burden for the rest of their lives. The long-term effects also tarnish the innocent children who are forced to witness such heinous murders.

On July 14, 2006, the killers of 25-year-old Samaira Nazir, a British Pakistani girl, were sentenced to life in prison. In a story unparalleled in the grotesque cruelty of its execution, Samaira, who had defied her family by marrying an Afghan immigrant, was held down by her mother while her brother stabbed her more than eighteen times. Her two nieces, aged 2 and 4, were made to watch as their young rebellious aunt was given the treatment deserved by girls who defy the will of their family. When the police arrived at the behest of a neighbour who heard Samaira's screams, they found her bloodied body in the hallway of her home. A silk scarf had been tied tightly around her neck and her throat sliced three times. The two nieces, their clothes spattered with blood, watched as their aunt's body was carried away to the morgue.[75]

The grief of an honor-killing victim's mother is surely as strong as the shame she would bear if her child were alive. Women who live in fear of honor killing, virginity tests, rape, and domestic violence—as well as the perpetrators—experience life as a dark, shameful nightmare.

Crimes against women in the name of honor and shame have been occurring around the world for a long time; only recently have the media given much attention to such crimes. Mass media usually cover such issues simplistically, blaming patriarchal culture and religious customs without giving any kind of cultural context or historical background. Traditions and customs of a society develop alongside its economic system and are intricately tied to the material changes. Adding fuel to this fire are the rigid, fundamentalist interpretations of religious texts that perpetrate misogynistic doctrine.

The physical being at no time is disconnected from the mental being. For many women in different parts of the world, the horror of honor killing, the mental anguish of being "proper" and not doing anything to arouse suspicion or generate gossip that could jeopardize their lives, is a terrible way to live. Women who carry the heavy mental burden of men's honor at the cost of their bodies are mentally drained; they pass the same toll to their daughters. Being a good mother means being complicit in the oppression of your own daughter—a dreadful legacy. Women who become sexually active too early in life, especially when coerced by traditional practices, carry an ineffable burden. Women who engage in revirginization do so out of guilt, poor self-image, and even fear of death. The exaltation of virginity dismisses a woman's individuality and humanity, essentially reducing her to a sexual organ with a price tag.

Consecrated virgins—as well as those innocent pubescent Punjabi girls who are forced to be the Brides of the Qur'an—must deny their human biology and chemistry, a sacrifice that some might question. In fact, any extreme action taken by a woman to protect her virginity for the reward of a husband, a better spot in heaven, or the highest bidder is a desperate relinquishing of control of her own body.

Sterility, Childbirth, Taboos, and Popular Religious Practices

In traditional societies, women face an array of restrictions and challenges around the issues of sexuality and reproduction. The problem of sterility holds especially tragic consequences; therefore, women make enormous efforts to become pregnant, with hopes of giving birth to a son. A unique set of accepted practices—the combination of religious doctrines, cultural taboos, and a belief in the supernatural—hold sway over a woman's reproductive life in traditional, patriarchal-based settings. This chapter focuses primarily on these popular religious practices, as they impact women in general and Muslim women in particular. It also deals with the dominance of male power structures over women's bodies, resulting in the use of medical technologies (e.g., the sonogram) to promote a widespread practice of gender preference. Also discussed are strategies that women adopt to survive, and often subvert, restrictive environments.

Religious vs. Cultural Norms

The gradual transmission of cultural taboos and folk beliefs from one generation to the next is a natural process in any given society. Therefore, it is not surprising to find traces of pre-Islamic customs and beliefs in Arabic culture and in those peoples who have been conquered and converted to Islam. The same holds true for many Persian (Iranian) traditions from pre-Islamic Iran. For example, traces of ancient Zoroastrian religious practices carry over to contemporary Iranian belief systems. Thus the reader should be aware that no culture ever dies completely to be replaced by an entirely new system of beliefs. Rather, cultures are modified to fit the needs of a society at a given time in history.

It is generally acknowledged that religion is a key factor in social and cultural outcomes, intertwined with issues of nationalism, human rights, ethnicity, gender dynamics, and (most recently) globalization. In recent years, one sees religious influence in the politics of abortion in the United States, the emergence of Hindu nationalism, communal violence in South Asia, the Taliban's rise to power in Afghanistan, and the bloody wars and ethnic cleansing among Balkan religious groups.

In many traditional societies, cultural norms are often mistaken for and, in fact, dictated by religious doctrine. A good example of this, as mentioned in chapter 1, is the practice of young Punjabi girls being "married to the Qur'an." In the Muslim world, these cultural norms have their roots in pre-modern patriarchal systems, which have been legitimized under the banner of "Islam." During the medieval period in Islam (seventh through thirteenth centuries), power and knowledge were concentrated in the hands of men. Men laid exclusive claim to political, religious, and social authority. Since medieval times, scientific and literary texts regarding sexuality and fertility have fallen under the domain of male authority. Then, as now, obsessive interest existed in a woman's body and her sexual self, an obsession far removed from the true practice of Islam. Cultural taboos mixed with Islamic doctrine have resulted in a plethora of texts, precepts, and popular "religious" practices, trapping Muslim women in an intricately woven net that is at once authoritative and arbitrary. Lila Abu-Lughod notes that "in any community of Muslims, individuals say and do a vast number of things, sometimes drawing on or invoking recognizable Islamic traditions and concepts, sometimes not."[1] She further emphasizes the need to examine how individuals make reference to Allah's will in one moment and do something totally different that contradicts Islamic doctrine in another.

Sadly, in recent scholarship on women and Islam, the focus is all too often restricted to the abuse of women, whether among Afghanistan's Taliban or in African nations, where atrocities such as female circumcision are often linked to cultural and religious beliefs. While these studies contribute to our understanding of part of the equation, they have neglected another dimension, namely, the agency of women within these social contexts. Not all women living in highly restrictive or repressive environments respond passively to patriarchal dictates. In fact, many find ways to assert their independence and to pursue what they believe will support their own interests. It is impossible to fully understand the status and quality of life of these women if one looks only at the established social, cultural, and religious institutions intended to control and govern their lives. The overall effect of these institutions is only part of the picture. Equally as important are the diverse and often subtle strategies women use to accommodate, alleviate, or even subvert efforts to control their minds, bodies, and lives.

Importance of Fertility

The historical importance of fertility in Muslim culture is expressed by the Arabic proverb "*Iilli khallaf ma maat,*" which means "one who reproduces does not die." It is widely believed that infertility is a fundamental failure, particularly in Muslim countries.[2] Concerning the importance of fertility among the women in Iran, Henri Masse wrote:

In the Orient, a sterile woman has always been the object of scorn. Chardin (4:441) shows this clearly: "Sterile women are the most superstitious of all, for since sterility is the greatest disaster in the Orient, there is nothing in the world that a woman will not do to be rid of her disability. I have seen women who did not know what saint to make their vows to next, and they even made pilgrimages to Christian churches. All the more reason, then, to go to the Islamic oratories and sanctuaries. . . . Sometimes they do not even hesitate to ask for an effective remedy from a Christian traveler.[3]

As evidenced by Masse, an infertile woman is considered disabled. In Persian (Farsi), the infertile woman is equated with a fruitless tree, *derakhte bi samar,* a metaphor for being useless.

From pre-Islamic times, among the Arab nomads, sterility served as justifiable grounds for divorce. Sterility was believed to be the woman's biological fault. After Islamic law, or Sharia, was introduced, stricter criteria for granting the divorce were instituted. For example, although the husband was allowed to take a second wife, the first (sterile) wife had the option of remaining in the household. Embedded in Sharia was a double standard, however. If the husband was infertile, the wife was not allowed to take a second husband, although she was allowed to apply for divorce. In general, these same criteria apply today, although regional differences exist in interpreting Sharia.

The emergence of Islam resulted in certain religious rules superseding nomadic laws. For example, according to religious law, a woman cannot be divorced if there is any chance she is pregnant. This Sharia was not intended to protect the woman, but rather to ensure that any child born would inherit the father's name and property. Another Sharia governing divorce still holds true for every Muslim: after divorce is finalized, the woman must still wait at least three months before entering a new relationship with another man. She must observe *ida* (abstaining from sex) for three months to ensure that three menstrual periods have passed, thus erasing all possibility of pregnancy. Not surprisingly, her husband is *not* restricted from having sex during this ida. He is free to marry another woman at any time. At first glance, this Sharia seems to protect the woman. If she becomes pregnant and has been divorced based on sterility, she can go back to her husband and refuse the divorce. Nonetheless, the rule of Sharia primarily benefits the husband. For example, in Shi'i Sharia, a man is allowed to take "temporary" wives during the ida, thereby using religious law to legitimize multiple wives.

While not every Muslim society practices one specific type of Sharia, the vagueness of Qur'anic verse allows for manipulation of religious rules that invariably subvert the first wife's position and power. Although an infertile woman may always be risking divorce, there are exceptions. Unni Wikan tells us that an infertile Omani woman has many other qualities as a person, qualities that are prominent in her husband's evaluation of her: "loyalty and faithfulness, tact and hospitality, love and considerateness."[4] Fertility is desired, but not a condition. "The whole person is not stigmatized by failure in any one particular respect."[5] In such cases, husbands may take a second wife [co-wife] who is able to bear children, and thus he remains married to his infertile wife. The author does not offer any findings regarding the psychological consequences for the infertile woman who must share her husband with a fertile co-wife. One can only imagine the heavy psychological burden on both women.

Sterility, Childbirth, Taboos, and Popular Religious Practices

Indeed, a recent study addressing the psychological and sociological outcomes of infertile women suggests that "while women may find it easier to recognize infertility as a 'problem,' many women still experience a strong desire to become mothers and motherhood is viewed as central, 'normal,' and an expected role for women."[6]

A separate study conducted in Pakistan by Bhatti, Fikree, and Khan places emphasis on the support typically provided to an infertile woman by her husband, his family, and her own family and friends.

> Generally speaking, spouses and in-laws were very supportive. . . . Only three men refused to go for semen analysis despite being strongly advised by the health care providers. The helplessness of women in trying to get their husbands to seek care is voiced by this 36-year-old Mohajir woman:
>
> "Now God forbid, if I say anything to my husband and then I conceive. Then he will ask where has this come from? I have heard stories like that. That's why I don't say anything to my husband. I am telling you this, or if it is any friend of mine, I tell her, but I have never let my husband know about this."

The authors of this study caution that the sampling of women *excluded* barren women deserted by their husbands. The following comments are also telling:

> Threats of second marriage or divorce either by spouses or in-laws were not mentioned by any of the respondents even when we specifically asked them. On the other hand, there seems to be considerable support from spouses and in-laws. The women that we have interviewed were all still in sexual union with their husbands. We did not interview any women who were either separated or divorced as a result of their infertility. Furthermore, we did not interview women whose husbands had opted for a second marriage. We feel that perceptions of these women would have enriched our results, especially reflecting on their mental well-being.
>
> Although infertility is one of the worst afflictions that can befall a woman and divorce or taking of a second wife is common among these couples, in our sample the majority of husbands and in-laws supported the infertile women. No threats of second marriage and divorce were mentioned by any of the respondents. In fact, a woman mentioned that she

was the proponent for her husband in a second marriage. However, social pressures usually lead these women to socially isolating themselves.

There can be no doubt that the limited sampling of women in this study skewed the findings. Had the authors addressed a larger number of women, surely the results would have been significantly different. This point is clearly noted by the authors themselves.[7]

Another study conducted in Israel reveals a deeper understanding of the negative psychological and emotional effects of infertility among Jewish women:

Infertility became a master status for these [infertile] women, undermining any other merits and achievements they might have. Most women fully internalized and endorsed the pronatalist discourse by way of pursuing long-term and burdensome infertility treatments, at any personal cost. The paper argues that resistance to the stigma of infertility is only possible where women dare question the motherhood imperative, which is clearly not the case with most Israelis. Material and mental resources needed for resisting the stigma of infertility are found among [only a] few educated professional women.[8]

In Yemen, a woman's self-identity as well as her claims to social status depend entirely on marriage and fertility. A study of Yemeni women underscores the importance of moving from the status of virgin to that of wife and mother. Rules and regulations regarding the physical appearance of unmarried women differ markedly from those for married women. Wives are expected to adorn themselves to demonstrate care for and sexual interest in their husbands. The author concludes that Yemeni women gain their full identity through reproductive sexual activity. Those who have achieved reproductive success are most apt to talk about sexuality and to display their jewelry and clothing during all-women gatherings.[9]

These studies from Oman, Pakistan, Israel, and Yemen underscore the hard reality of being a childless woman in societies that value women primarily for their reproductive ability.

Remedies for Infertility

For centuries, the belief that a woman's value depends on her ability to procreate has led women to seek remedies ensuring fertility. As folk and re-

2.1. Three examples of talismans engraved in brass used for love, affection, and fertility.

ligious beliefs have intersected, women have turned to "popular religious practices," including belief in the Elm-e Ramel, Funun-e Sehr va Jadu (the "sciences" of geomancy, witchcraft, and sorcery), belief in the power of various *jinn* (spiritual beings), and reliance on *hakims*,[10] the local religious "medicine men."

As evidenced by the proliferation of old manuscripts now available on the global market—manuscripts satisfying all levels of complexity and range of subjects—an interest in the supernatural and reliance on magical cures for infertility have hardly diminished. During a 2004 trip to Iran, I purchased a number of reprints of these old manuscripts from religious bookstores in Tehran. The manuscripts include cures for infertility and other sexual problems. Some are "magic" formulas based on numerology, specifically the Abjad numerical system. This system uses groupings of Arabic letters (appended to Hebrew, Syriac, Aramaic, and Greek letters). The letters themselves have no meaning independently. Rather, they are used exclusively as memory aids. Many of the formulas contain a chronogram—the numerical sum of the letters of a word. These chronograms hold specific meaning in terms of cure. I studied the basics of this "science" called *hurufi wa raqami* (science related to letters and numbers), and with the help of an expert, I was able to decipher some of the simpler charts. Reading more complicated formulas and charts requires significant expertise. Below is a "cure" for avoiding miscarriage, written in Arabic and excerpted from *al-Kabrit*:

> To make sure that a woman remains healthy during her pregnancy she should write [a talisman] on a piece of paper and hang it around her neck at all times, then she will have a safe and full-term pregnancy.[11]

Another publication, *Haftad Du Div* (Seventy-two demons), contains information on talismans and cures. Based on its narrative style and grammar, *Haftad Du Div* was most likely written during the early nineteenth century. Included are cures for infertility caused by jinns, spirit beings believed by Muslims to assume various forms and to exercise supernatural powers. The following excerpt deals with miscarriage:

> One of the jinns named Ghatis and one noble named Asef Ibn Barkhia came to Suleiman the Prophet of God (may peace be upon him); they said these Junun [pl. of Jinn] are wicked, thus Suleiman asked the 72 divs or Junun to come to see him one by one. He asked each and every one of them about remedies to protect humans from their wickedness. The following are the conditions in which the jinn will cause sickness in the human. One of the concerns is on becoming pregnant and the safe delivery of a pregnant woman.
>
> The third Div appeared. Suleiman asked him, "What is your name?" The Div replied, "My name is Sabasashat." His head was like a pig and his hands and legs resembled those of a cow. Suleiman said to him, "Oh, you miserable, damned creature, where do you live? And what kind of harm do you bring to these people?" Sabasashat replied, "I live in ruined houses, near fire temples. I will visit the pregnant woman carrying her second child. I cause her miscarriage. I breathe from my nostrils, so she can never have any other pregnancy." Suleiman said, "May Allah con-

demn you. What is the cure for the woman?" Div said, "Write down this talisman . . . then cover it in beeswax, put it in water. Then the woman should put a small amount of wolf's liver inside a date and eat it. She will be cured."[12]

Shaykh Baha'i, a Persian author from the sixteenth-century Safavid dynasty, was hired by the Safavid court to write as many texts as possible about the Shiite religion. Among these was a popular, multivolume book entitled *The Virtues of the Beautiful Names of Allah*. The following citation from Baha'i's book reveals the use of one of Allah's ninety-nine names:

> The cure for a sterile woman: the sterile woman must fast for seven days, then she must use the name al-Musawar [one of Allah's names in Arabic, meaning the creator, the sculptor, and the painter]. Write it on a glass filled with water and while writing the word al-Musawar, she must recite it thirteen times. Then she has to drink the water. Soon she will be pregnant with a male child.[13]

Another manuscript, *Kunz al Hussain,* also uses the name al-Musawar to offer the same cure for sterile women. Furthermore, the manuscript associates this particular name (al-Musawar) with a numerical value (336), with a group of angels (Ijma'il, Sar Hami'l), and with the element of fire. In this way, religious elements (e.g., Qur'anic names of Allah) have been associated with magic and prescribed as fertility remedies for women.

In Muslim culture, one constantly hears the word *Allah* (and especially *Inshallah,* or God willing) in daily conversation, suggesting that all actions and outcomes are reliant on God's intercession. The word *Inshallah* is placed at the end of almost every magic formula, thus releasing from liability those *hakim* (medicine men) who prescribe cures. In other words, the cure cannot be guaranteed absolutely, since all events are at the mercy of Allah and dependent upon His will.

The reader may be surprised to learn that Islam absolutely forbids black magic, sorcery, and witchcraft, so the aforementioned practices, at the very least, appear to contradict Qur'anic dictates. A. Yusuf Ali, in his 1983 translation and commentary on the Qur'an, notes that Qur'anic chapter 113, *al Falaq* (Dawn), "provides the antidote to superstition and fear by teaching us to seek refuge in God from every kind of ill arising from outer nature and from dark and evil plottings and envy on the part of others":

Say: I seek refuge
With the Lord of the Dawn,
From the mischief
Of created things;
From the mischief
Of Darkness as it overspreads;
From the mischief
Of those who practice
Secret Arts;
And from the mischief
Of the envious one
As he practices envy.[14]

2.2. A talisman from Egypt inscribed with Qur'anic chapter *Al Falaq* (The Dawn) (113: 1–5) used as a wall decoration or hung above doorways to protect the residents from the envious eyes of evil.

Sterility, Childbirth, Taboos, and Popular Religious Practices

Furthermore, Ali calls attention to:

> Those who practice Secret Arts: literally, "those who blow on knots," this having been a favourite form of witchcraft practiced by perverted women. Such secret arts cause psychological terror. They may be what is called black magic, or secret plotting[s], or the display of false and seductive charms, or the spreading of false and secret rumours of slander to frighten men or deter them from right action. There is fraud in such things, but men are swayed by it. They should cast off fear and do their duty.[15]

Both the translation of chapter 113, *al Falaq*, and subsequent commentary allude to witchcraft and black magic, insisting that man must refrain from believing in any other power beyond the absolute power of God. Indeed, God can be the only healer of man; any beliefs and practices that employ sorcery are sinful and strictly forbidden.

And yet manuscripts found in religious bookstores today still contain bizarre remedies—incorporating the practice of Secret Arts—to address infertility, such as those offered by *al-Kabrit:*

> To know if a woman can get pregnant or not the remedy is: the woman should insert peeled garlic in various parts [cavities?] of her body at night. When she wakes up the next day she should copulate with her husband. During sex with her husband, if she finds a taste of garlic in her mouth, she will be pregnant.
>
> The woman wishing to get pregnant should prepare the following mixture: some pieces of onion, gallnuts, a clove of garlic, and some cow fat. She should prepare the mixture with oil and wrap this potion in a clean piece of muslin and insert it like a tampon inside her vagina (after her period is over). She should keep the content of this tampon for three days inside her vagina. After the three days are over, she should copulate with her husband. She will get pregnant.[16]

Another manuscript (which includes no reference to its original printing) is *Shafaul Isteqam wa al Hazan,* reprinted in 1981. The text includes remedies for infertile women, including one magic formula to be copied on two pieces of paper and eaten every day. Inshallah (God willing), the woman will become pregnant. Further instruction suggests that the woman may wear the same formula around her neck or around her right arm. Apparently the potency of the formula is equally effective, regardless of technique.[17]

Once a woman becomes pregnant, further prescriptions are suggested, commingling folk and religious beliefs. For example, to ensure the birth of good-looking children, an expectant mother must recite the longest chapter in the Qur'an (Sura 36) forty times. She does this over forty thoroughly red apples, blowing on each apple after each recitation, and eating one red apple each day for forty days. Doing so will produce a child with a good complexion. This practice is prescribed in *Kolsum Naneh* of Mula Agha Jamal Khansari, one of the favorite clergymen of Iran's sixteenth-century Safavid court.

2.3. Qur'anic inscription on a piece of board. Pregnant women rinse these with water and drink the ink collected. This board was made for the photographer, Laurie Cook Heffron, in Dan Tchiao in the district of Magaria, Niger.

Sterility, Childbirth, Taboos, and Popular Religious Practices

Also mentioned in *Kolsum Nane* is the protection of women from evil spirits. In the sixth chapter, *Dar babe Zaeidan-e Zanan Zaou va Amal va Mutealeghate An* (On the subject and matters related to women's delivery), the author notes that in order to block the harmful effects of *āl* (similar to jinn),[18] the midwife must carry an uncased sword to the new mother's room, wave the sword in all four corners, and repeat the following lines:

khesh mikesham, khesh mikesham (I scratch, I scratch)
khesh haye khesh khesh mikesham (I scratch scratches)

According to popular Islamic belief, āl is afraid of the name of God. To make āl disappear, the believer should say, *"bism-e Allah"* (in the name of God). Jinns are supposed to be afraid of iron and other metallic objects, thus the necessity of using an uncased sword.[19]

According to *Haftad Du Div,* every child that is born has an invisible jinn attached to its spirit which is identical to that child in every way. What follows are instructions to a barren woman or to a woman who has failed to carry a child to full term. The instructions will prevent the child from being stillborn as a result of this particular jinn (*hamzad,* or jinn that is a birth twin). I offer a loose translation of pages 104–5 from this manuscript:

I bind the *hamzad* [that will kill the unborn child]
I bind the child him/herself . . .
[The barren woman or pregnant woman] must borrow flour from seven neighboring houses all situated to the left of her own house. From this flour she must bake bread, inscribe the talisman [on page 105] on this bread, and feed the bread to a female dog. When this dog gives birth, all of its puppies will be dead, and whenever the woman gives birth, Inshallah, her baby will survive.

Formulas for ensuring that pregnancy will be successful and that one's child will not be stillborn abound in other manuscripts such as *Asrar-e Ghasemi* and *Kunz al Hussain.*

Protection from the Evil Eye

One might assume that remedies and practices to divert evil spirits are found only in dated manuscripts from past centuries. In fact, these practices persist today in Islamic cultures. Commercial amulets to divert evil spirits

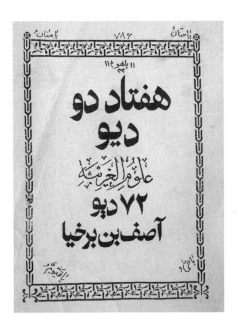

2.4, 2.5, 2.6. The cover and pages 104–5 of the book *Haftad Du Div* (Seventy-two Demons), which offer instructions for using talismans to increase a woman's chances of becoming pregnant and to prevent stillbirth.

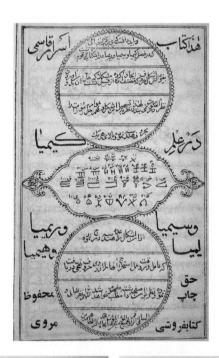

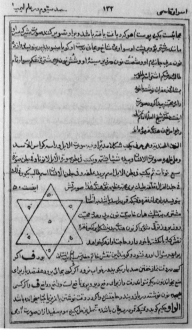

2.7, 2.8, 2.9. Cover page of *Asrar-e Ghasemi* and two pages (131–32) of directions for creating a talisman that will make someone fall madly in love with you.

2.10, 2.11, 2.12, 2.13. Cover page of *Kunz al Hussain* and three pages (252–54) offering other formulas to women for attracting husbands.

are sold openly in the markets of Saudi Arabia. I have accrued a substantial collection of gold and silver cases with Qur'anic inscriptions, purchased in Saudi Arabia. An incredible array of this type of talismanic jewelry is widely available in Saudi and other Middle Eastern markets, representing an impressive variety of decorative designs and functions.

2.14. (*left*) Indian amulet for girls and young women. Cowry shells, pierced buttons, the color red, and the small mirror all work together to guard against infertility and the evil eye. 2.15. (*right*) Silver amulets in the shape of hands or swords are designed to protect the woman from the evil eye.

2.16. Turquoise blue is one of the predominant colors found in protective amulets. Here are a few examples of Iranian and Turkish amulets in blue glass beads used as door hangings, wall decorations, or jewelry.

2.17. Two amulets in the form of jewelry worn by women in Afghanistan and Morocco. The silver square (Afghanistan) adorned with lapis lazuli stone (a natural semiprecious stone in a deep blue) is a case holding pages of the Qur'an to protect the woman. The silver triangular case (Morocco) is worn to protect a woman's reproductive organs from the evil eye.

Eleanor Abdella Doumato describes the critical view taken by Wahhabis regarding amulets and techniques used to appease evil spirits. They insist that such power "should belong to God alone." Wahhabis are primarily concerned with *shirk,* a religious term of Qur'anic origin signifying the act of associating with God; in other words, accepting the presence at His side of other divinities. Doumato cites the writing of Muhammad ibn Abd al-Wahhab as evidence for rejecting such practices: "The Prophet saw a man carrying a garment which he claimed protected him against fever. . . . He [the Prophet] tore it to pieces recalling the verse ' . . . most of them believe in Allah and still practice Shirk.'" Doumato also calls attention to the fact that in "the scriptural sources . . . used to validate condemning these acts, women are usually the culprits."[20]

Sterility, Childbirth, Taboos, and Popular Religious Practices

2.18. Three talismans worn around the neck. The larger two silver pieces are Saudi Arabian Qurʻan cases, holding either an entire miniature Qurʻan or a few small pages for protection. The other object is a piece of charcoal with silver protective ends; these ends are removable so that one can use the charcoal to write on a piece of paper. This charcoal pendant is worn by pregnant women or small children to protect them from harm by jinn. The author purchased this object from the city of Broujard in Iran.

Since the introduction of Wahhabisim to Arabia in the early twentieth century, the art of sorcery—including the use of talismans to divert the evil eye—has been strongly discouraged. Although women are not singled out as more likely to engage in (what is now the illegal practice of) witchcraft, Doumato writes, "When [magic craft is] performed correctly by a man, in fact, it could be [considered] a profession."[21] In contemporary Saudi Arabia, even in the realm of spirit engagement, gender discrimination is pervasive.

Helen Regis describes protective amulets for Fulbe children in North Cameroon; these amulets contain verses from the Qurʻan. Serving as talismans, they are placed around the infants' necks during the first two years of infancy. One man told Regis that his son's amulet was for protection against *mistiri'en* (witches).

It is a flat square leather pouch which suggests that it contains writing! This surprised me at first because the religious *mallums* (learned religious teachers) are said not to believe in *mistiraaku* (witchcraft). The writing of Arabic for *layaaji* (amulet string, often using verses from the Koran) is typically done by male clerics. Women use and manipulate Arabic writing also. The fact that the *layyaru* (amulet) contains writing does not necessarily indicate that it was produced from within the "orthodox" terrain of the *mallums*. I discovered that medicinal writing (*bindi*) is shared among women and copied again and again, often by people who have very limited knowledge of Arabic.[22]

2.19. Leather pouch filled with Qur'anic verses serving as a talisman. This pouch was made for the photographer, Laurie Cook Heffron, by the imam of Dan Tchiao, a small village in the district of Magaria, Niger. Dan Tchiao is inhabited by the Hausa ethnic group. This pouch is known as *laaya* in Hausa. The Hausa are mostly Muslim.

Sterility, Childbirth, Taboos, and Popular Religious Practices

As evidenced above, individuals misuse Qur'anic doctrine, adding to or omitting from selected verses, thereby transforming sacred text into a magical "science." The general population blindly follows, assuming that this "science" has religious legitimacy and is sanctioned by the rule of Islam.

In her study of Fulbe society, Regis underscores the strong influence of the evil eye. Women rely on "protection" poems to keep their babies safe from witches, spirits, and envious neighbors. One poem describes the child being born "on the edge of the flood waters. It came like flotsam and jetsam, garbage carried on the waves of the flood. The analogy to garbage suggests that the child was not wanted by the mother, implying that her child is undesirable [and thus undeserving of harm]."[23] By devaluing the baby, the mother invokes protection against all harm. Amulets serve as talismans and provide further protection. They may be hung around the neck or pinned on the garments of young virgins, new brides, pregnant women, or babies. Qur'anic verse from chapter 113, *al Falaq*, is frequently included in amulets to deter evil eye. Protection is sought from

> the mischief
> Of the envious one
> As he practices envy.

The reader should note that translations of this Qur'anic verse often change "envious *one*" to "envious *eye*." Local populations, such as those studied by Helen Regis in Cameroon, are frequently illiterate or poorly versed in the Qur'an—and therefore unable to detect irregularities.

Alan Dundes notes a striking similarity of evil eye reports across various cultures, leading him to suggest "that the evil eye belief complex depends upon a number of interrelated folk ideas in Indo-European and Semitic worldview." He further states, "In the event of a successful attack by the evil eye, there are prescribed diagnostic and curative procedures available. One may first need to ascertain whether or not it is a true case of the evil eye and second, if it is who is responsible for it. Sometimes, the agent, who was perhaps an unwitting one, is involved in the ritual removal of the evil eye and its ill effects from the victim. He may, for instance, be asked to spit on the victim's face."[24] Dundes records that not only is the evil eye considered a threat to female breasts (the source of milk for baby's nourishment), but it is also a potential danger to male and female genitals. Thus magical countermeasures are necessary to protect and defend against its damaging effects.

2.20. A silver armband made with leather straps inscribed with talismanic words to protect against the jinn and the evil eye. This talisman was purchased by the author in the city of Shiraz.

The following excerpt reveals contemporary attitudes toward sorcery and black magic, particularly in regard to pregnant women and their babies. The full article appeared in 2004 in *Sayidaty*, a popular Arabic women's magazine with global readership.

New concerns about sorcery and specifically the use of a "pouch" are terrorizing women in Mauritania. This type of sorcery targets pregnant women and breastfed babies. People believe that the "pouch," which is a mixture of coal ashes and bird feathers, causes miscarriages in women and kills babies.

Legend has it that sorcerers who kill a hundred babies or cause the same number of pregnant women to miscarry earn a golden treasure from the king of genies. These rumors have been widely circulated among the poor, especially those who believe in magic and witchcraft.

One woman said, "During my pregnancy, I was extremely frightened, even of my own relatives. This is why I spent most of my time inside my bedroom reading magazines and listening to music." Another woman said, "Whenever I feel pregnant, I go to the capital city Nouakchott because my city, Nawathibo, is full of sorcerers wandering the streets in broad daylight. I don't want to be a victim of their magical spells."

Later in the article, a religious affairs official comments on the "pouch" terror:

Belief in such things is against Islamic teachings, and I advise Muslims to get away from these places and beliefs because in God's book [Qur'an] there are verses that cure all diseases.[25]

In denouncing one set of folk beliefs, the religious affairs official promotes another set of contradictory beliefs; that is, an insistence on the Qur'an's magical, curative capabilities. Regarding a woman's fertility and nursing capability, Abu-Lughod discovered the following taboo prevalent in the Egyptian community of Awlad Ali:

2.21. The Imam Reza mausoleum in the city of Mashhad in Iran. This holy shrine is a place of pilgrimage for the world's Shi'as. Many pilgrims believe in Imam Reza's power to heal all kinds of ailments, physical and mental. It is not unusual to see the believers chain or tie up a sick patient and/or leave a scrap piece of the patient's clothing or a lock on the shrine as they pray for Imam Reza's soul, hoping to receive a miracle or a sign to cure their patient. When a scrap of fabric or a lock is secured to the bars of the mausoleum, it will remain there until the pilgrim returns to remove it. This is an oath taken with a promise of return to pay their respects to this Shi'i imam.

Sometimes [a person] who has just been to a funeral should not enter the room of a woman who has just given birth; people say that it will "block" (*kabs*) the new mother, either drying up her milk or preventing her from conceiving again.[26]

Abu-Lughod's example offers further evidence that folk beliefs remain fully operative within Islamic environments.

2.22 & 2.23. Cased window in the courthouse of Bibi Pakdaman, a female Shiʿi shrine Karbala Gamm-e-Shah in Lahore, Pakistan, showing how believers in the supernatural power of imams secure locks or ties on this window hoping for a curative and positive outcome through the power of sincere praying and using the imam as an intermediary. The author took this picture on her visit to this shrine.

Sterility, Childbirth, Taboos, and Popular Religious Practices

2.24 & 2.25. Lahore, Pakistan, two views of a Shiʿi shrine Karbala Gamm-e-Shah showing the mausoleum with fabric, ties, and locks secured on the metal bars. Rows of fresh
red roses are draped over the top of the mausoleum. The red rose is commonly known
as Gol-e Mohammadi (the flower of the Prophet). Since Shiʿi imams are all descendants
of the house of the Prophet, the red rose takes a metaphoric meaning of establishing this
relationship with the Prophet.

2.26 & 2.27. Two images of a model of the Shiʿi shrine Karbala Gamm-e-Shah of Imam Hossain. This model is kept inside the shrine. Here devotees can attach threads, scraps of fabric, and padlocks to the posts of the model. They can also inscribe their wishes on the cardboard on which this model sits, as well as on the model's flat surfaces. The author found a few written wishes in Urdu asking that Imam Hossain grant them baby boys.

Dr. Noor Kassamali, an Egyptian physician who has worked in Africa and Central Asia (Afghanistan and Tajikistan), developed a growing "awareness of the role that healing rituals play in the lives of many of [her] patients." In her study of Muslim women émigrés, for example, she found that "Muslim women living in the greater Boston area incorporated religious and cultural beliefs into their health and well-being practices." Dr. Kassamali documented healing rituals related to the prophet Muhammad's daughter, Fatima Al Zahrah (also known as Bibi Fatima), who is venerated by Shi'i and Sunni Muslims alike.

An important point in Dr. Kassamali's research relates to the manner in which those Muslim Somali women (living in the Boston area) ask for help from Fatima Al Zahrah during childbirth. This ritual of *sitaat* (plural of *sitt*, meaning "lady" in Arabic) refers to those ladies, or women, in the household of the prophet Muhammad. In the *sitaat* ritual, specific songs are performed, asking Bibi Fatima to facilitate the woman's labor and delivery. The supplicants believe that since Bibi Fatima was a mother herself, she can understand and empathize with the woman's pain and suffering during childbirth.[27]

Below is an amulet from Egypt used to divert the evil eye. It contains Qur'anic chapter 114: 1–6, *Nas* (Mankind):

> Say: I seek refuge with the Lord, and Cherisher of Mankind
> The King (or Ruler) of Mankind
> The God (or Judge) of Mankind
> From the mischief of the Whisperer
> (Of Evil), who withdraws (After his whisper)
> (The same) who whispers
> Into the hearts of Mankind
> Among Jinns
> And among Men.[28]

Clearly, within patriarchal-based societies, not only must a woman reproduce successfully but—to strengthen her value to family and community—she must also demonstrate the ability to bear a male child and keep him safe from harm.

Preferred Gender

While the issue of gender preference is not tied to any particular religious teaching, the birth of a male child is always a cause for celebration in societies where patriarchal dominance holds sway. Benedicte Grima's ethnographic study of Paxtun women of Afghanistan sheds further light on this phenomenon. Grima cites two events that she personally witnessed when living in Afghanistan, events that demonstrate striking differences in attitude toward male and female births. In a small village (Ahmadi Banda), a boy and a girl are born in a single week. Grima notes that the birth of a child is classified in two categories: *xadi*, or happiness for the birth of boys, and *gham*, sorrow for the birth of girls. News of the boy's birth spreads quickly, while that of the girl is given far less attention. The two mothers are schoolteachers, both of whom Grima visits. The author documents the number of visitors, the types of gifts received, and the visitors' reactions to, as well as engagements with, the infants and their mothers. The mother of the baby girl receives far fewer visitors and gifts. Moreover, the atmosphere in the baby girl's house is quiet and somber. Visitors do not ask to see the baby girl. In contrast, visitors to the baby boy always ask to see him; the atmosphere is gay and celebratory. Grima describes the attitude of the baby girl's mother: "She seemed very evasive, and continually drifted from the answers [about the visitors and the gifts she received] to say, 'If only God had given me a son.'" The author concludes that the new mother's evasiveness is a result of "shame and embarrassment associated with the infant [girl]." Grima also relates a personal experience vis-à-vis her own daughter. Women in the village teased her with statements of surprise such as, "You really like her [your daughter], don't you?" Some even reproached Grima, insisting, "That one is not even pretty! Stop doting over her and get a son." This ethnographical encounter reveals the difference in value between male and female children from the moment of birth. Although Islam teaches that all are born with equal goodness and are equally valuable in the eyes of Allah, gender preference is irrefutable, deeply rooted in the dominant patriarchal culture of the land.[29]

The majority of manuscripts I accessed from Tehran's religious bookstores are reprints from Pakistan. These manuscripts most likely originated in Quetta, Pakistan, on the border with Afghanistan, where refugees fleeing from the Taliban settled. One manuscript previously cited, Sarbazi's *Shafaul Isteqam wa al Hazan*, directs a woman desiring male offspring to inscribe a specific formula with musk and saffron on deer skin. Sarbazi states that she must wear this around her neck at all times when having intercourse with her husband. Once again, *inshallah* (God willing), she will become pregnant with a male child.[30]

In *Kolsum Nane,* one finds a popular prescription for new brides to follow in order to conceive a son. After a newlywed couple's first night together, the women in the family gather. They pass the bloody napkin of the bride on a silver or gold tray, the napkin being proof of her virginity, or *neshaneh*—which in Persian means "a sign." Then, if the newlyweds are fed a mixture of cardamom seeds and rosewater, their firstborn will certainly be male.[31]

The same manuscript describes methods for determining whether a pregnant woman is carrying a boy or a girl:

> Call the pregnant woman and watch her steps. If she comes forward using her right foot first, the baby is a boy, and if she uses her left foot first, then the baby is a girl. Another way to know the gender of the unborn baby is to see if the right breast of the pregnant woman gets larger first, then the baby is a boy. If the left breast enlarged first the baby would be a girl, if the nipple of the pregnant woman becomes red in color her baby would be a boy and if it becomes darker and blackish in color then the baby would be a girl. Another way to know the gender of the unborn child is to observe the pregnant woman's mood. If the woman is agile, happy, and in a good mood, she is pregnant with a boy, and if she is lazy, sleepy, and not in a general good mood, then the child would be a girl.[32]

The reader should note that the expectant mother is blessed with an easy, felicitous pregnancy if carrying a boy. Just the opposite holds true if the child in utero is female.

One of many articles dealing with reproductive norms involves Jordanian women. L. Sawalha reports that from the beginning of a woman's marital life, she is pressured culturally and socially to conceive a son. In Jordan, as elsewhere in the Islamic world, a woman's value is linked to her ability to produce a male heir. Infertile women face divorce; fertile women must have spousal permission to use contraception. Sawalha emphasizes the inadequate reproductive, prenatal, and menopausal health care provided to Jordanian women.[33]

Among the Shi'a of Iran, women traditionally appeal to a particular Shi'i saint or imam, asking to be blessed with a son. This practice is still observed today, although primarily in small villages and among the more "traditionally religious" families who firmly rely on imams for curative purposes. If a male child is born, steps are taken to acknowledge the blessing. For example, a woman who previously had only daughters will vow to pierce her son's ear. Thus if she gives birth to a son, she will put rings in the child's ears. This procedure is a form of consecration, known as Ali Haydari Kardan, meaning to devote the son to the first Shi'i Imam, Ali. Another popular vow entails naming the child after the Imam Ali, or his son, Imam Hossain. The boy is named Gholam Ali, meaning the servant of Imam Ali, or Gholam Hossain, the servant of Imam Hossain. Sometimes the devotee makes a pilgrimage to the tomb of the saint and—if her wish for a male child is granted—the child will also be taken to the tomb and given the saint's name. Many names such as Gholam Reza (servant of Imam Reza) or Gholam Hassan (servant of Imam Hassan) are very popular among the Shi'is in Iran.

The sad reality of gender preference extends beyond Middle Eastern borders. In August 2004, the *Hindu,* an Indian magazine published in English, included the article "No Girls, Please, We're Indian." The author, Kalpana Sharma, asserts that "India now has the dubious distinction of being known as the country that likes to ensure that girls are never born":

> The 2001 census figures of the 0–6 years sex ratio are a stark illustration of this reality. We are facing a national emergency and epidemic that will have far-reaching social consequences. The adult sex ratio in India has been declining for several decades. . . . Sex-detection and sex-selective abortions are today spreading like an infectious disease, from the rich to the poor, from the upper castes to Scheduled Castes (SC) and even to the Scheduled Tribes (ST). No one wants girls anymore. Eliminate them now instead of dealing with the problems of raising a girl, goes the thinking behind the deadly actions.[34]

The article goes on to highlight dangerous sex ratios (national average of 927 girls to 1,000 boys), with the most distressing statistics emerging from the districts of Punjab and Haryana. Modern technology (the sonogram) originally devised to detect genetic abnormalities, as well as to determine the sex of the child, is now used to support gender preference in India. Substantial data reveals that both private and governmental facilities perform sex-selective abortions, despite legislation forbidding this practice.

Abortion is legal in India. When a woman seeks an abortion, the physician has no way of knowing which factors impact the woman's decision. Equally as disturbing is the assumption that both education and economic factors will influence women to make sensible reproductive choices. Apparently this is not the case. Sharma's article continues:

A survey by Action India of women in Delhi revealed that even highly educated women have resorted to as many as eight abortions to ensure that they only give birth to a son. In this country, education and economic progress seem to make no dent on attitudes. On the contrary, these are getting more embedded.[35]

In addition, surveys from Haryana and Punjab indicated that some of the women supported gender-selective abortion based on the faulty logic that fewer females in the future would automatically enhance their value. The reality is that men are taking brides from other states in India and from neighboring countries, and that these same women are becoming increasingly vulnerable to violent acts, especially in areas reporting the lowest (female) sex ratios. When gender preference is ensured through the use of sonograms and subsequent abortions, women of all castes and from all religious and educational backgrounds unwittingly promote genocide of their own gender. Enslaved by cultural and social attitudes, these women are being used as pawns to ill effect; that is, fewer women for every man, sanctioned misogyny, and the continuation of a patriarchal-based system that devalues female children.[36]

China is equally guilty. The latest figures show that China's birth gender ratio has risen to about 117 boys to 100 girls, compared with 108 boys to 100 girls in 1982. China's persistent bias in favor of male children continues to fuel gender-based abortions. In addition, an alarming number of baby girls are being abandoned at hospitals or placed in local orphanages for adoption.[37]

In exploring the issue of gender preference in cyberspace, I found multiple sites listed on Google.com. One Web site from India offered advice for predicting the gender of an unborn child.[38] If the conception process is easy, then the baby will certainly be a boy. If a woman has difficulty conceiving, she will likely give birth to a girl. The site insists that one must engage in as much sex as possible—even to the point of excess—in order to ensure conceiving a boy. In addition, dietary suggestions are presented: the woman must consume a diet high in salt and potassium and low in dairy products. The authors of this information choose to ignore medical research linking adequate intake of calcium to strong bone formation in the early stages of fetal development. Also missing is the fact that dairy products contain an especially significant form of calcium, one that can be digested and absorbed efficiently in the bloodstream. As for salt intake, medical research warns that immoderate salt consumption during pregnancy may result in high blood pressure and excessive water retention. The Web site goes on to suggest that a woman's chances of conceiving a girl may increase if the woman or her partner is in a stressful job or they smoke. In other words, the more negative your life experience, the more at risk you are for conceiving a girl. Although the article ends with a disclaimer, it is unsettling to consider the naïve individuals duped by this site. The potential harm that such sites hold for pregnant women and their unborn babies cannot be dismissed.

In cyberspace as in nonvirtual reality, the phenomenon of gender preference crosses cultural lines. A Web site hosted by an American woman speaks openly about the preference for a male baby, especially in regard to one's firstborn child. The site supports women using medical technology to determine the sex of their child, ending with remarks that are shockingly inaccurate:

> I thought I would give you a few links for preplanning the gender of your baby. After all, why leave anything up to chance! Actually, there is about a 51% chance that everyone will have a boy! Older mothers are also more likely to have boys, according to some recent studies.[39]

The World Wide Web holds no monopoly on disseminating information that may be used to further gender-selective purposes. A national report aired on July 12, 2005, on News Channel 5 in Austin, Texas, alerted viewers to the following:

> Medical Breakthroughs, Blood Test Can Detect Gender of Unborn Baby
> A new blood test for women can tell at five weeks into pregnancy whether they're having a boy or a girl. That's much earlier than the traditional ultrasound method used to determine gender. Ultrasounds aren't usually taken until eighteen weeks or later. The blood test can be taken at home. Some people worry that women will use the information to terminate pregnancies early. The same concern has come up before with the introduction of other gender tests. The company marketing the test in the United States, Pregnancystore.com, said the product has nothing to do with family planning; it's designed to answer an age-old question.[40]

A user-friendly blood test administered in the comfort and privacy of one's own home is not the problem. Who will use the test and to what ends—those are the troubling aspects of this news report. How many unborn females will be aborted, simply based on their gender? That the practice of gender preference continues into the twenty-first century, crossing over national boundaries from east to west, reveals the level to which "modern" women are held hostage by cultural and social norms based on centuries-old patriarchal dogma.

The Role of Fuqaha:
Birth Control and Abortion

To reconcile contradictions between government policy and religious doctrine, Islamic jurists throughout the Middle East often redefine Sharia (Muslim law) and reinterpret *ahadith* to fit their personal or government's fundamentalist needs. Some *fuqaha* are more restrictive than others when interpreting Sharia.[41] Religious rulings differ widely, depending on the various schools of thought within each region. Sunni Islam, for example, supports four major schools of interpretation. Shiites reject some of the rulings of these Sunni schools, favoring their own interpretive views.

Muslim scholars first look to the Qur'an when dealing with issues of birth control and abortion. According to chapter 81, *al-Takwir* (The folding up), the pre-Islamic practice of female infanticide is condemned as a capital crime. Man is asked to consider what his response will be on Judgment Day, "when the infant girl, buried alive, is asked for what crime she was slain."[42] This particular verse not only denounces female infanticide but also presents the question of whether *ijhad* (abortion) can be considered an act of murder. Muslim nations gathering at Cairo's 1994 International Conference on Population and Development further investigated this question.

Not surprisingly, consensus proved impossible. The sticking point around abortion centers on the "ensoulment" of the fetus, that is, when the fetus is "infused with life." Some ulama insist that ensoulment occurs at conception, while other jurists conclude that the fetus is ensouled—and therefore human—after 120 days. In chapter 23, *al-Mu'minun* (The believers), Qur'anic verses 12–14 describe Allah's creation of man. The order of development includes *nutfah* (sperm), *'alaqah* (blood clot), and finally *mudghah* (embryo):

Man We did create[43]
From a quintessence (of clay)
Then We placed him
As (a drop of) sperm
In a place of rest,
Firmly fixed;

Then We made the sperm
Into a clot of congealed blood;
Then of that clot We made
A (fetus) lump; then We
Made out of that lump
Bones and clothed the bones
With flesh; then We developed
Out of it another creature.
So blessed be God,
The Best to create!

More detailed information about creation is recorded in the Prophet's hadith: "The fetus is held as a drop of sperm for 40 days, as a blood clot for another 40 days, and then as an embryo for a final 40 days, at which point the fetus is created." Based on this particular hadith, some religious scholars consider the 120th day as the time that the soul enters the fetus. Other jurists cite 40 days as the time of creation. Still others hold fast to 80 days.[44]

One thing ulama agree upon is the permissibility of coitus interruptus, or ʿazl, as a contraceptive technique. However, both abortion and ʿazl are considered makruh (a detested practice but not forbidden.) From a woman's point of view, the problem with ʿazl is that the man controls the decision making and therefore all the power. Rulings grant men the right to use coitus interruptus if the woman agrees because "they [ulama] believe she has an overwhelming interest in bearing a child, and waives her own interests by consenting to contraceptive use."[45] Rulings based on a woman's wish to avoid pregnancy when the man refuses to practice ʿazl are conspicuously absent.

A review of abortion laws in Egypt, Kuwait, and Tunisia reveals "a correlation between the inflexibility of the criteria for allowing abortion and the centrality given to the Sharia as a source for legislation." In other words, the more conservative the Islamic state, the less likely it is that abortion will

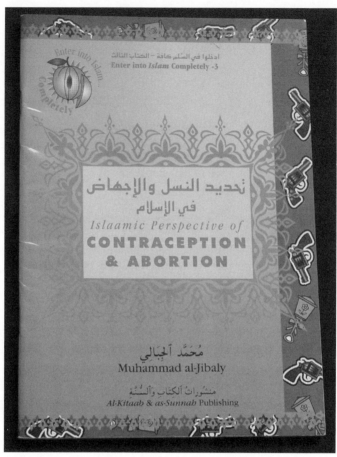

أدخلوا في السلم كافة – الكتاب الثالث
Enter into *Islam* Completely -3

تحديد النسل والإجهاض
في الإسلام
Islaamic Perspective of
**CONTRACEPTION
& ABORTION**

مُحَمَّد آلجِبَالي
Muhammad al-Jibaly

منشوراتُ ٱلكِتَابِ وَٱلسُّنَّةِ
Al-Kitaab & *as-Sunnah* Publishing

2.28. An example of contemporary Islamic text on birth control and abortion. Notice the border design of handguns and baby rattles.

be sanctioned. The Egyptian penal code stipulates, "Anyone who induces an abortion . . . [including] a pregnant woman willingly aborting her fetus is . . . subject to imprisonment. Physicians, pharmacists, surgeons, and midwives who perform an abortion are subject on conviction to hard labor."[46] In this type of repressive environment, women seeking abortion literally put their lives at stake. According to a 1998 study in *International Family Planning Perspectives,* approximately 216,000 women were hospitalized in Egypt in 1996 for treatment of abortion-related complications.[47]

Kuwaiti law offers a slightly less restrictive approach, allowing abortion if approved unanimously by a medical commission consisting of three Muslim physicians. Tunisian abortion law, based on a 1973 constitutional amendment, provides the most liberal framework of the three states. However, even in Tunisia, where abortion laws are fairly progressive, women still seek —and frequently suffer—the terrible results of unsanitary back-alley abortions. According to Oren Asman, "As long as Islamic society deems abortion as culpable and prohibited by religion, women will be afraid to undergo an abortion in an open way, under suitable medical supervision, even when the law approves of it."[48] Bowen makes an especially strong case pointing to the dilemma women face in every Muslim nation: "Over the centuries, men have formulated the discussions in Sharia on abortion and have interpreted these sources for the community. Although women bear the children, and sometimes abort fetuses, they have had no input into the debate on the permissibility of abortion."[49]

In the Islamic Republic of Iran, the issue of birth control—including the permissibility of abortion—has demanded creative strategies on the part of the state. After gaining power following the 1979 revolution, the ruling clerics dismantled Iran's relatively new family planning program and introduced pro-natalist policies.[50]

Currently Iran boasts one of the most progressive family planning programs in the developing world. What forces spurred this about-face in policy? After the overthrow of Mohammad Reza Shah Pahlavi, the fundamentalist clerics opened a Pandora's box by encouraging procreation. The Islamic Republic needed a vast army of young men to defend the homeland against Iraq. However, even with the catastrophic loss of life suffered in the war, Iran's burgeoning population placed undue stress on the nation's economy. From 1976 to 1986, the population increased by approximately 14 million— supplemented by an influx of refugees from neighboring Afghanistan.[51] The ruling clerics, painfully aware that their tenure in office was secure only as long as the economy remained stable, feared loss of power, status, and ultimately income. Claiming a sacred right to amend policy, even when their pronouncements ran contrary to long-held religious doctrine, they adopted a host of progressive policies. These new policies not only sanctioned the use of birth control pills and condoms but also made hysterectomies and contraceptive implants accessible to all women. Vasectomies became available to men.

At present all *official* positions on abortion still deny decision-making authority to the woman herself. However, while the Islamic regime "forbids" abortion, the clerics generally look the other way. In short, abortion is allowed within Iran as long as a woman is willing and able to jump through multiple hoops. She first must obtain a letter from her physician providing a "medical" justification for the procedure. Then she must procure her husband's consent. Finally, she must personally present the physician's letter to the magistrate. This charade suggests that those clerics presiding on the Sharia court retain ultimate judgment; in reality, abortion is a private matter between the woman and her physician.

Today, public discussion of sex in Iran remains taboo. The government forbids any advertising or mention of sexually related topics on state television or radio. Yet sex education classes instructing and encouraging men to use condoms properly are mandatory for all couples desiring a marriage license. Moreover, one is free to read—without any restrictions—governmental policies adopted to control the population and reproductive health of the population. The Ministry of Health provides informational pamphlets through free clinics and physicians. Quoting from a 2003 WHO international conference on the reproductive policies adopted by the Islamic Republic of Iran:

> The Government has taken policy measures, made legislative changes and institutional changes at the national level to enforce reproductive rights. Selecting the best method of contraception freely and with the best possible knowledge during the counselling process was adopted as the best policy for family planning services at the national level. Also, reproductive health needs of women, men, and adolescents/youth are explicitly recognized as priorities in the Health Sector Reform Package.[52]

In an interview on the subject of condoms in Iran, National Public Radio (NPR) reported that female employees at condom factories attempted to hide their occupation from friends and family. When asked what the factory manufactures, the women's responses were vague. Some insisted that they worked in a governmental latex factory manufacturing rubber gloves. On the one hand, cultural norms drive these women to shame and embarrassment while, on the other, Iran's government proudly boasts the only state-supported condom factory in the Middle East. In fact, Iran claims to be the biggest producer of condoms in the Middle East, supplying 90 percent of Iran's needs. The Keyhan Bod Condom factory, located about two hours from Tehran, produces nearly 45 million condoms a year, in thirty shapes, flavors, and colors. "About 80 percent of our production is plain condoms destined for the Health Ministry," says general manager Kamran Hashemi. "The fancier ones go to the private sector. The favourite colour is pink and, for flavour, mint."[53]

Inarguably, economics lies at the heart of the massive effort to reform reproductive policy in Iran. Politico-religious leaders understand that people will not tolerate prolonged periods of unemployment, poverty, and lack of opportunity. This fact is underscored in the May 2002 *Journal of Population Research:* "The Iranian experience raises some doubts about the efficacy of policy pronouncements by government or fatwa by religious leaders in modifying the actions of the populace, if these pronouncements are out of tune with emerging trends."[54]

It is interesting to note that in the radically fundamentalist environment of Iran, dedicated social workers and researchers have been able to make positive changes in public attitudes toward the use of condoms, not only for family planning but also for HIV/AIDS prevention.

2.29. Kayhan Bod's marketing team cleverly makes use of the Farsi word *nike,* meaning kindness. Consumers mistakenly assume this product is a division of Nike Sportswear.

Sterility, Childbirth, Taboos, and Popular Religious Practices

2.30–2.36. Front and back of various condom packages manufactured under the auspices of the Islamic Republic of Iran. The use of the English language only on external packaging gives the impression that this product is imported. Even the insert information is written in English/Persian. One must read the small print to see that the condom is indeed made in Tehran.

2.37. Kayhan Bod's insert information in Persian (and English on its reverse side) guiding the user in the proper way to wear a condom.

In 2005 questionnaires were sent to the "most influential Shiite Muslim clerics to elicit their views on condom use, the government's role in AIDS prevention, and how society should deal with HIV-infected Iranians. . . . Nearly all were in favor of the government's efforts. The UN AIDS office plans to compile them [results of the questionnaires] into a book to be distributed at mosques."[55] It is refreshing to learn that mosques can be used as centers for education where the public can obtain important information relating to health.

Dr. Arash Alaei is one of Iran's most respected AIDS researchers and the main architect of Iran's national HIV prevention program, a program that is being exported to Afghanistan, Lebanon, Iraq, Syria, Sudan, Pakistan, North Africa, and other Muslim nations. In fact, the World Health Organization named Alaei's clinics the best-practice model for the Middle East and North Africa. With the election in 2005 of the ultraconservative president Mahmoud Ahmadinejad, many AIDS workers feared a reversal of their hard-won progress. Ahmadinejad's health minister told a news conference that AIDS wasn't a priority for the government. The education minister stopped the printing of pamphlets for young students, saying the pamphlets needed revisions. It was uncertain whether distribution of these pamphlets would proceed. However, Dr. Alaei indicated that he was optimistic about the Islamic Republic's AIDS program and believed that progress would continue.

Whenever religious law substitutes for secular law, as is the case in Iran, women are invariably at risk. Even in the Republic of Turkey, which fosters a façade of secularism—primarily to curry favor with the West and to gain admission to the European Union—women suffer under a criminal code that includes discriminatory provisions relating to sexual and reproductive rights. Moreover, they are denied access to resources impacting their very survival. According to Dicle Kogacioglu's research on honor crimes (the murder of a woman by family members who do not approve of the woman's sexual behavior), "In modern-day Turkey, with a population of seventy million, there are a total of eight women's shelters and no twenty-four-hour hotlines for any form of violence against women."[56]

Against this deplorable backdrop, third world and first world feminists have banded together to lobby against a plethora of laws in the Turkish Penal Code, including legislation that deals with honor crimes and abortion rights. Particularly active in this struggle is Women for Women's Human Rights (WWHR), an international organization with multiple bases throughout the

Middle East and Africa. Although honor crimes are referred to as "crimes of tradition," Kogacioglu insists that feminists working for legislative reforms in Turkey should target institutional policies instead of focusing primarily on (Islamic) tradition. For it is the men and the male-dominated institutions (i.e., the European Union as well as the Turkish state) that promote suppression of women's basic human rights while claiming to make efforts to contest tradition.

Women in Malaysia, for example, from housewives to prostitutes, are especially at risk for HIV because Malaysian men refuse to wear condoms. While Muslim clerics in Malaysia will not step forward and sanction condom use, they do welcome healthcare professionals filling this role. The most hopeful development and perhaps the answer to protecting Malaysian women from contracting HIV from their partners or husbands is the marketing of a new condom designed for and worn exclusively by women. This newly designed product finally will give women the power and control they have customarily lacked.

Muslim religious authorities and imams in Bangladesh serve as excellent role models for other Muslim nations, in that these individuals participate in training programs regarding issues such as HIV/AIDS and gender equality. Senegal also must be acknowledged for its efforts to recruit religious Muslim leaders in sharing responsibility for educating the public about AIDS prevention.

Establishing sane reproductive and societal rights for all women in the Muslim world is surely a daunting task. However, it is women advocating for women through organizations such as the WWHR that will ultimately reverse repressive religious, political, and economic policies.

Vanguards of Change:
Women Supporting Women

Remarkably, Muslim women living in highly repressive societies still manage to find ways to assert sexual independence and protect their legal interests. To fully appreciate the creative strategies women have developed, one must look beyond the patriarchal, social, cultural, and religious institutions intended to control their lives. Instead, attention must be afforded to the ways in which women support each other through education, advocacy, community, and role modeling.

Beginning in nineteenth-century Egypt, Muslim women attempting to move toward feminism and modernity met with iron-fisted resistance. Even today, it is not unusual for oppressive governments to dismiss, imprison, assassinate, or issue fatwas against outspoken women who champion human rights and who attempt to educate other women regarding feminist issues. Nawal Saadawi, an Egyptian physician, novelist, and activist, is a prime example. Dr. Saadawi has written twenty-seven books, focusing particularly on Arab women's sexuality and legal status. Her 1972 publication, *Women and Sex,* aroused the wrath of political and theological authorities. As a result, Dr. Saadawi lost her position as chief editor of a health journal and as assistant general secretary of the medical association in Egypt. In 1980, after fighting steadfastly for Egyptian women's social and intellectual freedom, she was imprisoned for alleged "crimes against the state." Saadawi explained, "I was arrested because I believed Sadat. He said there is democracy and we have a multi-party system and you can criticize. So I started criticizing his policy and I landed in jail."[57] Despite imprisonment, Saadawi continued to fight against women's oppression and created the Arab Women's Solidarity Association in Egypt in 1982. This NGO was dissolved by Egyptian authorities in 1992, accused of violating the rule of law and public order and morality.

Saadawi belongs to an ever-expanding group of individuals using the written word to empower women. By continuing to disseminate her ideas and knowledge in the Arab world and beyond, Saadawi leads a cadre of brilliant, progressive thinkers who will not be silenced in their efforts to educate their "sisters."

In the field of journalism, many Muslim women are actively advocating for women's rights. Like Saadawi, they are doing so even at the risk of arrest and imprisonment. By keeping readers well informed and by creating forums for intelligent and meaningful discussions regarding important political and social issues, these journalists are making critical contributions to the velvet jihad. In the Islamic Republic of Iran, Shahla Sherkat, editor of Iran's *Zanan* (Women), was sentenced to four months in prison after attending a conference in Berlin that focused on the future of political change in Iran. Enraged conservatives labeled the conference "un-Islamic," citing that during the event a woman danced with bare arms and a male protester disrobed. Nine other Iranian moderates attending the conference, including several journalists, were also handed prison terms, ranging from four months to nine years. Sherkat appealed her sentence. On January 28, 2008, Sherkat's magazine was shut down. According to the government's statement, Sherkat was accused of "offering a dark picture of the Islamic Republic through the pages of *Zanan*." Her monthly publication had addressed serious social issues, including the unequal treatment of women under Iranian law and the difficulties women faced in obtaining divorce. Sherkat had exposed and documented the sexist statements of male lawmakers, explaining, "I keep careful track of all the unfair things legislators say about women. . . . And then, when they run for office, I publish all the quotes alongside their pictures so women will know not to vote for them." The 2005 Class of Nieman Fellows at Harvard selected Sherkat as recipient of the 2005 Louis Lyons Award for Conscience and Integrity in Journalism.[58]

Another risk-taking advocate for Muslim women's rights is Samia Farhad. Along with her colleague Sheeba Masoodi, Farhad launched the first women's magazine (*SHE*) in Kashmir, a Muslim majority state and site of Islamic revolt against Indian rule since 1989. The magazine *SHE* shows the new face of "Kashmiri women who are eager to experiment with some of the social changes sweeping the Indian subcontinent while maintaining their Islamic identity and values." Farhad, who has shunned the veil, "knows her task to set Kashmiri women debating about their rights is not an easy one."[59] As political tensions run high at this border state between Pakistan and India, women have as usual become the target of fundamentalists. While acknowledging the tremendous obstacles she faces in persuading Kashmiri women to resist fundamentalist ideology, Farhad remains determined and hopeful that she can effect positive change.

A world apart, in the United States, Tayyibah Taylor, a Muslim woman of color, publishes the magazine *Azizah*. As editor-in-chief, Taylor makes every effort to cast Muslim women in a positive light. In short, she sees *Azizah* as a catalyst for women's empowerment. The magazine gives voice to American Muslim women's accomplishments and opinions, publishing articles with titles such as "Muslim Women in the Male-Dominated Field of Engineering Blaze a Trail for All Women." Taylor notes that *Azizah* "is the first written by and for Muslim women in North America. It is also one of the first Muslim magazines with no affiliation to an Islamic ethnic group or school of thought, for example, Sunni or Shiite."[60]

Many Muslim women in developing countries devote their time to education and to service, establishing or supporting organizations that promote

Sterility, Childbirth, Taboos, and Popular Religious Practices

better living conditions for the disadvantaged and oppressed. To describe each individual and every organization, both in indigenous Muslim nations and in the West, is not my objective. Instead, I will offer a few examples to illustrate their diversity and significance.

Perhaps the most moving examples are the anonymous Afghan women who, throughout the Taliban's reign, risked their lives by transforming their homes into underground networks of schools for girls. Through solidarity and mutual trust, these women defied constant danger, conducted classes in strict secrecy, and managed to educate entire communities of young women.

In contemporary Afghanistan, the Revolutionary Association of the Women of Afghanistan (RAWA) is steadfastly working to expose crimes of violence. Again, during the Taliban reign, members of RAWA risked their lives to secretly film violence perpetrated against women by the Taliban and then disseminated this information to the outside world. RAWA continues to provide shelter, vocational training, and education to homeless women and prostitutes in Herat, Kabul, Mazar-e-Sharif, and Jalalabad.

Two organizations advocating for women's rights in Pakistan are Shirkat Gah and the Aurat Foundation. With a keen eye to government policies directly impacting women—and how these policies are implemented at the grassroots level—the Aurat Foundation attempts "to develop an enabling environment for women's empowerment at all levels through participatory democracy and good governance in Pakistan."[61] On Shirkat Gah's Web site, one finds excellent links to information and publications in Urdu and English on the subject of women, law, and rights.[62]

In Bangladesh, cottage industries have been established to promote financial independence for women. For example, Jahanara Cottage Industries, created by Mrs. Jahanara Begum, is a rural-based handicraft training center. The artisans are offered childcare, low-interest loans, and adult literacy classes. Also, women's micro-credit savings and loan cooperatives have been established in some of the poorest states of India, such as western Gujarat and Orissa. The Self-Employed Women's Association (SEWA), based in Ahmedabad, operates sixty literacy classes in both rural and urban areas for girls and women throughout the region. SEWA also "has trained grassroots activists to go out and offer help to women with their most pressing problems—from small loans, to minimum wages, access to water, health insurance, work skills, and childcare."[63]

Another successful effort at grassroots organization, this one in a first-world environment, is the Canadian-based Federation of Muslim Women (FMW). In 1997, Mariam Bhabha assembled ten women to discuss issues pertaining to the Muslim community, women, and children. A year later this small group formed FMW. Their grassroots objectives include educating the Muslim and mainstream communities about Islam and taking every measure to alleviate poverty. This organization "believes that its work is important, as it provides a voice to those who are voiceless and a face for those who are hidden. FMW has been fortunate to have been able to work with many partners on various projects."[64]

Women Living Under Muslim Laws (WLUML) "is an international solidarity network that provides information, support, and a collective space for women whose lives are shaped, conditioned, or governed by laws and customs said to derive from Islam." With branches in more than seventy countries, this organization strives for women's equality and rights, "especially in Muslim contexts." WLUML also publishes a scholarly journal with articles relevant to the organization's objectives.

WLUML focuses on laws and customs and the concrete realities of women's lives. This includes the often diverse practices and laws classified as "Muslim" (resulting from different interpretations of religious texts and/or the political use of religion) and the effects these have on women, rather than on the religion of Islam itself.

We are especially concerned about marginalized women. This includes non-Muslims in Muslim majority states, especially where spaces for religious minorities are rapidly dwindling; Muslim minorities facing discrimination, oppression, or racism; women whose assertions of sexuality—including but not limited to sexual orientation—are either criminalized or are socially unacceptable.[65]

Visiting the WLUML Web site, one can search for information according to nineteen regions or by themes such as sexuality, violence against women, and reproductive rights. Their news articles (all pertaining to women's issues) are reprinted from nonprofit, UN, and academic publications, to name only a few.

Another educational and charitable Muslim women's organization, Muslim Women Lawyers for Human Rights (KARAMAH), supports Muslim communities in America and abroad in the pursuit of justice. KARAMAH "stands committed to research, education, and advocacy work in matters pertaining to Muslim women and human rights in Islam, as well as civil rights and other related rights under the Constitution of the United States."[66]

Baitul Hemayah (House of Protection) was established by Sa'idah A. Sharif in 2003. Based in Newark, New Jersey, this organization's mission is "to empower the women of our community in order to confront the cycles of domestic violence, abuse, exploitation, and ignorance. We strive to build a movement that works to end violence against women."[67] Because these same issues also affect non-Muslim communities, Baitul Hemayah does not limit its services to Muslims.

Although I have mentioned numerous organizations dedicated to bettering women's lives, perhaps no other NGO is as representative of the newly emerging global paradigm for training and nurturing women's leadership as Women's Learning Partnership (WLP). Working with autonomous and independent partner organizations in eighteen countries,[68] particularly in Muslim-majority societies, the WLP "creates culturally adapted leadership training curriculum and implements leadership and empowerment programs" for women at the grassroots level. The important point is that WLP has learned the value of working with and respecting existing cultural norms rather than imposing external norms on indigenous cultures. Furthermore, the WLP "ensures that gender equality remains on the agenda of policy makers and civil society leaders through . . . advocacy and networking activities."[69]

While national and international women's organizations continue to grow in number and influence, women also participate in less formal community-based efforts to lend support and comfort to each other. A good example, as I will discuss in chapter 6, is the *sofreh-e-nazri*, a banquet held by women and for women only:

The sofreh is more than a ritual banquet for the fulfillment of a religious obligation. There is much to learn from such gatherings of women. The sofreh, held by women for other women, serves to unify the women in a community. It is a way for women to be hopeful for their future and to be compassionate towards each other. The sofreh provides a place where women with similar beliefs, social status, and state of mind can meet. At a sofreh, women can be comforted psychologically, escape the boredom of daily life, strengthen religious beliefs, and offer hope for better days ahead. The sofreh is an important part of Iranian women's spirituality that offers both comfort and community and provides an opportunity for them to participate in their religion in a way that is open to them, since most leadership roles are not.[70]

Beyond the sofreh, Muslim women assist each other in numerous ways at the community level. For example, they develop and share home remedies to enhance libido, reverse infertility, and promote successful abortions. During research trips to both Iran and Morocco, I witnessed an unmistakable "sisterhood" shared among women, particularly in those situations where women in desperate circumstances received not just curative recipes but also genuine affection, understanding, and sympathy.

THREE

Even Dolls Must
Wear Hijab

A particular genre of religious writing on Muslim ethics has been in existence for at least three hundred years. These manuals or guidebooks for leading a moral life are written for a popular audience and give specific advice on a variety of subjects such as clothing and religious participation. Among the earliest such books are *Holliyyat al-Mottaqin* (The adornment of the pious), written in Persian by Allameh Mohammad Baqer Majlesi, a well-known Shi'i scholar of the seventeenth century, and *Behishti Zewar* (Heavenly ornaments), written in Urdu by Mulana Ashraf Ali al-Thanvi, a Sunni scholar in early twentieth-century India.[1] They have a large readership and have often been reprinted.

In recent times, with the religious resurgence in parts of the Islamic world, there has been a proliferation in the publication of similar books. Like their precursors, they are meant to be guidebooks, but they tend to be primarily concerned with the conduct and proper moral behavior of women in public and private spheres. Books such as *Az-Zaujus Salih* (The pious husband) and *Al-Mar'atus Salihah* (The pious woman) are actually full of folk practices passed off as religious orthodoxy that are intended to influence people's belief systems and behavior.[2] Ironically, some women who are more educated than their mothers buy into the teachings of these manuals, while less educated women often reject them—the opposite of what one might expect. The manuals often promulgate patriarchal cultural traditions meant to control women, but because they claim to be based on religious teachings, many women are captivated—or perhaps held captive—by these writings.

Holliyyat al-Mottaqin

Allameh Mohammad Baqer Majlesi published three hundred works on various religious subjects.[3] With his grand title of Allameh (most learned, highly educated person), Majlesi is credited with popularizing Shi'i rituals and culture in Iran, thus spreading Shi'ism among Muslims. Majlesi's writings were in Persian and used Arabic religious terms that the layperson could understand. The language of *Holliyyat al-Mottaqin* is simple enough for the average believer to understand. Hence the pious do not need the expert knowledge of the *ulama* (religious scholars) in order to follow the right path in their daily rituals and religious practices described in *Holliyyat al-Mottaqin*. Perhaps it is the relative simplicity of his writings that made them so popular.

Majlesi wrote at a time when Shi'ism was promoted as the official religion of Iran by the Safavid kings. He was hired by the Safavid court to research, collect, and write Shi'i manuscripts. So it is not surprising that the enormous body of scholarship in Iran on Shi'ism dating back to the Safavid era was authored by Majlesi. His importance went beyond his home country. Soon his teachings were followed by other Shi'i ulama outside Iran, many of whom wrote similar manuals for Muslim women because they believed that women lacked sufficient moral knowledge and needed to be educated in that regard. *Holliyyat al-Mottaqin* was a source of religious inspiration for the Shi'i masses following the 1978–79 Islamic revolution in Iran, and reprints have been in demand ever since.

Behishti Zewar

Behishti Zewar has been translated from Urdu into English and published in India and Pakistan. I rely mainly on Muhammad Masroor Khan Saroha's translation. I also like a 1990 book by Barbara Daly Metcalf called *Perfecting Women: Maulana Ashraf 'Ali Thanawi's Bihishti Zewar, a Partial Translation with Commentary*. There are countless Web sites with translations, commentaries, and references to the work, but I cite only those with attributed authorship.

Even Dolls Must Wear Hijab

Thanvi's *Behishti Zewar* was an important part of Muslim culture on the Indian subcontinent during British colonial rule. In fact, Thanvi wrote the book partly, I believe, because he feared a decline in religious and cultural values due to British rule. *Behishti Zewar* provides detailed examples of everyday domestic life and attitudes about Muslim women of the subcontinent and is also a textured, detailed presentation of the major themes of Islamic reform during Thanvi's time.

When he published *Behishti Zewar*, Thanvi had a particular goal in mind: to educate Muslim women in all aspects of their religion. He writes, "I have for some time . . . realized that in order to manage women, it is absolutely necessary to teach them the science of religion."[4] The book was published at a time when women were not expected to know more than the bare essentials of religion, nor were they encouraged to explore the deeper meanings of religious practices. They were expected to follow the religion obediently without questioning the authority of males who told them what to do.

Behishti Zewar emphasizes Muslim women's roles in moral leadership, social alliances, and economic prosperity, while preaching piety and religiosity. The implication is that if women follow Thanvi's guidelines, they will achieve heavenly rewards. The book was also meant to assist South Asian Muslim women in matters related to weddings, marriage, childbirth, etiquette (*adab*), and dress, so it was often given to Muslim women as part of their dowry in early twentieth-century India. Muslims interested in "reformist visions" of Islam have rediscovered this book, and today *Behishti Zewar* is among the most influential works of religious guidance among Sunni Muslim women in South Asia.

At first, it seems that Thanvi implies that women are essentially the same as men, being neither endowed with a special nature for spiritual or moral virtue nor handicapped in any way by limitations of intellect or character. Unfortunately, a closer reading of this text indicates otherwise. Despite his best intentions, he was not able to separate his gender-biased attitude (which was the norm during his era, and still is, to a large extent) from his preaching to women.

Thanvi's teaching that adultery extends beyond actual sexual relations to thought, sight, hearing, and touch, has been distorted to the point where now jurists demand that women be secluded so that their voices may not be heard, their jewelry not seen, and their perfume not smelled. In mainstream Islamic thought, permitted sexuality is seen as positive, but deviation from what is permitted is abhorred. To prevent deviant sexual behavior, women were removed from public spaces, including mosques, where men are present. Some of the modern guidebooks extend this to barring women from business dealings as well. They put a double burden on women by preaching old ideas of morality borrowed from the earlier writings while ignoring contemporary conditions of women who are heads of households. Many women cannot remain segregated because they must work to support their dependents.

Contemporary Sources

Az-Zaujus Salih (The pious husband) and *Al-Mar'atus Salihah* (The pious woman) by the Mujlisul-Ulama (assembly of religious scholars) of South Africa are among the most popular of the modern publications of this genre. There are many other books and pamphlets—mostly written by fundamentalist men and women—intended to correct female behavior, such as Huda Khattab's *Muslim Woman's Handbook*. Khattab writes about personal hygiene, marriage, and divorce, and addresses issues like menstruation, *hijab* (veiling), and the Muslim woman's role in her family, community, and society. The publisher's online ad for this manual claims, "This book is of immense value to Muslim women and teenage girls, especially those who are discovering or rediscovering the relevance of Islam to their lives—a book to read and reread, and to be kept near at hand at all times."[5]

Many of these guidebooks sold in Islamic bookstores around the globe (including online) are not concerned with a deep knowledge of religious scholarship and have nothing new to offer to improve the lives of the millions of women who read them. Most of them are little more than copies of previously published texts arranged in a different order and recycled for the mass market. Nowadays, with desktop and Web publishing, anyone who considers himself pious enough (or has the computer skills) can crank out these guidebooks regardless of religious training (or lack thereof). Thus many "pious" engineers, businessmen, and physicians have made the dangerous decision that, in addition to their professional careers, they can be part-time religious authorities as well. Theology is a discipline that requires proper study for credentials. Many of these self-appointed religious experts do not understand the historical context in which those old guidelines that they recycle were drafted. The Persia of Majlesi and the colonial India of

Thanvi are so different from our times that their guidebooks have no relevance to the lifestyle of Muslim women today.

Because so many of these guidebooks devote an inordinate amount of attention to women's apparel (clothing, cosmetics, jewelry, and other accessories), this chapter will focus primarily on that topic and on the effect of such writings on a woman's mind and body. Women are dressed, undressed, and redressed to fit political, economic, and religious agendas. Women are told they must follow sartorial strictures in order to function properly, to avoid temptation that would cause *fitna* (chaos), to prevent gossip, and to walk safely in public without drawing attention.

Such a large swath of Muslim ethics is fixated on women's apparel that one is not surprised to discover a blogger wondering whether dolls have to wear hijab. Indeed, an entire cottage industry that mirrors this fixation has emerged from the world of toys. Razanne, Farah, Laila, and Sara are some of the properly dressed, good Muslim, anti-Barbie dolls sold with accessories and spin-off toys by Islamic stores and Web sites or, in the case of Iran, at the Institute for the Intellectual Development of Children and Young Adults.

3.1. (*left*) This doll is wearing a black Islamic hijab, appropriate for outdoor activities.
3.2. (*right*) This doll, engaged in *salat* (praying) and sold with stylish red boots, is particularly appreciated by pious Muslim parents. Photo by Christopher Rose, Center for Middle Eastern Studies, University of Texas at Austin.

3.3. This Fulla Doll, sold with prayer beads and a prayer rug, is the moral version of the immoral Barbie. Photo by Christopher Rose, Center for Middle Eastern Studies, University of Texas at Austin.

3.4. (*left*) Islamic doll in elegant outdoor veils. 3.5. (*right*) Sara, the national doll of Iran, in Iranian Kurdish folk costume, dressed in accordance with the hijab dress code.

Not even the youngest child is immune from the online marketing of "Islamic" products, including toys, dolls, and games.⁶ Perhaps the most extreme example is Leen, the first Islamic talking doll. According to the Hedeya Web site, the Leen doll can recite Al-Fatehah, the first surah in the Qur'an, or sing a nice Arabic song about her mother."⁷ Manufacturers of such items feed off fundamentalist users, whether those users are in Iran, Pakistan, or Saudi Arabia. In the Kingdom of Saudi, for example, because the religious police declare Barbie dolls a threat to public morality, manufacturers of Muslim dolls now market modest alternatives to the decadent, immoral Barbie. The indoctrination of young girls as to proper attire begins long before they can read the guidebooks that are the focus of this chapter.

Apparel Guidelines
in *Holliyyat al-Mottaqin*

Majlesi bases much of *Holliyyat al-Mottaqin* on *ahadith* (plural of *hadith*), or sayings of the Prophet. However, the *isnad*, or chain of authentication (list of those who transmitted the sayings) of the ahadith he cites, is questionable. Like many others, Majlesi probably cited apocryphal ahadith when it suited his purposes. So the reader should approach the work with some skepticism.

Majlesi says that according to authentic ahadith, it is a tradition to adorn one's body with jewels and to wear clean, expensive clothes if the means to obtain them was provided from honest and *halal* (religiously lawful and permissible) earnings. One's dress should be in accordance with one's status, which will please Parvardgar (a Persian term for God). If people cannot obtain such luxury items from halal sources, they should be careful not to spend too much time on clothing because that may prevent them from devoting time to Parvardgar. If people have wealth, they should dress well, eat well, spend well, and give to their fellow pious Muslim sisters and brothers.

Majlesi cites Imam Ja'far Sadegh as the source of a hadith which says that whenever God blesses people, it should be reflected in their sartorial finery. Then Khoda (another Persian term for God) will be pleased with them, and they will be considered friends of God. If people do not show the blessings of God in the way they live, then they fail to acknowledge God's gift to them of good fortune and are considered an enemy of God.

Majlesi cites Amir al mu'menin (a reference to Ali, first Shi'i imam as well as cousin and son-in-law of the Prophet) as saying that a man should dress in elegant clothes for his Muslim brothers just as he would dress himself for his non-Muslim enemies. He should impress both friends and enemies with his clothing and neat appearance. He should dress in the best clothing that he has at his disposal and wear fragrance at all times, since God said:

> Say: Who hath forbidden
> The beautiful (gifts) of God
> For His servants
> And the things, clean and pure
> (which He hath provided)
> For sustenance?[8]

In *Holliyyat al-Mottaqin*, Majlesi speaks of the "wisdom of glamour and adorning one's body." At first, he addresses both men and women about topics such as forbidden garments or colors, but later his exhortations apply to women only. Majlesi justifies the exaltation of beauty in apparel on religious grounds by citing verses in the Qur'an which declare that cleanliness is next to holiness. He concludes that one must try to be neat, well dressed, well groomed, and perfumed to please God. Thanvi, on the other hand, believed that piety in women was dependent upon the segregation of the sexes and that hijab extended to a woman's voice, jewels, and scent, all of which could be considered evil because they could arouse a man's interest in her. Clearly, these two ulama have different opinions regarding apparel and adornment.

Citing another hadith without proper isnad (authentication from the actual Companions of the Prophet), Majlesi says that a well-known Sufi came to Masjid al Haram (the Dome of the Rock in Palestine) and saw that his holiness Imam Ja'far al Sadegh was in the mosque, dressed in beautiful and expensive garments.[9] The Sufi said, "I swear to Allah that I have to tease him, for he is dressed in expensive garments." Then the Sufi went to Ja'far al Sadegh and said, "Oh, you, the descendant of the Prophet of Islam, the Messenger of God, I swear to God that the Prophet himself never wore such extravagant clothing, and none of your previous fathers wore such clothes either." The imam said, "During the time of the prophet Muhammad, the situation was different. People did not have enough to get by, but today times have changed, and people are better off compared with the time of the Prophet. And it is well deserved and justified to spend on yourself when you are a pure person." Then he recited the above-mentioned verse from the Qur'an (7:32) to reiterate his point. He went on, "We [descendants of the Prophet] are the most deserving people [because of our purity] for spending from the *baraka* [blessing] bestowed on us from God." Then he lifted the bottom of his garment and revealed a garment he was wearing underneath. He said to the Sufi, "I have worn this coarse, thick garment for myself. My soft, elegant outer garment is for people to see." Then he walked over to the Sufi and lifted his coarse woolen outer garment to reveal a thin garment worn underneath. He said, "You have worn the undergarment for your personal enjoyment and comfort and the outer garment to fool people."

I believe the moral of this story is that God loves for his servants to reveal His blessings to everyone. Majlesi says that the story exposes the hypocrisy of people who have wealth but who never reveal it to the public. Such people claim that they do not have enough and pretend to have less than they actually do. For example, many of the *akhounds* (mullahs or clerics) in Iran are well-to-do, but they pretend to be less fortunate than they really are. There are two attitudes about personal appearance among the clerics: one group believes that the religious man should dress himself in his finest attire when he is in public, while the other group is more ascetic and believes in a simple lifestyle that includes avoiding luxury and indulgence in clothing. Both groups justify their beliefs according to the religious interpretation that is most appealing to them.

When Ayatollah Khomeini rose to power with the Islamic revolution of Iran, he set the tone for personal appearance with his simple cleric's outer gown, or *aba* (which, by the way, was made of fine, expensive camel down). In his sermons, Khomeini stressed the idea that one should cultivate personal piety and engage in religious good deeds, not accumulate worldly goods. He emphasized the concept of *sadeh zisti,* or simple living. Ironically, many of his followers maintained a very plain appearance but garnered every type of privilege and material good. But it is easy to see why the masses would follow Khomeini's speeches so seriously. They interpreted his exhortations to mean that if people looked unkempt and dressed down, they were literally more holy. During the previous government, the shah's regime was always associated with Western attitudes of greed for material goods and opulent lifestyles. A common epithet in postrevolution Iran is *taghoot* (literally, tyrant); it refers to those who continue the decadent lifestyle associated with the reign of the shah. Recently, former president Khatami (known as *ruhani e khoosh poosh*, or the well-dressed religious man) was attacked by the extreme religious media of Iran for his extravagant clothing. Khatami's defense was similar to Majlesi's Sufi story about the pretentious attitudes of wealthy clerics who pretend to be humble and poor in order to fool the public with their unkempt appearance. He also said that as a religious person, a political leader, and a good Muslim, he is displaying God's kindness to him publicly. He also provided religious justification by citing the same verse of the Qur'an (7:32) to prove his point that Islam does not teach that one should look poor and unkempt in public.[10]

Apparel Guidelines
in *Behishti Zewar*

In the *Behishti Zewar*, we are constantly reminded that Islam is a religion that eschews asceticism, while also rejecting the opposite extremes of luxury and self-indulgence. Thanvi claims that it is as impermissible for women to wear very fine and thin clothes (such as muslin) as it is for them to go naked. He alludes to a hadith with questionable isnad that "on the Day of Judgment many women will be naked. It is more awful if the shirt and scarf of a woman are very fine and thin." Fine silk clearly wouldn't be an option, since it is even more fine and thin than cotton muslin. The only other choices would be wool or coarse, thick cotton or silk fabrics. Again we are reminded of the Sufi in Majlesi's story who denounced luxury. Thanvi (a Sufi himself) was referring to transparent clothing, which reveals skin underneath, an offensive public behavior. His comments reflect the cultural belief that women's hair and breasts are considered to be sexual and will provoke temptation in men. Thus Thanvi's preaching is intended to keep men pious so they do not stray by seeing women in revealing clothes. In other words, women are made responsible for keeping men on the virtuous path. He also says that women are forbidden to put on male shoes or dress. He attributes this proscription to a hadith; although he doesn't give the source, it is from al-Bukhari (chapter 61, hadith 773).[11] According to Thanvi, "It is permissible for women to wear ornaments, but not too many.

One who did not love [ornaments] in this world, she will get much to wear in the hereafter. Wearing of jingling ornaments is not permissible. Rings of metals other than gold or silver are not permissible for women."

Although gold and silver are considered more precious than iron, brass, or copper, I believe this teaching may have roots in Indian cultural taboos. Hindus and Muslims in South Asia believe that one should wear only "suitable" metals and stones next to the body because unsuitable ones may bring misfortune or cause harm to the wearer. Furthermore, some minerals and metals have undesirable chemical reactions with the body. Thanvi's writings mix cultural beliefs with religious advice, which seems natural for both the writer and the intended reader who is familiar with the culture of the subcontinent. But his guidebook eventually spread far beyond India, so that readers unfamiliar with Indian culture and history tended to accept his advice as purely religious.

In another example involving jewelry, Thanvi again conflates culture and religion, claiming, "Some women and grown-up girls get bangles worn by male bangle merchants; it is immodest. The merchant holds the hands of women. This should not be done, as it is improper and a matter of great shame."[12] Thanvi may be right that Islam does not permit related men to touch women outside their family, but many of the women buying colorful glass and metal bangles in the Indian bazaar would not have been Muslim. If they follow Thanvi's teachings, many Muslim women, particularly those who are illiterate, who lack true knowledge of the religion, or who are not exposed to other religious or cultural traditions, unintentionally follow taboos and traditions of another culture via religious instruction. More important, Thanvi's teaching ignores the principle of "intention," which is greatly valued in Islamic law and is entirely relevant to this situation: the women intend to buy bangles, not to be touched by strangers.[13]

Thanvi constructed a puritan world of cleanliness, order, regularity, and self-control. Reformists placed their hopes in his teachings as a safeguard for Islam against British colonialism. The *Bihishti Zewar* rapidly became a classic gift for Muslim brides, who "entered their husband's home with the Holy Qur'an in one hand and the *Bihishti Zewar* in the other."[14] Thanvi was sought out for his erudition, his passion for reform, his integrity, and his spirituality as a Sufi leader. He offered followers a range of commitments and meanings that were not tied to the institutions and values of the colonial state. He is remembered as a forceful personality who insisted on directness and frankness in all personal aspects of life. His successors (*khulafa*, or leaders) and their successors continue to be influential among Muslims of the subcontinent. Nowadays, the Tablighi Jama'at, an offshoot of the Deobandi (the Sufi order to which Thanvi belonged), remains highly influential throughout the Muslim world. Tablighi is a Muslim missionary movement that provides instruction in basic social and religious duties. Among its followers in Great Britain and South Africa, *Behishti Zewar* is required reading.

The Pious Woman: Modern Guidelines

How do contemporary guidebooks for Muslim women compare with the historical ones? Has there been any change in terms of women's progress regarding how they should dress themselves and run their personal affairs, according to the culturally influenced religious interpretation of male authors? Following the tradition of conservative Muslim families of the subcontinent of presenting a copy of *Behishti Zewar* to the bride on her wedding day, *Al-Mar'atus Salihah* touts itself as "the perfect wedding gift which will ensure for the bride a life of blessing and happiness if she gives practical expression to its advice, which is the advice of the Qur'an and Sunnah."[15] Both books are intended to guide the reader—especially the bride—on the path of high moral values.

The way to achieve happiness in married life, according to *Al-Mar'atus Salihah*, "is not the way of demand [i.e.,] demanding fulfillment of rights. . . . The way to achieve happiness is for the wife to offer humble submission to her husband."[16] The contemporary Muslim woman is advised to ignore her rights, including her religious rights, and give in to her husband's demands in the emotional, moral, and practical matters of marital life, no matter how unfair they are, and to be patient rather than take action. Even when victimized by her husband, a wife must not take any legal action or show her dissatisfaction. She must sublimate her feelings and present a pleasant façade. If her husband is having an affair with another woman, the wife is advised to resign herself to God's will and to pray "earnestly and constantly. . . . She should, therefore, not allow her grief—which is normal and natural—to give rise to frustration, impatience, and un-Islamic behaviour."[17]

Adding insult to injury, *Al-Mar'atus Salihah* warns the wife against alienating her husband from the other woman by reminding the wife that

Even Dolls Must Wear Hijab

"adopting a bullying, quarrelling, nagging, and unwomanlike attitude will result in the opposite of the desired effect." Instead, "to achieve success for her marriage the wife must be submissive, humble, walk the path of piety. If she seeks to emulate her western *Kuffar* [irreligious] equality [the author here means those Western feminists who believe in gender equality], then she should understand that she is treading the road to divorce, which is a daily occurrence among Western couples."[18] Not only must a proper wife be submissive, docile, and self-sacrificing, but she must also be invisible.

Al-Mar'atus Salihah, like the earlier works, advises that hijab must go beyond covering the body with clothing. It extends to concepts of morality and includes the voice, sound, and scent of a woman deemed to be disruptive and tempting to man. According to this group of authors, who are ulama from South Africa, a woman's voice must be controlled:

> It is not permissible for a woman to unnecessarily make heard her voice to males. This *purdah* [seclusion] for the voice can be gauged from the Shariah's instruction to a woman who corrects the Imaam. If women happen to be performing *Salaat* [praying] in *Jamaat* [the congregation], and the Imaam commits an error in recitation, a woman cannot rectify the Imaam by reciting the relevant portion. The method the Shariah has chosen for her on this occasion is the clapping of hands. She should draw the attention of the Imaam to his error by clapping her hands once. Such clapping, which is an excessive act in relation to Salaat, is not permissible for men. However, in view of the restrictions the Shariah places on a woman's voice, clapping hands even in Salaat has been tolerated for her, but not reciting the relevant part of the Qur'anic *aayat* [verses] aloud. This order of clapping hands applies even if the Imaam happens to be her husband or any other *mahram* [man with whom contact is permissible].[19]

Such admonitions are not much different from Thanvi's. In fact, this manual credits many direct quotations to Thanvi. For example, the section "Advice by Hakimul Ummat Hadhrat Maulana Ashraf Ali Thanvi (Rahmatullah Alayh)"[20] tells what Thanvi said about relationships, demands, piety of wives, and many other subjects.

The authors of *Al-Mar'atus Salihah* also echo the teachings of guidebook writers from centuries past when they advise the pious woman not to ask for maintenance above her husband's means. "Be satisfied with whatever he gives. If sometimes you fancy some jewelry or garment, then do not hanker after it if your husband cannot afford it, nor regret for not being able to [acquire] it."[21] And, like Thanvi, they are worried about Western influence on Muslim culture, especially on women.

> Among the evil ways of the *Kuffar* [sinful, unbeliever] acquired by "liberated" Muslim women of these times is the evil habit of adorning and beautifying themselves for others. While Islam commands the Muslim wife to adopt adornment solely for her husband, the modern Muslim wife has chosen to do just the opposite. She will reserve adornment for others when she has to leave the home precincts. But with regard to her husband, she is not at all concerned with her untidy and shoddy appearance.
>
> It is the obligatory duty of the wife to beautify herself for her husband. On the other hand, it is *haraam* [religiously forbidden] for her to embellish herself for others. A woman who adorns herself for others is severely reprimanded and criticized by Islam. Rasulullah (Sallallahu Alayhi Wasallam) has compared such a wife to "the darkness of the day of Qiyamah" [Day of Judgment].[22] Such a woman, says Rasulullah (Sallallahu Alayhi Wasallam), is without any *Noor* [light]. In one narration, Nabi-e-Kareem (Sallallahu Alayhi Wasallam) said: "*A woman who applies perfume and passes by a gathering is like an adulteress.*" Among the rights that the husband holds over his wife is her adorning herself for his sake."[23]

Clearly, when referring to women in this context, "liberated" is not considered positive; rather, it is equated with sinfulness and evil.

Automobiles didn't exist in Majlesi's time, and the issue of women drivers would have been essentially moot in Thanvi's milieu. But *Al-Mar'atus Salihah* takes on the issue with gusto and puts it in the same context in which it addresses women's apparel: Western women are immoral and profligate, and good Muslim women should not emulate them; rather, they should hide.

> Undoubtedly, for Muslim women to drive cars is contrary to the spirit and teaching of the Quraan and Sunnah [Prophet's tradition]. The Quraan Shareef [honorable Qu'ran] commands Muslim Females: "And remain within your homes and make not a display (of yourselves) like the display of the (time) of jaahiliyyah [pre-Islamic era]."
>
> The Quraan and the Ahadith place restrictions upon the emergence of females from the home. Islam exhorts and commands its female adherents to conceal themselves, hence Rasulullah (Sallahhahu Alay Wasal-

lam) said: "Woman is *aurah'* (i.e., to be concealed).[24] When she emerges [into the public], shaitaan [Satan] casts surreptitious glances [evil glances] at her."

Islam emphasizes purdah [segregation and/or concealment]—concealment for women, but western culture in a variety of ways and means (of which women driving cars is one) emphasises "self-expression," i.e., exhibitions of *jaahiliyyah*. Islam lays stress upon modesty and shame (*hayaa*) whereas driving destroys the *hayaa* of a woman. By means of driving woman places herself in the forefront of exhibition. She barters away her *hayaa* by aping the ways and mannerisms of males in the driving seat. Her place is not in the driving seat to wander around, putting herself up for public gaze and display. Her place is the home—to live in dignity, respect, *hayaa,* and honour. The greater her self-exhibition, the greater the destruction she brings to her natural modesty.

And about this *hayaa*, Rasulullah (Sallallahu Alayhi Wasallam) said: "*Hayaa* is a branch of *Imaan* [religious belief or belief in God]."

It is virtually impossible for a woman who drives to observe the Islamic laws of *Hijaab* [veiling]. Even if she is a bit conscious of Islamic *Purdah* restrictions, her constant projection and exhibition which driving entails corrode her *hayaa* and reduces her to utter shamelessness. She then qualifies for *Quraanic* description of *tabarruje jaahiliyyah,* "exhibitions of the times of ignorance."

The arguments advanced in favour of women driving are all fictitious and designed to appease the lowly *nafs* [soul] of man. Those women who are observant of the Divine restrictions and prohibitions, those women who remain within the confines of Islamic *Hijaab* will, *Insha' Allah* [God willing], not be confronted with fictitious "emergencies" and exigencies imagined and sometimes confronted by the women of exhibition. Those who have Trust (*Tawakul*) in Allah Ta'ala will be well cared for."[25]

I quote this section at length as an example of the fundamentalist, absolutist interpretation of the Qur'an and ahadith of the Prophet so often employed by writers of religious guidebooks. It also provides an interesting counterpoint to certain cases where fundamentalist interpretations of Islam conflict with quotidian exigencies, such as getting a driver's license. There have been several cases in the United States of Muslim women being denied a driver's license. The women claim that Islamic law forbids them to be photographed unveiled, while state law mandates that driver's license photos must show the full face of the driver. In 2003, a woman who had recently converted to Islam insisted on wearing her *nighab* (face veil) for the driver's license photo, arguing that a Muslim woman is obligated to wear the face veil in any picture. Apparently, her "exigencies" were not fictitious or imaginary, but she couldn't have it both ways: she couldn't both adhere to a fundamentalist interpretation of "display" *and* abide by state requirements for getting a driver's license. However, the fundamentalist interpretation of this issue, as stated in *Al-Mar'atus Salihah*, contradicts the true teachings and authoritative position of the highest mufti:

> Muhammad Sayid Tantawy, the highest cleric or mufti in the theology school of the University of Al-Azhar in Egypt, the oldest and most respected Islamic seminary in the world, states that the covering of a woman's face with a veil is not a requirement of Islam. According to the mufti, "Wearing a face veil or covering the hands with gloves are not required by Islam, but we will not discourage those women who choose to do so."[26]

Women as Dolls:
The Fundamentalist Legacy

The old-fashioned genre of guidebooks addressing moral behavior and proper dress, those guidebooks popularized by early authors such as Majlesi and Thanvi, seem to be making a big comeback, encouraged by the resurgence of fundamentalist Islam and facilitated by global electronic communications and commerce. Curiously, the new online entrepreneurs taking advantage of this conservative revival include a number of women.

Among these Internet entrepreneurs, Farhat Hashmi stands out for her remarkable ability to tap into the growing global market catering to Muslim girls. Farhat Hashmi is a religious scholar from Pakistan who arrived in Canada in 2004. With a doctoral degree in Islamic studies from the University of Glasgow, Hashmi teaches her female students an extreme brand of Islam, promoting the practice of polygamy as well as utmost subservience to men.[27] Challenging liberal Muslims, her reactionary teachings represent a retrogressive interpretation of Islam.

Hashmi's school in Toronto, Al-Huda, attracts young, middle-class women from mainstream Muslim families, especially those living in Canada, the United States, and Australia. A shrewd businesswoman and opportunist, Hashmi goes where the money is; in other words, she goes where people can afford her fees. She has built a lucrative business selling lecture notes, DVDs, videos, and audiotapes over the Internet. She also profits from the sale of a specially designed conservative black hijab (Saudi Arabian style) and an ever-expanding line of burqas. During the 1990s, Hashmi established religious schools in Pakistan. Taking her *wahabbi* (Saudi brand of fundamentalism) teachings to Canada, Hashmi opened her Toronto-based private school. After the devastating 2005 earthquake in Pakistan, Hashmi was quoted by a correspondent of the Toronto-based newspaper *Globe and Mail*: "The people in the area where the earthquake hit were involved in immoral activities and God has said that He will punish those who do not follow His path." In response to Hashmi's pronouncement, Tarek Fatah, communications director of the Muslim Canadian Congress, asked, "What sort of a sick mind would suggest that the over 20,000 Pakistani and Kashmiri children who were buried alive in their schools were 'involved in immoral activities'?"[28] It is interesting to note that Hashmi was ordered to leave Canada by immigration authorities on September 30, 2005. As of this writing, almost two years later, she continues to ignore the immigration order and remains in Toronto illegally, providing unlawful sanctuary for her husband and children as well.

Hashmi has amassed considerable personal wealth while exploiting countless young women who suffer under the yoke of patriarchal dogma and superstitions. In guidebooks and in lectures such as those Hashmi offers, the religious justification for controlling Muslim women's clothing is to prevent *fitna* (chaos). It seems to me that if women can cause chaos unless they are invisible and caged, then they must have awe-inspiring power indeed and men must be very weak. But neither Hashmi nor the guidebooks talk about men's weaknesses; rather, their lessons regarding women's proper attire and behavior rationalize the social and civil barriers to Muslim women's physical movement and intellectual growth. These oppressive strategies are justified by a narrow interpretation of the Qur'an and ahadith and are often rooted in pre-Islamic beliefs, customs, and collective cultural practices.

Considering the eras in which Majlesi (seventeenth century), Thanvi (early twentieth century), and the Ulama of South Africa (late twentieth century) wrote their guidebooks, the contemporary *Al-Mar'atus Salihah* is the worst offender. Has there been no progress or evolution in human thought over four centuries?

Only a misogynist would be so blind to the emotional needs of women, especially those married to cheating husbands. The senseless advice given by contemporary *ulama* of "pouring the emotional pain inside" will cause physical symptoms such as ulcers, insomnia, and drastic weight change, not to mention clinical depression and suicide. It will also result in marriages brimming with resentment, disrespect, mistrust, and lies. Rather than being an ideal wedding gift, guidebooks like these bring harm to millions of women worldwide. They should be packaged in a plain brown wrapper with a warning: "Reading this book may be hazardous to your mind, body, and spirit."

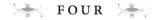

FOUR

𝒜rts and 𝒜thletics

STEPPING OVER
BOUNDARIES

In Islamic culture, women's bodies are mandated and controlled. Fundamentalist ideology claims that women are to be "shielded" from the prying eyes of lustful men. Based on this notion, and relying on the interpretation of religious texts, fundamentalist Islamic authorities ban women from participating publicly in virtually every genre of performance art and every athletic arena. Nevertheless, many Muslim women believe that sharing their beauty, creative talents, and athletic skills with the wider world is no crime, and they have found innovative ways of doing so. Especially when patriarchal restrictions become untenable and unreasonable, women rise up to form their own dance troupes, musical ensembles, theatrical groups, and even their own Olympic games. The more oppressive the male-driven policy, the more creative the women's response.

Women in Performance and Visual Arts:
Halal or Haram?

In Arabic, the word *jamal* means "beauty," and it is one of the ninety-nine names of Allah, known as Asma al Hussni (beautiful names). There is a well-known saying both in Persian and Arabic: God is beautiful and loves beauty (*Khodavan zibast va zibaei ra doost darad* [Persian], and *Allah jamil wa yuhibb al-jamal* [Arabic]). Many Muslims believe that beauty is the embodiment of God; if so, one questions why the display of a woman's beauty, as well as her artistic expression, must be forbidden. The transcendent quality of a woman's song, her lovely image recorded on film, the fluid motions of her graceful dance, and the inspired sounds she creates on musical instruments—all are considered taboo.

The issue of Muslim women participating in performance art conjures up widely opposing viewpoints: is it *haram* (forbidden under Islam) or is it *halal* (permissible under Islam)? An examination of the Qur'an and other Muslim religious texts as to the more general issue of music may serve as an apt departure point for discussion.

When considering various interpretations on this issue, Lois Ibsen al-Faruqi warns that one must be "aware of the multitudinous collections of often contradictory statements, both oral and written, on music that have come from various regions and periods of Islamic history." He also cautions against zealous critics who have not considered differing circumstances when disapproving certain musical activities, thus grossly distorting the original intent of the original sources. In his opinion, terms such as *haram* (forbidden) "cannot be properly applied to musical performance in any part of the Muslim world in any period of time. . . . Instead, we should realize that we are discussing, for the most part, ethical rather than legal judgments."[1]

Among all Muslim cultures, one form of music is accepted without dispute—the recitation of the holy Qur'an in solo vocal improvisation. Although Qu'ranic recitation varies from region to region, virtually every Muslim agrees that it is the most sublime example of musical expression.

Historically, performance artists—whether singers, dancers, or instrumentalists—have not been held in high esteem among Middle Eastern/Arabic cultures. In fact, for centuries, these individuals were generally viewed with suspicion, even considered immoral. To a certain extent, this prejudice still exists in remote areas and small villages, where little distinction is made between a professionally trained musician and a local street performer.

Today, essentially four viewpoints frame Islamic thought in regard to musical expression. The first, or "purist," view opposes every form of musical expression. The second view allows for recitation of the Qur'an and the call to prayer (without instrumental accompaniment). The third, more moderate viewpoint, held primarily by scholars and musicians, makes no distinction between secular and religious music. Thus if musical recitation of the Qur'an is allowed, then all modes of song should be sanctioned. The final viewpoint, embraced by the mystical branch of Islam (Sufis), believes that music, dance, and chanting are essential parts of religious ritual, a means of unity with the Divine.

To sample the purist viewpoint, one turns to Mustafa Sabri (1869–1954), a scholar from the Ottoman era, who wrote:

> Firstly, music is a useless activity, which in fact is a state of passiveness. Secondly, the benefit and pleasure taken from music involves a meaning of deep slavery in passion.
>
> Although it might be difficult for some to realize the fact that music has a sense of passiveness, those with a subtle mind would not hesitate to accept it, as it is not possible to imagine another worldly benefit of music. . . . One should not ask hastily: how could this be claimed while there are many singers, instrument players in the West, for example, making a living or even a fortune? To make a living would not be proper unless it is done in a way which does not harm human dignity since it would not be at ease with conscience otherwise. . . . The acts of pure entertainment are considered low-level professions in the eyes of unpolluted human nature. . . . Likewise, a lot of respect is usually paid to some ladies in order to take sexual advantage of them.[2]

In the last sentence, musicians are equated with prostitutes. According to Sabri, both serve the public and are paid for a service that brings temporary pleasure.

Another religious scholar, Abu Bilal Mustafa Al-Kanadi (1950–1989), offered commentary on the topic of music and singing. Primarily, he elaborated on the possible meaning of interpretations by Al-Qurtubi, Al-Tabari, and Ibn Abbaas. His commentary cited verse from the Qu'ranic Sura XVII, *Al-Israa* (Children of Israel):

> Another verse alleged to be proof of the illegality of music, singing, etc., is mentioned in Sura Al-Israa: 61–64 as follows: After Iblees (Satan) refuses to bow before Adam as ordered, he requests that Allah grant him respite until the day of resurrection, so that he may misguide all but a few of the descendants of Adam (peace be upon him). Allah, the Glorious and exalted, addresses Satan thus:

"Lead to destruction those
Whom thou canst among them
With thy (seductive) voice;
Make assaults on them
With thy cavalry and thy
Infantry; mutually share
With them wealth and children;
And make promises to them."
But Satan promises them
Nothing but deceit.

It is related that some of the commentators from the generation of the *taabieen,* such as Mujahid and Dahhaak, interpreted Satan's exciting mankind with his voice to mean through the use of music, song, and amusement. Ad-Dahaak said it was the sound of wind instruments. However, according to Ibn Abbaas, the voice mentioned in the verse refers to every form of invitation to disobey Allah, the Exalted. After mentioning the various interpretations of the commentators, Al-Tabari says, "The most correct of these views expresses that verily, Allah, the blessed and Exalted, said to Iblees, 'Excite whosoever of Adam's progeny you can with your voice,' and he did not specify any particular type of voice. Thus every voice which is not an invitation to Allah's worship and to His obedience is included in the meaning of Satan's voice which is referred to in the Qur'anic verse."

In his commentary, Abu Bilal Mustafa Al-Kanadi concluded that this verse is "too general in its meaning, and is not by itself an explicit and unequivocal proof of the prohibition of music and singing, except in the case that such singing and music invites or leads to disobedience to Allah." However, Al-Kanadi then referred to Qur'anic verse from Sura XXXI, *Al-Luqman* (The Wise):

And there are among men those who purchase idle talk in order to mislead others from Allah's path without knowledge, and who throw ridicule upon it. For such there will be a humiliating punishment.

Al-Kanadi quoted Ibn Jareer al-Tabari's opinion in his *Jaamiul Bayaan,* stating that "the interpreters of the Qur'an differed as to the meaning of the term *lahwal hadeeth* (idle talk). Their views regarding its meaning can be formulated into three basic categories." Al-Kanadi cited the categories as singing and listening to songs, the purchasing (hiring) of professional male or female singers, and the purchase of instruments, namely, the drum (*tabla*). In short, according to these conservative Islamic interpretations, music and song are taboo.[3]

For a more contemporary ruling on the issue of music, one need only turn to Mufti Ebrahim Desai, a respected South African mufti with authority to issue *fatwas* (religious decrees). Desai is in charge of a popular Web site, www.ask-Imam.com. Rulings regarding music, dance, singing, and entertainment are posted in a depository of fatwas. What follows are a few examples of the questions and answers appearing on this Web site.

Question: Is music halal in any circumstance, and how do you classify singing? Most of the naats [religious songs praising the Prophet] and nasheeds [Sufi chants with music] I hear today are like rap songs with Music. Is this permissible? How far is the Duf [drum] permissible?

Answer: To assert on the basis of some Ahaadith that to listen to Islamic songs with music in the background is incorrect. Several Ahaadith clearly prohibit the use of the drum as well as other musical instruments.

Consider the following Ahaadith:

Hadhrat Ibn Mas'ood (Radhiallaahu Ánhu) reports that Rasulullah (Sallallaahu Alayhi Wasallam) declared every wine, gambling, beating of drums, and every intoxicant as Haraam. (Abu Dawud)

Hadhrat Ali (Radhiallaahu Ánhu) narrates that Rasulullah (Sallallaahu Alayhi Wasallam) prohibited the beating of drums. (Kanzul Ummaal) The Kubah (drum) is Haraam. (Bayhaqi; Musnad Bazzar)

In contemporary times there is no need to use the drum to announce any occasion, nor is it used for such purposes. In these times, it is used commonly as a musical instrument. The use of the drum as a musical instrument is expressly forbidden, as has been clearly ascertained from the Ahaadith mentioned in the beginning. Also, music itself is expressly forbidden in Deen [religion]. . . .

Rasulullah (Sallallaahu Alayhi Wasallam) mentioned, "When singing girls and musical instruments becomes common, wait for red winds, earthquakes, the earth swallowing people, disfiguring, and many more punishments." (Mishkat 470)

Question: Is regular singing and listening to music forbidden in Islam? Has music been considered "Haraam" in Islam? If it has been, then is listening to it a minor sin, or is it among the "Kabeera" sins?

Answer: Music is expressly prohibited in many Ahaadith. Among the dominant purposes of our beloved Prophet (Sallallaahu Alayhi Wasallam) was to destroy musical instruments. (Mishkat vol. 2)

Another fundamentalist Web site, devoted to Muslim "sisters," provided a forum for contributing articles and advice, entering chat rooms, and receiving support from other sisters in Islam. A 2006 posting on this Web site dealt with the subject of Islamic rulings on music and singing. The author of this article claimed that she had based her material on a book written by al-Kanadi. She emphasized that Muslims should read this excellent book on music and singing in Islam. After reviewing her voluminous article, I concluded that this "sister" served as a convenient mouthpiece for her fundamentalist "brothers."

Nothing in her article was original. It was merely a restatement of dogma that "brothers" have been handing down for centuries—with a new twist. That is, the "sisters" appear even more rigidly fundamentalist than the "brothers." In brief, "The Sisters' Club, Sisters in Oman," speak on the following issues:

Musical instruments (*Ma'aazif*): The use of all musical instruments is forbidden.

Singing (*Ghinaa*): The narration of Al-Haakim described the singing voice coupled with music as imbecilic and sinful. Naturally, singing to musical accompaniment is forbidden, since it is coupled with music.

Dancing: Dancing to musical instruments is prohibited, since that which is coupled with a prohibited thing becomes forbidden.

Throughout human history, dance, music, recitation—indeed, all performance arts—have proven to be vehicles of social and cultural change, transforming the very fabric of a society. Even as conservative Islam forbids women to perform in public and as clerics relegate the status of female performance artists to prostitutes, many talented women continue to transcend this repressive attitude, becoming national treasures in their Muslim homelands.

One such legend is the Egyptian singer Umm Kulthum (1904–75), referred to in the Arab world as "the star of the East" and "the diva of Arabic songs." Umm Kulthum is remembered not only for her vocal excellence but also for promoting traditional Arabic music. She became the spokesperson for various worthy causes, endowed a charitable foundation, advocated government support of Arabic music and musicians, and always stressed the importance of honoring indigenous Arab culture. After the Egyptian coup of 1952, she recorded numerous songs in support of the new Egyptian government and became an ally of President Gamal Abdel Nasser. Following Egypt's defeat in the Six-Day War (1967), she toured the Arab world, donating concert proceeds to the coffers of the Egyptian government. More than a musician, she became "the voice and face of Egypt."[4] During her lifetime, Umm Kulthum was feted by numerous heads of state. Upon her death, she received an honorary state funeral, attended by four million people.

In Nigeria, Siti binti Saad (1880–1950) was revered by her people. She was the first star of the musical genre of *taarab,* which traces its background to the sultan of Omani.[5] Taarab, which is also popular in Tanzania and Kenya, is Arabic in origin. The verb form means "to delight" or "to entertain." It came into English in the form of *troubadour,* a wandering musician. Taarab uses instruments from many cultures, especially those with a historical presence in East Africa. Siti binti Saad was the first Muslim woman on the continent of Africa to perform publicly without a veil. As one of the first East African female politicians, she also embedded political messages in her songs. In the late twentieth century, the Nigerian government began to support taarab musicians and clubs.

By 1950, two sisters—Bibi Azizi and Bibi Nuri—had introduced the *lele-mama,* an East African dance, to taarab performances. This particular dance genre "was part of the Africanisation of the music and dance, a process that continued as new dances and new rhythms were introduced."[6] According to Flavia Aiello, "A modern taarab concert is in fact a very spectacular event, where . . . women display their elegance (dress, jewelry, hairstyles, and henna) and dancing abilities." Perhaps one of the most important components of this art form is the lyrics, which serve as a vehicle for addressing social issues, such as the relationship between co-wives. Taarab "poetry allows the expression of polemic argument or erotic references only through *mafumbo,* a sort of language and imagery difficult to decipher and thus not disturbing the sense of dignity and respect (*heshima*)."[7]

Another example of Muslim women performing in public may be found in the Hausa community of northern Nigeria. In her book *Muslim Women Sing: Hausa Popular Song (African Expressive Cultures)*, Beverly Mack examines the culture of Hausa women, who enjoy a long tradition of oral poetry. Hausa women perform mostly for all-female audiences, although it is not forbidden for the audience to include men. Similar to the taarab performance, song and poetry themes tend to reflect contemporary issues. The Hausa women sing about cultural concerns, such as the Islamic woman's role in society. Themes range from politics to AIDS prevention, childcare, and hygiene. The Hausa musical genre allows women to express ideas relevant to issues impacting their lives and communities.

Village women in Bangladesh are an excellent example of velvet jihadists confronting patriarchal attitudes. These Muslim women singers, all from impoverished rural environments, have traditionally performed songs during celebrations. Ranging in age from seven to seventy, the performers write their own lyrics. According to Nabamita Mitra, the lyrics often contain satire and cover many issues: social, religious, and political. Some of these women have been known to leave their husbands for the love of singing, and they are able to earn their own livelihoods doing so. One of these Bengali singers, Namuna Bibi, is quoted by Mitra as saying, "My husband did not like me singing. I left him for that, as I cannot give up my singing."[8] What sets these women apart is their fearlessness; they are not afraid to criticize (in public) interpretations of Muslim Sharia. Nor are they timid about targeting religious hypocrisy. Needless to say, the Bengali *maulvi* (clerics) have been targets of these songs and therefore have railed against the women's public performances.

Historically, women have always performed for each other. In the absence of male audiences, they sang and danced at all-female gatherings. Because men were forbidden to invade women's spaces at such times, rebellious messages could be encoded in the songs. Laura Lengel suggests that rebellion (*nushuz*) against hegemonic Islamic values can be communicated through song, but go largely unnoticed. In "Performing In/Outside Islam," Lengel notes, "It is not just men who are unwelcome in these performance spaces. The women who support these men most passionately—their mothers—are often excluded. The songs are subversive texts that allow women to insult the mother-in-law, talk of leaving their husbands or taking on a lover, and ignore what a 'good Muslim girl' should be."[9] Openly stating such opinions would carry dire ramifications for these women; weaving such notions into song has allowed them at least a modicum of expression.

Arts and Athletics: Stepping over Boundaries

Monia Hejaiej, who studies Tunisian women's performance of folk narratives, refers to the women-only space as "a door or a window open."[10] Muslim women have always welcomed other women to share stories and struggles, seek and receive comfort, and express their opinions safely.

In the Iranian culture, for example, women participate in private performances known as *bazi*, a comedic and sometimes lewd form of entertainment allowing women full dramatic expression. Sexual freedom is explored in the genre of such songs and activities. Kaveh Safa-Isfahani suggests that it is not unreasonable to assume that these performances "represent a continuing world which is parallel to the everyday world of Iranian women—and which interpenetrates it at various junctures—in daily interactions and communications among women—and which is ever ready to intrude more dramatically and systematically by restructuring women's experiences through actual performance."[11] Such exclusive spaces remain a far cry from concert halls and other public performance venues. Women who dare to be heard and viewed publicly run the risk of being regarded as little better than prostitutes.

Fatemeh Habibian, who performs publicly in the Islamic Republic of Iran, perhaps best exemplifies the exception to this rule. Not only does she perform in public in front of mixed gender audiences, but Habibian also assumes the role (and therefore the manners) of men. She does this with the tone of her voice and with masculine gestures and expressions. The reader may ask: how is it possible for her to go against the hadith of the Prophet?

Narrated Ibn Abbas: Allah's Apostle [the Prophet] cursed those men who similitude [imitate] women and those women who similitude men.[12]

When nationalism and patriarchy merge, it is not unusual for fundamentalist Islam to take a back seat. In fact, nationalism trumps fundamentalism every time.

Born in 1978 in Ahvaz, the southern region of Iran, Fatemeh Habibian goes by the stage name Gordafarid, a female heroine from the ancient Persian epics. She trained with Murshid Turrabi, master of Naqali, the art of storytelling. Naqali particularly relates to stories from the Persian epics found in poetry collections of Shahnameh Ferdosi (940–1020).[13] Habibian began her training at the age of twenty-two. Recalling her early days of training, which took place primarily in traditional Iranian coffeehouses, she says on her Web site:

Because I was very shy and was feeling embarrassed [about being the *only* woman in a coffeehouse full of men], my master recited the following poem to me: "If you are seeking the path of Love, do not think about your reputation. Be assertive and project yourself. Be a Warrior."[14]

As previously mentioned, her audiences are mixed gender and of all ages. Habibian performs fully covered, according to the dress code of the Islamic Republic. However, her costuming becomes irrelevant once the performance begins. With dramatic flair and a mesmerizing voice, Habibian transforms herself into an indescribably powerful presence. She also encourages all audience members to read these epics and therefore become familiar with their pre-Islamic heritage. Because of her immense popularity, the University of Tehran School of Dramatic Arts has instituted classes in the traditional performance of Naqali.

In Tunisia, a remarkable group of women have managed to form their own choral group and orchestra. El'Azifet, the first all-women's orchestra in North Africa, has given women the rare opportunity of performing in public together.

In Afghanistan, with its long tradition of storytellers of religious myths and legends, as well as vaudeville entertainers who perform at weddings, performance art is returning in the wake of the Taliban's "departure." Women are not only writing plays but also acting and directing. Their subject matter reflects the daily realities of Afghan women, the array of social problems they face, and their lives under the Taliban. Female performers are still required to wear a *hijab,* the traditional head covering. Nevertheless, at the 2004 Kabul Festival, women were allowed to perform in front of mixed gender audiences, and their voices were well represented.[15]

Needless to say, Islamic radicals are challenging the emergence of Afghan women in the performing arts. Many Afghans continue to regard theater as inappropriate for women, and they view it as a practice forbidden by Islamic precepts.

From one Islamic region to the next, tolerance levels regarding women and public performance strikingly differ. For example, after the 1979 implementation of hijab in Iran, women were entirely sealed off from public expression of any kind. The Islamic Republic followed extremist Qur'anic interpretations, such as those advocated by Imam Qurtubi of the thirteenth century. The hijab decree effectively silenced the female voice. Overnight, female vocalists became haram, religiously forbidden. This ruling was met with disbelief by most Iranians, resulting in a mass migration of vocalists, musicians, and actors.

Today Iran's popular music industry remains active in Los Angeles–based recording studios. The recordings produced are often heard in Iran within the first day of release (due to downloading from the Internet). Indeed, the Islamic Republic of Iran's attempts at censorship did little to reduce demand for popular music. Although the mullas continue to label these songs as *moseghiye-moftazah*, the shameful music,[16] their censorship efforts have unexpectedly given rise to a genre of traditional Iranian music known as *moseghiye sunnati*. This newly revived art form, popularized at first by male singers using classical Persian Sufi poetry as lyrics, proved to be a safe approach. Not even the ulama could accuse Mulana Rumi, Sa'di, or Hafez of Shiraz—giants of Persian poetry—of composing anything shameful.

Very gradually female vocalists began to make their way back, circumventing the hijab of voice by singing in the chorus—where individual voices could not be detected. Numerous Iranian women formed ensembles that performed only for women.

In response to this creative strategy, the authorities were at a loss. Sold-out concerts ensued. Later, groups of female performing artists also began appearing onstage with their male counterparts. This trend continues to enjoy popularity in both classical and pop genres, even as CD covers still feature female artists adorned in proper hijab.

Mahsa Vahdat, a singer born in Tehran in 1973, is one of the voices on the 2004 compact disk *Lullabies from the Axis of Evil*. She participated in the 2005 Freemuse conference on freedom of musical expression in Beirut. During the conference, she was interviewed about musical censorship in Iran and, specifically, the status of female musicians and singers. Vahdat emphasized that silencing the voices of women must never be regarded as a religious issue, for it is entirely political.

Censorship also impacted the film industry in Iran. Following the shift from monarchy to Islamic Republic, movie producers were handed rigid guidelines. No unveiled woman could appear in Iranian films. After twenty years of censorship, actresses gradually began to carve a niche for themselves in the movie industry. In fact, women are now behind the cameras, shooting and directing films. From Iran to Malaysia, Muslim female filmmakers continue to struggle with hard-line clerics.

For example, Yasmin Ahmad, a controversial, award-winning film director from Malaysia, has defied the rising tide of conservatism in Malaysian society by directing films such as *Muallaf* (Convert). In this award-winning film, the lead actress had her head shaved for the role, and she performed opposite a Chinese Christian—both taboos from the Muslim clerics' perspective. Although "music, dance, and now films have suffered because they are frowned on by the strict interpretations of Islamic law," Ahmad has declared that only God will stop her from making movies.[17]

In the mid-1980s, the Ajoka Theatre was created in Pakistan, one of several groups to emerge as part of a broader movement for the restoration of democracy. A controversial play produced by Ajoka Theatre was entitled *Barri,* meaning "to be released from prison." Written by Shahid Nadeem, a Pakistani exile living in London and working for Amnesty International, the play was based on true stories of women incarcerated under the infamous Hudood Laws,[18] and it illustrated the injustices being perpetrated on women of the lower socioeconomic classes. The lead actress was Fawzia Afzal Khan, now a professor in the English Department at Montclair University in New Jersey. She has written at length on this and other plays in *A Critical Stage: The Role of Alternative Secular Theatre in Pakistan.*

Unfortunately, in nearby Afghanistan, the fate of women participating in media and performance venues has proven inexpressibly tragic. Shaima Rezayee hosted a popular music show, *Hop,* on Afghan Tulo TV. In March 2005, Ulema Shura, a government council of religious scholars, criticized Tulo and other stations for transmitting "programs opposed to Islam and national values." Shaima Rezayee was dismissed from her job, and two months later, she was murdered.[19]

Afghanistan's history of violence against female vocalists, musicians, and TV celebrities is well documented. Two singers, Bakht Zamina and Khan Qarabaghai, were both killed by Islamic extremists in Kabul in the early 1990s. TV personality Saima Akbar was murdered a decade earlier by mujahedin loyalists.[20]

Despite this history of violent reprisal, women continue to brave the odds. Three Afghans known as the Burka Band have recorded a song entitled "Burka Blue" and have been received enthusiastically by European audiences. Their song deals with the way women feel when forced to wear the *burqa,* a form of veil particularly worn in Afghanistan that is also known as *chaduri.* The names of these three young women remain secret in order to ensure their safety. As one of the band members explains, "It would be quite dangerous if the group's identities were revealed to the public. If people in Afghanistan knew who the members of the Burka Band were, we could be attacked or killed because . . . of religious fanatics."[21]

One might assume that Muslim women have a better chance of thriving as performing artists in the West. An August 2005 online report challenges this assumption. According to the report, female vocalists and string players were prevented from participating in Ontario's 2005 Muslimfest. The festival, billed as "promoting diverse culture from the Islamic world," created dissension in the Muslim community after its "organizers insisted that all participants adhere to 'Islamic' etiquette and sharia Islamic law." A prominent Canadian visual artist responded to this interdiction. Asma Arshad, a local artist whose multimedia installations have been displayed at the Royal Ontario Museum, objects to the Islamic ban on sitar and guitar music, the depiction of faces in artwork, and even clapping.

> What is un-Islamic material exactly? I received an invitation to participate last year, but they would not have asked me if they had seen my work, which is very political. Why do they call it Muslimfest when their interpretation of Islam is so narrow?[22]

The Progressive Muslim Union of North America (PMU), based in the United States, also condemned Muslimfest's decision.[23] They voiced strong opposition, arguing against restrictions on Muslim women performers:

> forbidding them from singing in front of mixed audiences, requiring that they wear hijab if reciting poetry, or that they refrain from motions that might be mistaken for dancing, etc. We reject the fundamentalist argument that Islam considers a woman's voice to be part of her "awra" (the part of a person that should supposedly be "covered"), as the Qur'an and hadith have many examples of women expressing themselves in public. . . . Misguided solidarity with extremists who demand the exclusion of women performers, or serious restrictions on their creativity, is not an argument for this kind of gender inequity and repression.[24]

The concept of haram, that which is forbidden, permeates patriarchal Islamic thought. From a young age, children are taught that many behaviors related to music and performance are considered haram. Diana Harris wanted to know why some music teachers in England were experiencing difficulties teaching music to Muslim children. She discovered that conservative interpretation of Sharia deems music to be haram. As a result, Muslim children feel reluctant to learn about or participate in musical activities. They associate music with sex, drugs, and alcohol. For many Muslims, music lessons are considered *mubah,* an action neither forbidden nor recommended, in relation to the religious law. Yet for cultural reasons, they still prefer that their children not take part in music education. Although 90 percent of the Muslims in Harris's study are from the Gujarat region in India and therefore cannot be accepted as the norm for all Muslims, her study sheds light on how rigid interpretations of Islam affect an entire community of believers. The school's director told Harris that several militant governors from the local mosques had stated a preference for banning music education. The school's director also indicated "in many cases it was not the parents who were objecting but the 'uneducated imams.'" Because final authority rests in the hands of imams, it is no wonder that Muslim children, both male and female, are burdened psychologically with skewed perceptions as to the value and beauty of music and the propriety of public performance.[25]

Religious authorities who engage in rhetorical debate concerning women's participation in the arts are also busy issuing fatwas against such activities. I recently visited the official Web site of the Grand Ayatollah Sayyid Ali Husaini Sistani, an impressive site translated in six languages: Urdu, Turkish, French, English, Farsi (Persian), and Arabic.[26] The following questions and answers are excerpted from a section entitled "Current Legal Issues, Entertainment, Music, and Leisure."

> *Question:* Some schools in Western countries compel pupils to learn dancing. Such dancing is not accompanied by singing and it is not for pastime, rather a component of the curriculum. Is it haram for the parents to permit their children to attend such classes?

> *Answer:* Yes, if it contravenes religious upbringing ... as a matter of *ihtiyat* [caution].

The following is another example:

> *Question:* Is dancing prohibited in Islam (that is, dancing with a group of people like bhangra [Punjabi dance], by oneself, or dancing with females)?

Dr. Salim Ahmad Salamah, dean of the faculty of Usulud-Deen at the Islamic University, Gaza, replies:

Men and women dancing together is absolutely haram in all cases, except when a wife dances in front of her husband. The reason behind this prohibition is that with mixed dancing bodily contact is close and improper sexual desires are aroused. This has been strictly forbidden by Islam in an attempt to block the way against evil. If men and women were permitted to dance together, a lot of haram acts could occur. That is why mixed dancing is not allowed.

Dance is only one of many forms of artistic expression that radical Islam attempts to stifle. In the visual arts, as well, Muslim women resolutely continue to defy fundamentalist interpretations. Female photographers and filmmakers are using their talents to reveal what is really happening behind the iron curtains of Islam. For example, Iranian visual artist Shirin Neshat's photography and video clippings are replete with political messages. Neshat's work, shown in fine art galleries throughout Europe and the United States, serves as an exposé of the absurdities and hopelessness endured by women trapped in a closed society.

Sharareh Attari records the alarming realities of life in the Islamic Republic of Iran. She has directed a provocative documentary about the plight of Iranian transvestites and transsexuals in Muslim society. Based on a fatwa issued by Ayatollah Khomeini, sex change operations have been legalized in the Islamic Republic of Iran. Attari's film, *It Happens Sometimes,* recounts the plight of Iranian transsexuals who face disapproval from parents, relatives, and society. Renowned director Khosro Sinayee, who was among the select audience at the premiere, praised the young filmmaker's "courage and determination" in tackling such a delicate issue.[27]

According to Parvez Sharma, whose 2008 documentary, *A Jihad for Love,* deals with the sensitive topic of homosexuality and Islam, the struggle of gay Muslims (also referred to as the "invisible minority") is to continue embracing a religion that frequently persecutes them. Sharma insists that while non-Muslim filmmakers have created commendable films about Islam, in fact "Islam needs us to step out as Muslim artists and take back the discussion of our faith."[28]

Another brilliant Muslim filmmaker, Shebana Coelho, is perhaps best known for her 2006 documentary, *Against All Odds: Women Partnering for Change in a Time of Crisis.* Produced with Rakhee Goyal, this film tells the story of women activists from the Middle East, Africa, and Asia. Their narrative portrays the challenges and successes inherent in coalition building, as well as the value in sharing cross-generational experiences and skills and creating contextual, intercultural approaches to the empowerment of women and girls.

As Muslim women continue to push against the forces of fundamentalism in order to express their artistic talents, they do so in memory of those women who have gone before—including many who have paid with their lives. Gender discrimination in the performing and visual arts will surely continue until all Muslim communities embrace gender equality as an ethical imperative central to Islam.

The Body as Battleground:
The Female Athlete

Muslim women are making their presence felt not only in the arts but also on athletic fields and in sports arenas. For decades, theological debate has centered on how much of a woman's body should be seen in public. In those nations governed by conservative clerics, it is no exaggeration to say that more time and energy has been devoted to this single issue than to economic development or scientific research.

Few would argue that participation in athletics helps an individual develop invaluable skills, including teamwork, leadership, decision making, and self-discipline. A close examination of the Qur'an reveals no admonitions that could be interpreted as barring the believer from physical exercise. In tracing the history of Islam, one discovers that in the Prophet's time, numerous contests were held, including foot races and wrestling. Furthermore, the influential second caliph, Umar Ibn al-Khattab (584–644), stated, "Teach your children swimming and archery, and tell them to jump on the horse's back."[29] Khattab's instruction reveals no mention of teaching athletic activities to male children only.

In pre-Islam, women participated in sports such as archery and horseback riding—not only in public against other women but also in competition with men. The Persian epic *Shahnameh of Ferdosi* records a Persian woman fighting the leader of a rival army. During the invasion of the Tuoran troops in the land of Iran, Sohrab, the brave young Touranian commander, wishes to capture Dezh-E-Sefid, the border fortress of Iran. But he encounters the resistance of a strong hero in a face-to-face struggle.

> In the midst of the battle, when the helmet falls down from the anony-
> mous Iranian hero, the astonished Sohrab finds the Iranian brave fighter
> is a girl by the name of Gordafarid. Gordafarid rescues herself by promis-
> ing Sohrab to open the gates of the fortress, only to escape into the castle,
> close the gates, and ridicule [the commander] and his army.[30]

While physical competition comes as naturally to women as it does to men, women's participation in athletics has been frowned upon by the Islamic patriarchy. Breaking from tradition, Algeria's Hassiba Boulmerka competed for and won the 1996 Olympic gold medal in the 1,500-meter race. She competed wearing a standard runner's outfit.[31] Boulmerka's vic-tory enraged a Muslim preacher in Algeria, who condemned those daring "to display their nudity before the whole world." Death threats followed. Boulmerka became an outcast, afraid to return to her own country. Later, to her credit, she was elected to the Athletes' Commission of the International Olympic Committee and became the first woman from an Arab or African nation to win a world track championship.

The issue of women and athletic participation has become fertile ter-ritory for Internet fatwas. For example, in 2004 a young Muslim woman, eager for guidance, asked for an online religious ruling on participating in sports and received the following response:

> This is what is clear in the fatwa issued by Sheikh Faysal Mawlawi, deputy
> chairman of the European Council for Fatwa and Research. It goes as
> follows: The requirements to be met for a Muslim woman to practice
> sports relate . . . to her duty to cover the 'awrah (parts of the body that
> are not supposed to be exposed to others; vis-à-vis women, her 'awrah
> is from the navel to the knee; as for men, it is all of her body except the
> hands, feet, and face). Thus, if there is a sport that woman can practice
> while adhering to this requirement, then it is permissible for her to do so
> as long as all other religious requirements are fulfilled. In addition, there
> should be no kind of photographing or televising that may broadcast
> these scenes.[32]

Shedding more light on this issue, Dr. 'Ali Muhyy Ed-Deen Al-Qara Daaghi, head of the Department of Principles Jurisprudence (Usul Al-Fiqh) at the Faculty of Shari'ah, Qatar University, adds:

It is an undeniable fact that woman's practicing sport is, in principle, Islamically accepted. However, there are many conditions to be met in this respect. They are as follows:

1. Women must not adorn themselves for the purpose of being seen by men.
2. They must not unveil any of their private parts that Islam orders them to cover.
3. They must not intermingle with men in any way that brings them physically close together.

It is reported that when the Prophet (peace and blessing be upon him) had a race with A'ishah (may Allah be pleased with her), he made sure that men were in the front and A'ishah in the back. This has two significances: first, the permissibility of woman's practicing sport and second, the legal requirements that are to be met in this respect. . . . May Allah guide you to the straight path, and guide you to that which pleases Him, Amen. Allah Almighty knows best.[33]

According to religious scholars, then, women are not barred from participating in sports per se. However, the imposition of a restrictive dress code (in compliance with hijab) as well as the interdiction of mixing with men (i.e., no woman can be trained by a male coach or be present in the same arena or sports facility as men) handicaps Muslim women athletes in ways that their Western counterparts cannot imagine.

In many Muslim countries, including Iran and Egypt, state-owned television limits coverage of events featuring Olympic women athletes. According to Amir Taheri, a reporter for Gulf News, a circular from the Ministry of Islamic Guidance and Culture in Tehran [Iran] asks TV editors to make sure that women's games are not televised live. "Images of women engaged in contests must be carefully vetted," says the letter, leaked in Tehran. "Editors must take care to prevent viewers from being confronted with uncovered parts of the female anatomy in contests."[34]

Shaikh Yusuf Al Qaradawi, an Egyptian theologian based in Qatar, claims that female sport is exploited as a means of undermining "divine morality." Ayatollah Emami Kashani, one of Iran's ruling mullahs, goes further. In a 2004 sermon he claimed that allowing women to compete in the Olympics was a "sign of voyeurism" on the part of the male organizers.[35]

Predictably, self-appointed "mullahs" and "religious scholars" remain preoccupied with issuing Internet fatwas and condemning female athletes who participate in international competitions. The fatwas target women who appear in regular athletic uniforms, claiming, for example, that their legs are indecently exposed by wearing runner's shorts. Instead of being welcomed home as Olympic heroes, female athletes must live in constant fear for their personal safety, as mentioned earlier regarding Algeria's Hassiba Boulmerka.

In 2004, a fatwa was issued against Sania Mirza, an eighteen-year-old Indian tennis player:

"Half-naked" Sania Mirza comes under attack

"Sania Mirza is a Muslim and she stands half-naked on the tennis court while playing, which is against Islam," Siddikulla Chowdhury, secretary of the Jamiat Ulama-i-Hind in Kolkata, told AFP by telephone. "She is trying to ape some Western tennis players who dress in a similar way," said Chowdhury, whose group has a strong base in two eastern states. "The dress she wears on the tennis court not only doesn't cover large parts of her body but leaves nothing to the imagination of voyeurs," another cleric, Maulana Hasheeb-ul-Hasan Siddiqui, told the *Hindustan Times* daily.

"She will undoubtedly be a corrupting influence on these women," said Siddiqui, general secretary of a group called the Sunni Ulema Board, which is influential in Mirza's hometown, the southern city of Hyderabad.[36]

Nida'ul Islam (Call of Islam) is an Australian society. A 2006 article appearing in its magazine addressed the topic of "Muslim Women in Sports." Young Muslim women who participate in sports are advised: "The clothing must be Islamically acceptable. This would therefore exclude shorts, T-shirts, leotards, swimming costumes, etc." The author of the article, Sister Hikmat Beiruty, insists that, when swimming, even the wearing of body suits is not sufficient, nor is the female-only swimming complex appropriate for Muslim women. She bases her argument on the following hadith:

Some women from Homs or from Sham (now the area of Damascus) came to A'ishah. She asked, "Do you enter the public baths? I heard the Messenger of Allah saying that a woman who undresses anywhere else other than in her own house tears off the satr (shelter) [coverage] which lies between her and her Lord."

Beiruty further states that *satr* is not the only problem; the act of "reveal[ing] hair, arms, etc., is permitted only to a Muslim woman's husband, father, mother, and so on. . . . Although many women-only gyms have become popular, we have the same problem as with baths: being in the presence of non-Muslim women. However, as long as loose clothing is worn along with proper head covering, this problem can be avoided."

Beiruty emphasizes that "public showers at female schools are totally forbidden," as is using deodorant: "Many sisters will also apply deodorants after a work-out. What must be kept in mind is the Prophet's warning on fragrant perfumes: 'The woman who perfumes herself and passes through a gathering is an adulteress.'"[37]

On March 29, 1979, Ayatollah Khomeini announced that all of Iran's beaches, public swimming pools, and sports events were to be segregated. Iranian public beaches now have signs guiding female visitors to segregated areas. Private beaches are frequently patrolled to make sure that no one strays beyond gender-restricted zones. The same gender-exclusive regulations apply to ski resorts, hiking trails, and bike trails. Initially women were warned that riding bicycles would be religiously forbidden. Because a bicycle is constructed in the same way as a horse's saddle, requiring women to spread their legs, this activity was deemed unladylike and unfit for Muslim women.

After several years of struggling with the ulama, however, women finally regained the privilege of riding bikes. The government allocated specific times for females to ride in public parks, when men were absent. Because most Iranians are under the age of thirty—and because both youth and women have managed to present united fronts—the ulama have, on occasion, been forced to compromise on rigid decrees. Therefore, it is not unusual to see young women riding scooters in Iranian cities, using them not only as a means of transportation but also as a form of sport and recreational activity.[38]

The ulama have also been forced to back away from rigid decrees based on the efforts of one particularly impeccable velvet jihadist, Faezeh Hashemi Rafsanjani.[39] Perhaps no other individual in Iran has worked as tirelessly to ensure that women have access to athletic activity. Along with other determined Iranian women, Rafsanjani organized the first Islamic Countries Women Sports Games in Iran in 1992. At this first event, 480 female athletes from eleven countries participated. In the second event in 1997, more than

1,000 female athletes from twenty-four countries participated. Upon opening the games, Rafsanjani declared, "It has always been by and through the efforts of women themselves that their rights and legitimate wishes were respected. In order to prove our rightfulness and with regard to our participation in social and sports activities, we Muslim women have no intention whatsoever to resemble men. We practice sports because it guarantees our health and grants us joy and strength, but not at the cost of damaging reverence and sanctities."[40]

Her carefully crafted speech—socially and politically correct—emphasized that women's sports should not be perceived as competition with men. In order to comply with, respect, and honor the dictates of Islam, only female spectators were present at the games. No reporters or photographers were allowed to attend events, since the athletes wore requisite (and therefore revealing) sports uniforms. Only when the women athletes were fully dressed in their hijab could photographers be admitted to record the awards ceremonies.

4.1. Faezeh Hashemi Rafsanjani delivering a speech at the opening ceremonies of the second Islamic Countries Women Sports Games.

4.2., 4.3., 4.4. Athletes from Kazakhstan participating in the second Islamic Countries Women Sports Games.

4.5. Champion athletes from Indonesia at the second
Islamic Countries Women Sports Games.

Against astounding odds, these women managed to create an environment where Muslim "sisters" could participate in international sports competitions. At the second games, Rafsanjani commented, "Our priority was
solidarity between Muslim women. The foundation is strong. We know the
goals and ideals. We are experienced and essential. With God's assistance
we shall reach to our ultimate. The future is more brilliant than the present.
Of this we are sure."[41]

In anticipation of the 2005 Islamic Countries Women Sports Games, a
clash occurred between Rafsanjani and Mahmoud Ahmadinejad, who was
elected president of the Islamic Republic of Iran that same year. In liaison
with the religious authorities, Ahmadinejad complained that the cost of
the games was prohibitive. Furthermore, stricter dress codes would have

4.6. A group photo of track and field participants at the second Islamic Countries Women Sports Games.

to be observed: the athletes would be obliged to wear headscarves in all sporting events except for swimming competitions. Rafsanjani responded, "The games will take place despite radical political change in the country," warning that "some forces currently in power would like women to abandon sports."[42] This overt reference to Ahmadinejad and his radical Islamist supporters stirred up controversy, to say the least, and caught the Islamic world's attention.

While rules and regulations regarding women's participation in athletics differ from one Islamic country to the next, the position of the Islamic Republic of Iran remains pivotal. Increasingly, other conservative Muslim nations look to Iran's policies as an example of accepted protocol.

In Iran, women have refused to sit quietly by and accept exclusion from public spaces. In 2002 a grassroots effort was organized to protest a ban on women attending soccer games. According to the publication *Jane,* Zohreh Solemiani and several thousand women arrived at Azadi Stadium to watch the World Cup in which the Iranian soccer team was playing. Authorities refused them entry, stating that "soccer matches are too rough for women." The women, however, stood their ground, led by older, working-class women who shamed the guards by reminding them that "they'd raised these boys and it was their hard-won right to join the celebration." The authorities finally gave in.[43]

In 2005, the *International Herald Tribune* reported another seminal event. Mahboubeh Abbass-Gholizadeh, a leading women's rights activist, suffered a broken leg when she and other women were charged by militia as they tried to push their way into the national stadium in Tehran. The *Tribune* quoted Abbass-Gholizadeh:

"We consider this [allowing women to attend live soccer games in stadiums] a victory for the women's movement," she said on Radio Free Europe. "Before Mr. President issued this order, we were planning on creating some solidarity among Iranian women who live abroad. We were busy working on a campaign to attend matches at the World Cup and chant slogans and have placards. But it appears that before people outside Iran could hear about the campaign, the president was informed and issued this letter."[44]

In a surprising move in 2006, Ahmadinejad announced that women would be allowed into sports stadiums for the first time since 1979. After the Islamic revolution, women had been prevented from entering stadiums and from attending soccer matches because men were wearing shorts.[45] In fact, Ahmadinejad ultimately criticized those who linked social corruption to the presence of women in public, saying, "Some consider women as the source of corruption, and this is a very wrong attitude."[46] The last word, however, came from Iran's supreme leader, Ayatollah Ali Khamenei. In late spring of 2006, he ruled that women would not be allowed entry to soccer games, not even to sit in a segregated section. Ahmadinejad remained powerless in the face of this ruling. But Iranian women continued to make their presence known. According to a May 2006 Associated Press report, female soccer fans showed up at the fence surrounding Tehran's soccer stadium chanting, "We will be inside someday." A few men in the stands answered, "Sisters, don't give up!"[47]

4.7. *Zanaan,* March/April 2006, cover photo of two Iranian soccer fans, protesting against the ban on women entering Azadi Stadium. The young woman protesting on the right has wrapped herself in Iran's flag. Their sign reads, "Azadi, the stadium with a 100,000 boys? Where are our seats? Where can we cheer?" Because the Persian word *azadi* means "freedom," these individuals are implying that no freedom exists for them simply because they are women.

Arts and Athletics: Stepping over Boundaries

Sportswear Tailored
to the Modern Muslim Woman

In 2004, Nike Go and the United Nations High Commissioner for Refugees (UNHCR) entered into partnership.[48] Their stated mission: to effect positive change in the lives of Muslim girls by facilitating healthy involvement in sports activities and competitions. The first phase of this project provided trained coaches to work with Muslim girls and to teach them health and hygiene. Gyms and sports arenas were created especially for practice and training.

The second phase, the phase that deserves closer scrutiny, entailed the creation of a line of sportswear for Muslim girls. A video produced by UNHCR and Nike Go (*Together for Girls, Designers on Mission*) featured several Nike Go associates discussing the importance of creating this line of sportswear. Their designer clothing did in fact meet the religious requirements of modesty—featuring adjustable length, which may be ankle length for street wear and shortened for sports activities. The savvy comment of the head designer is particularly revealing: "The design construction should be a Muslim girl's friendly garment; they should like it. Whether we like it or not is unimportant." Aside from Nike's altruistic pose, their shrewd marketing strategies promise huge returns. Considering that there are 500 million Muslim women in the world, one-fourth of the world's female population, the profit potential seems impressive.

Also tapping into market potential is Ahiida, an Australian women's sportswear company run by a Muslim businesswoman, Aheda Zanettie. This company features a line of fashionable, high-priced lifestyle gear for Muslim women; swimsuits range in cost between $150 and $175. This includes a hood-shaped Hijab design called the Hijood (a clever name combining both *hijab* and *hood*) and a hybrid of the Islamic burqa and the Western world's bikini called a Burkini. According to FrontPageMagazine. com, "The [Burqini/Burkini] lycra two-piece bathing suit covers its wearer from head to foot, showing only the hands, feet, and face."[49] Yet another start-up company is Splashgear, based in Huntington Beach, California, which began offering conservatively designed bathing suits for the Muslim woman in 2007. This particular swimwear line emerged out of the owner's personal need for modest scuba diving gear.

4.8. Islamic bathing suit, called the Hijood, made in Australia by Ahiida. Courtesy of Aheda Zanetti, Ahiida Company.

Turkish clothing manufacturer Hasema also produces modest swimwear for Muslim girls and women. Mehmet Sahin, creator of Hasema's swimwear line, began by designing swimsuits for men. Sahin explains, "As a pious Muslim, I wanted to wear a bathing costume that did not cling to my genitals." A shrewd businessman, Sahin claims that the material used for the bathing suits even allows solar penetration, "Customers who want a tan can now get one without undressing."[50]

While manufacturers exploit the predicament of Muslim females, asking only whether their products have sufficient market potential, few are asking the more important questions: Are fundamentalist policies that place unreasonable clothing restrictions on Muslim females necessary? Are these policies promoting the good health, self-confidence, success, and personal happiness of these girls and women?

Some would argue that the situation is not so bad. After all, at the beginning of the 1979 Islamic revolution in Iran, women were barred completely from swimming at public beaches. The government finally gave in to women's demands, at least in part. Segregated public beaches were created, allowing women to swim and exercise far from the lecherous eyes of

4.9, 4.10, 4.11. Islamic bathing suits produced by the Turkish clothing manufacturer Hasema. Courtesy of *Cumhuriye Daily News,* Turkey.

men. On a trip in 2004 to the Island of Kish, located in the Persian Gulf, my daughter, my female relatives, and I frequented one of these segregated beaches. From the lifeguards to the restaurant employees, all were women. We saw no specially designed bathing suits, but did see a significant number of topless and nude bathers. In Egypt as well, at the elite Mediterranean resort of Marina La Femme (one of three women-only beaches), a growing business now caters to the "new class of religious Egyptians who are hip, rich, and young. These secluded strips of sand are an attempt to reconcile liberal and conservative, worldly and heavenly, fun and piety."[51] On my trip to Tel Aviv in the summer of 2006, I encountered two public beaches along the Mediterranean Sea with signs in Hebrew and English: "The Separated Beach Bathing Days for Women: Sun, Tue, Thu. Bathing Days for Men: Mon, Wen [Wed], Fri." I did a double take, reminding myself that I was in the Middle East, although certainly not on Islamic soil.

Whether or not beaches throughout the Muslim world continue to be segregated, and whether or not Nike Go realizes its projected profit margins, the fact remains that Sharia-driven policies, holdovers from a different time, continue to jeopardize the basic rights of contemporary Muslim women.

4.12. A swimming schedule posted at a Tel Aviv beach.

4.13. Kish Island in the Persian Gulf. A sign posted reads: "Ladies' beach only, entry of gentlemen is forbidden."

Sarah J. Murray acknowledges that fanatical fundamentalists are not exclusive to Islam; they exist in every religious group. However, she voices special admiration for Muslim women, given the enormous barriers to their full participation in athletic competition.

Murray explains that the Women's Sports Foundation exists because of its belief in the power of play in girls' and women's lives, including the many benefits derived from sports. She states:

> To promote truly global growth of female athleticism, we must sow and nurture the seeds of recognition, empowerment, and equality in Muslim countries as we do at home. . . .
>
> We [American women] have struggled for decades to provide women with equal opportunity in sports and have overcome both the prejudices and extremist discrimination that keep Muslim women's sports unexposed and underdeveloped today. For the sake of unity and humanity, it's time to unveil the myths and truly celebrate the glorious participation of all women in sports.

Murray underscores the sad reality that "many Americans have been conditioned by politics, media, and prejudice to associate women of Islam with notions of oppression and indignity." Murray labels this perception as "disempowering and largely misdirected." Given the unparalleled efforts and successes of female Muslim athletes, there can be no doubt that, in tandem with grassroots activists, these determined women are leveling the Islamic playing field, positively impacting access to and full participation in the public arena of sports competition.[52]

God Is Beautiful and Loves Beauty:
Allah jamil wa yuhibb al-jamal

In the Holy Qur'an, Sura XCV, *Tin* (The Fig), verse 4 alludes to the perfection of human beings. According to A. Yusuf Ali, humankind (which includes both men *and* women) has proven to be Allah's most perfect handiwork.[53] The *barakat* (blessings) Allah has bestowed upon human beings—including the ability to convey emotion through voice and dance and to express the joy of being alive through physical activities—are countless. Islam encourages the "believer" to make maximum use of these numerous blessings. Muslim women are doing just that, expressing themselves artistically and athletically.

As noted by Fedwa Malti-Douglas, in the Arabo-Islamic tradition, a woman's voice and body are inextricably related to each other.[54] And Fatima Mernissi goes straight to the heart of the matter by asking:

> How did the [fundamentalist] tradition succeed in transforming the Muslim woman into that submissive, marginal creature who buries herself and only goes out into the world timidly, and huddled in her veils? Why does the Muslim man need such a mutilated companion?[55]

Mernissi provides a convincing answer to her own question:

> The downward slide, as far as women are concerned, took place under the Abbasid dynasty.[56] That period which is regularly presented to us as the Golden Age (8th and 9th centuries) was the period of international conquest for the Muslims and also of the arrival of the *jawari* (women slaves) coming from conquered countries: "Men gave each other *jawari*: Persians, Romans, Turks, etc." With the economic boom and expansion of the cities, "the Arabic woman was completely marginalized; she had lost all her freedom and pride. . . . Then she began to be treated with contempt. . . . "
>
> The *jawari* turned to learning and poetry to better their condition and attract the attention of powerful men who paid well for the company of beautiful, learned women who could provide them with diversion.[57]

These same slave girls of the Islamic Middle Ages, according to Malti-Douglas, were highly trained in music, entertaining "at social occasions where men were present." In fact, the singing slave girls were sex objects and great courtesans who wielded enormous seductive power. Thus the association of prostitution with public singing dates back to the eighth century. According to treatises from the classical period, the legacy that Muslim women face today dates back to this specific historical era and is clearly documented.

However, if one returns to the source of all Islamic wisdom, the hadith of the Prophet, one finds that singing and music were sanctioned, especially to celebrate the human spirit. Among many companions of the Prophet, as well as second-generation Muslim scholars that followed, none of these men saw anything immoral about women singing and making music.

A'ishah narrated that during the days of Mina, on the day of 'Eid al-Adha, two girls were with her, singing and playing on a hand drum. The Prophet (peace be upon him) was present listening to them with his head under a shawl. Abu Bakr then entered and scolded the girls. The Prophet (peace be upon him), uncovering his face, told him, "Let them be, Abu Bakr. These are the days of 'Eid."[58]

Perhaps the fundamentalist attitude has more to do with the eighth century than it does with the teachings of the Prophet and his companions. Equally as important, the issue of women's participation in sports and athletics can be traced back to the actual life experience of the Prophet. As narrated by Ahmad and Abu Daoud, A'ishah commented on her own foot race with the Prophet. This comment is particularly telling because it explicitly shows that Muhammad requested women to run:

I raced with the Prophet (peace be upon him) and beat him in the race. Later, when I had put on some weight, we raced again and he won. Then he said, "This cancels that," referring to the previous occasion."[59]

Banning women from the athletic arena and silencing their artistic expression should not be debated from a religious perspective. Rather, these restrictions are entirely political. The term *Islamism* underscores this reality. According to Wikipedia, it is defined as "a set of political ideologies holding that Islam is not only a religion but also a political system." Only when Islam is taught in its true spiritual context can Muslims guide humanity toward a more equitable, benevolent world community.

FIVE

Gender Preference

AN ISLAMIC VIEW

Due to the patriarchal structure of Islam, female sexuality has always been viewed through a distinctly myopic lens. The idea that women would be interested in securing intimate sexual relationships with other women has largely been dismissed. Nowhere in the Qur'an does one find mention made of same-sex love between women. One can only assume that the patriarchs perceived this issue as a phenomenon unworthy of serious moral consideration. In large part, this may be due to female physiology. Anatomically a woman cannot penetrate another woman, and since penetration is requisite for procreation, all other forms of sexual behavior seem inconsequential. Historically, Muslim men have cultivated a narrow perception of what constitutes sexual activity, ignoring the wider concept of "pleasure" while focusing exclusively on the single act of male/female copulation. The same male egocentrism prevails today, although attitudes toward lesbian behavior vary significantly among contemporary Islamic societies.

Homosexuality: Qur'an and Ahadith

In contrast to other monotheistic religious traditions, Islam sheds a positive light on sexuality, celebrating it as a positive expression of Allah's will. Sex and sexual desires are neither sinful nor shameful. The Qur'an is very clear on this point. Adam and his nameless female companion (referred to in Qur'anic verses only as "his wife") are viewed as divinely perfect. Contrary to commonly held beliefs, Islam views sexual desire as a natural part of creation, reflecting Allah's purpose to secure continuity of generations.[1] The Qur'an depicts a sensual, sexually blissful heaven where the righteous will reside. In Sura 52, *Tur* (The Mount), verse 20, note the reference to *Hurin*:

> They will recline (with ease)
> On Thrones (of dignity)
> Arranged in ranks;
> And We shall join them
> To Companions [Hurin] with beautiful
> Big and lustrous eyes.[2]

According to Yusuf Ali's commentary, men and women alike will share the joyful bliss provided by Allah.[3] Thus, in an Islamic paradise filled with joy and pleasures, God blesses both genders equally.

Although the Qur'an does not mention lesbianism, Sura 95, *Tin* (The Fig), verse 49, does emphasize the majesty of human beings:

> We have indeed created man
> In the best of moulds.

According to Yusuf Ali, this mould (*taqwim*) is interpreted as "There is no fault in God's creation."[4] In Sura 15, *Al-Hijar* (The Rocky Tract), verse 29, the spirit of God is addressed:

> When I have fashioned him [man]
> (in due proportion) and breathed
> Into him of My spirit,
> Fall ye down in obeisance Unto him.

A number of Qur'anic interpretations refer to man as the *khalifa* (agent) of God on earth, including the writings of Ibn 'Arabi, who discussed the idea of *al-Insan al-Kamil,* the perfect man. Al 'Arabi states that God created the whole world like a mirror that has not yet been polished.

> [In order that] He might be perfectly manifested in it, it was necessary by means of divine Order (*amr*) this mirror should be made clear . . . and Adam became the very clarity of this mirror and the spirit of this image." Therefore the Prophet says that God created Man in His image; that is to say, that Adam is the prototype who synthesizes all the categories of the divine Presence, essence (*dhat*), attributes (*sifat*), and actions (*af'al*).[5]

Examining a wide array of religious commentaries written by scholars across time, one finds this concept of the "perfect man" addressed repeatedly. Given the universal interpretation that each individual contains God's spirit and has been created perfectly in God's image, it is not unreasonable to argue that whatever sexual tendencies with which one is born perhaps reflect God's intention as well. This issue, like any other, can be argued from opposing viewpoints.

The tendency toward homosexuality, especially male homosexuality, has been addressed in detail by Islamic jurisprudence. In contrast, the ahadith have (historically) hardly touched the issue of lesbianism. One exception was the medieval religious scholar Ibn Hajar Haytami (1504–67) of the Shaf'i school of Islamic law, who wrote the *List of Enormities* in which sexual offenses are enumerated, including homosexual behaviors between women. Haytami labeled this "female tribadism (*musaahaqat al-nisa'*)—which is a woman doing with a woman something resembling what a man would do with her"[6]—and referred to it as a forbidden practice. It is not difficult to find many *sahih ahadith* (authentic sayings of the Prophet) addressing homosexual behavior between men, but again, with the exception of Haytami, there is practically no mention of lesbian behavior in any hadith collections of which I am aware.

While traditional orthodox Muslims generally agree that sahih ahadith contain the authentic pronouncements of the prophet Muhammad, a majority of liberal Muslims remain skeptical. The liberal faction, some of whom have been exposed to fraudulent ahadith (for example, commentary developed and collected two hundred years *after* the Prophet's death), wonder what the man Muhammad would have said on the issue of homosexuality. According to Murray and Roscoe, "In Mohammad's homeland of Arabia, male-male sexual relations were apparently ridiculed," but there were no officially sanctioned punishments.[7]

A liberal Muslim must question the severity of punishment for the act of *liwat/lutiyya*.[8] All too often, the type and intensity of punishment for this behavior is dependent on the Sharia and customary law practiced in the village or region where the "crime" occurs. For example, punishment for homosexual behavior in Istanbul or Beirut differs significantly from punitive measures meted out in Riyadh or Tehran. The *Western Journal of Medicine* reports that sodomy between men is punishable by death in eight countries around the world. These eight Muslim nations, where the constitutions are based on Sharia, are Afghanistan, Iran, Mauritania, Pakistan, Saudi Arabia, Sudan, United Arab Emirates, and Yemen. The rulings on homosexuality in these countries often result from clerics manipulating Qur'anic verse to fit their own personal attitudes and moral preferences.[9]

For example, one Qur'anic verse in particular—Sura IV, *al-Nisa* (The Women), verses 15–169—condemns the act of homosexuality between men (in addition to what is normally cited in various Qur'anic chapters and verses about Lut):[10]

> If two men among you
> Are guilty of lewdness,
> Punish them both.
> If they repent and amend, Leave
>   them alone; for God
> Is Oft-returning, Most merciful.[11]

As noted in the verse itself, there is no mention of execution or death. The word *punishment* is open to interpretation; also, the verse leaves ample room for repentance and redemption. The same chapter (verse 15) directly refers to lewdness and women, but falls short of addressing sex between two women.

> If any of your women
> Are guilty of lewdness
> Take the evidence of four
> (Reliable) witnesses from amongst you
> Against them; and if they testify,
> Confine them to houses until
> Death do claim them,
> Or God ordain for them
> Some (other) way.

While this verse refers to heterosexual sex outside of marriage, including fornication and adultery, clearly no mention is made of sexual acts between women. Moreover, the form of punishment set for the unchaste woman is ambiguous: "Or God ordain for them Some (other) way." This ambiguity leaves the type and severity of punishment open to interpretation.

Although the ahadith provide some instruction about same-sex behavior, these dictates appear inconsistent, and their authenticity seems questionable. Countless scholars have offered various interpretations, each bringing his personal perspective and prejudice to the issue.

Regarding acts of homosexuality, including lesbianism, Al-Bukhari is often quoted in the hadith of the prophet Muhammad:

> Narrated Ibn Abbas: Allah's Apostle [the Prophet] cursed those men who similitude [imitate] (assume the manners of) women and those women who similitude (assume the manners of) men.[12]

If one accepts Al-Bukhari's collection as authentic sayings of the Prophet, two points are clear: the act of cross-dressing is condemned, as is the behavior of adopting opposite gender roles. However, there is no mention of punishment, let alone execution. Reading this hadith carefully, the term *manner* is wide open to interpretation by any religious authority to include or exclude a plethora of sexual behaviors.

In Islamic-dominated countries, it seems unlikely that equal rights for gays and lesbians will be achieved by logical secular arguments—arguments that do not adhere to the sacred text of the Qur'an or to hadith of the Prophet. However, the Feminist Sexual Ethics Project (a study from Brandeis) suggests that, at least for lesbians, instituting a legal same-sex relationship might be a possible resolution.

> Islamic jurisprudence has never addressed the question of same-sex sexual behavior (male-male or female-female) except as illicit contact outside of a legally sanctioned bond [marriage]. This raises an important question: is homoerotic sexual activity always forbidden? Or might the impermissibility be the result of the lack of a legal relationship between the same-sex pair? . . . If there were such a thing as a lawful relationship between two women or two men, then would the verdict about sexual activity between them differ? Whether such a licit same-sex relationship can exist is a different legal issue . . . but it is one that Muslim jurisprudence has not addressed.[13]

Khalid Duran, a Muslim scholar, has addressed the issue of homosexuality from the perspective of human rights. He bases his argument on general ethical readings rather than on restrictive (textual) readings of the sacred texts. Duran's example suggests taking a closer look at the beliefs attributed to the prophet Muhammad throughout his lifetime, especially the ethical principles he preached and followed as a human being.[14]

Whether from a theological, legal, or ethical standpoint, the issue of homosexuality in Islam is not likely to be resolved in the near future. Prerequisite to the process of resolution would be the collective awareness of, and admission to, inevitable ambiguities in interpretation resulting from each interpreter's personal, moral, and religious bias.

Homosexuality and Medieval Islam

Volumes of Sufi poetry dating from the thirteenth century reveal affectionate expressions of love between men. Many believe that the Islamic philosopher and Sufi mystic Jalal al-Din Rumi (1207–73) took a male lover, Shams Tabrizi, for whom he composed many volumes of love poetry.

The love of and appreciation for manly beauty—especially that of an older man for a handsome boy—is a familiar theme in Persian poetry. The idea that a charming face or figure, whether male or female, could stir desire in the male psyche was universally accepted. In fact, responding to the natural beauty of the human form, regardless of gender, was in no way considered improper in medieval Islam.

To discover how and when this attitude began to change—specifically, in Iranian culture—one need look no further than Afsaneh Najmabadi's book *Women with Mustaches and Men without Beards*. Describing this shift in attitude from a historical perspective, Najmabadi writes:

> By the seventeenth century . . . some texts on ethics define an adult man's desire for the adolescent as an illness as well. Whereas the thirteenth-century *Akhlaq-i-Nasiri* called such desire excessive attraction, the seventeenth-century *Akhlaq-i-'almara'* transformed it into an illness (*maraz*). This, however, did not become a dominant mode of thinking.[15]

Najmabadi also refers to identity categories—labels that emerged over time to describe the "homosexual as a species," especially the categories of "gay" and "lesbian."[16]

Literature discussing the era of Turkish Ottoman rulers (1299–1922) includes copious references to homosexuality, while devoting hardly a footnote to the subject of lesbianism.[17] Perhaps lesbianism was not afforded the same attention simply because of the cultural tendency to guard female sexuality as a very private matter. Given that female sexuality has always been tied inextricably to a man's honor in Islamic society, revealing or discussing women's sexual preferences would have been a taboo topic, and it remains so today. Literacy is another factor that might explain the scarcity of lesbian literature throughout history. Without permission to read or write, Muslim women were effectively prevented from recording or reflecting on their own lives. Any contemporary scholar or historian striving to understand these women's lives within their respective societies must rely on history written exclusively by men.

The widespread practice of gender segregation in most Islamic societies created unparalleled opportunities for women to gather privately together, affording them time to experience and experiment with all aspects of life, including exploration of their sexuality. Such conditions may have even encouraged and contributed to same-sex love among women. As mentioned previously, men apparently considered sex to be limited to the act of copulation, and since women engaging in sexual pleasures with each other were never at risk of becoming pregnant, women with lesbian tendencies could remain "honorable" and "pure" from the perspective of family and community.

Historical literature describes life in large Muslim societies as surprisingly colorful and rich in sexual motifs. Examples of this literature include *Arabian Nights*, originally known as *One Thousand and One Nights* (*Alflailah wa-lailah*), written by Ibn Battuta in the fourteenth century, and *The Perfumed Garden of the Shaykh Nefzawi*, written by Umar ibn Muhammad al-Nefzawi in the fifteenth century. Both of these medieval texts, translated by Sir Richard Burton, amply satisfied Burton's Victorian preoccupation with homosexuality and sexual deviance.

In their study of classical Arabic literature, Wright and Rowson discuss the same-sex theme in detail.[18] They point to intimate relationships between rulers and their male lovers, a commonplace practice in medieval Islam. Saleem Kidwai describes this practice as a "tradition . . . well established among the elite since the inception of Muslim rule in India." Saleem Kidwai cites numerous Indian kings with homosexual leanings, including Sultan Mahmud of Ghaznah, who in the eleventh century fell in love with his male slave Ayaz.[19]

In medieval Islam, then, influential men—especially those men at the top rungs of political power—were connoisseurs of every kind of beauty, seeking a wide variety of sexual experiences. Their communities apparently neither frowned on this behavior nor labeled their exploits negatively. For the most part, officials looked the other way, endorsing tolerance of male sexual preferences as private choices. Undoubtedly, women's sexual experiences were just as colorful, though rarely recorded in the literature.

The plethora of surviving historical documents describing Muslim culture suggests that taboos regarding same-sex love did not exist with the same virulence as they do today. With the exception of orthodox Muslim theologians in India, who requested the harshest punishments for homosexual sodomy in the seventh and eighth centuries, the majority of Islamic theologians based their judgments on the Qur'anic verse that suggested forgiveness in the face of repentance and lenience where punishment was considered. Kidwai points out that "compared to Christian Europe, trials and punishments for homosexuality are rare in the history of Muslim peoples in medieval times."[20] Kidwai cites the Urdu poets Najmuddin Shah Mubarak (known by his pen name, Abru) and Mir Taqi Mir (1723–1810) as noteworthy for their homoerotic verse; both were highly regarded by their contemporaries and successors.

Ruth Vanita states that, in pre-nineteenth-century India, same-sex love between women and between men, while not encouraged, was certainly not persecuted. According to Vanita, no record exists in India of any individual ever being executed for the act of homosexuality. She further notes that those who preferred to have same-sex love in place of heterosexual love had to display "tremendous creativity in shaping their own lives as well as patterns of community." In other words, by living a double life, one could satisfy sexual desires and proclivities while safely keeping the larger community at bay. Vanita calls attention to the fact that the manuscripts she studied—texts from the Kamasutra, the Puranic, and Katha literature, and popular folk tales—all contained reference to sexual interaction between men and between women in the same sections. Thus she concludes that same-sex love, treated equally in all of the manuscripts, would have been equally prevalent among men *and* women.[21]

Again, according to Vanita, in late medieval Urdu poetry, depiction of sexual relationships between women is unmistakable. She notes a particular genre of poetry called Rekhti, which characteristically employs terms denoting sexual activity between women and describes women given to such activity. This form of poetry, written by men, used a female voice. According to Vanita, during the recitation of Rekhti poetry, a poet often recited the poem imitating the feminine voice in order to emphasize the female persona in his poetry. Some of the poets would dress like a woman or wear a veil. Some of these poets also took a female pen name, including some very suggestive names such as the Dogana, meaning "two-ness" or "doubling." In fact, the Urdu term *dogana* refers both to homoerotically inclined women and to lesbian activity. Another term prevalent in Rekhti poetry is *chapti*, a word still in use in the Urdu language that means sticking, clinging, or rubbing together. Lesbian women are called *chaptabaz,* or "given to the activity of chapti."[22]

In his introduction to *Suppressed Persian*, Paul Sprachman states that among the many Persian literary traditions of poetry and prose, there were writers who "violate[d] a fundamental Islamic taboo against obscenity."[23] This "forbidden" genre of Persian literature—beginning with the mystic and poet Sanai of Ghazna (1087–91) and expanding through the centuries to Iraj Mirza (late nineteenth century, a member of the Qajar royal family)—grew alongside "forbidden" Arabic literature. Sprachman calls attention to the fact that "Arabic and Persian writers of the medieval period generally did not use circumlocutions when referring to private parts and functions in literary work; however, contemporary theologians determined that any such references were anathematic to Islam."[24]

Sprachman's allusions to bawdy literature, within the bilingual and bicultural contexts of Persian and Arabic, include numerous references to the theme of same-sex love among men. Although no mention is made of same-sex love among women, Sprachman does include the eleventh-century poetess Mahasti Ganjavi (born in Ganja in Azerbaijan) in his anthology. Ganjavi's poems protest against religious prejudice, hypocrisy, and conservatism while exploring—from a woman's perspective—what it means to lead a completely free and therefore happy life.

Another poetess, Walladah bint al-Mustakfi, who lived in eleventh-century Islamic Spain, composed poetry openly in praise of Muhjah, her female lover. According to As'ad AbuKhalil, most of this poetry was not saved or referenced because of the explicit sexual language. AbuKhalil makes this claim based on a study by Hoenerbach, who refers to Walladah as the woman who broke ibn Zaydun's heart.[25]

One cannot easily deny the pervasive theme of same-sex love in the literature of the Muslim subcontinent, from medieval times through the eighteenth century. Persian poetry, which was influenced directly by the Sufis—and which was responsible for shaping and inspiring Urdu poetry in India—is rife with references to the *shahid*, or beloved. This "beloved" is invariably associated with the male gender. While Sufi scholars may argue that the "beloved" was merely a symbol of sublime union with the Creator (as noted by Schimmel),[26] ample historical evidence exists of homosexual practices—especially among the ruling elite, among artists and poets, and likely among women sequestered and secluded in tightly knit families and community groups—to counter this argument with some credibility.

In fact, according to the Feminist Sexual Ethics Project, there is no question whatsoever that same-sex sexual activity between women prevailed in medieval Islam:

Despite current conventional wisdom to the contrary, same-sex sexual expression has been a more or less recognized aspect of Muslim societies for many centuries, as can be seen through literature, history, and law. Medieval Arabic literature, including both belles-lettres works (in the genre of *adab* [etiquette or proper behavior]) and copious amounts of erotica, discusses same-sex sexual activity frequently and explicitly. Most often it is sexual activity between men that is discussed, but these literary works also include discussion of sexual acts between women.[27]

Other evidence points to the fact that lesbianism existed as an accepted practice in Iranian society as early as the seventeenth century. Sadegh Hedayat (1903–51), a well-known twentieth-century Iranian author, writes about the concept of *khahar khandegi* (adoptive sister) in his 1933 work, *Neyrangestan*.[28] The following translation is of particular interest:

Khahar Khandegi

When two women want to become *khahar khandeh* with each other, they should find a woman whom they both trust, who has a reputation of being a *pa sabz*, to perform the initial rite of introduction.[29] In the beginning, the two women do not meet face-to-face. Instead, the pa sabz, or intermediary, will create a small figurine made of wax in the shape of a woman.[30] The wax figurine will be placed in the center of a large tray on which various types of sweets are placed. The woman who wishes to be a khahar khandeh will send this tray to the woman she desires (sending this tray is like sending a proposal to the other woman to become her lover). If the receiver of the tray places a black chador (veil) over the wax figurine, she has refused the proposal, but if she places a necklace on the figurine and tips the messenger who brought the tray, then she has accepted the offer.

Ceremony of Khahar Khandegi

The day of Qadir-e Khom (Eid-e Qadir-e) is designated as the proper day on which the two women will be officially recognized as khahar khandeh, or companions.[31] This initiation will take place at one of the local shrines where women will gather [as witnesses to the ceremony] to drink sweet drinks and play tambourines. One of the women [in the couple] will say *Be hagh-e shah-e Khaybar gir* (swear in the name of the king and the conqueror of Khaybar),[32] and the other woman will reply *khodaya matlab-e ma ra bar avardeh be pazir* (Oh God, grant us our wish and accept us). Then the two women will perform a ritual which requires twelve scarves tied differently, each scarf with a particular name. Then these women will send gifts to each other, according to what is inscribed in Kulsom Naneh's book.[33]

Bahram Choubine also refers to the practice of lesbianism as an accepted phenomenon in seventeenth-century Iran. According to Choubine, although unmarried women were not allowed to enter an open lesbian relationship, no secret was made of married ladies having female lovers. Indeed, it was possible for two women (married or unmarried) to perform the ceremony of khahar khandegi, allowing them to become intimate lovers and to remain partners for a lifetime.[34] Choubine states that prior to any such commitment, the women would often take a short trip together and afterwards spend about six months deciding whether they were compatible. On occasion, husbands would not agree to such open lesbianism, and the couple would end up in divorce. Whether divorce ensued or not, usually the two women remained committed to each other in terms of emotional and financial support.[35]

The lesbian ceremony of initiation vividly described by Sadegh Hedayat and Bahram Choubine demonstrates an unmistakable creativity on the part of Iranian Muslim women. By juxtaposing a cultural tradition (which obviously grated against existing religious rules) with sacred pronouncements and religious references, women were able to use the Islamic framework to further their private agendas and to engage in behavior that might otherwise have been forbidden. By doing so, they successfully kept the tradition alive while protecting their status as respected members of the larger society. The openness and acceptance of same-sex activity between Muslim women (in Iran), dating from the seventeenth century, is all the more surprising when contrasted with the strictly enforced social and sexual taboos of contemporary Islam.

In the literature of *Kulsom Naneh,* specifically chapter 15, Agha Jamal Khansari states the following:

> All the ulama [religious scholars] are in agreement that [every] woman should have khahar khandegi, and if a [female] person dies without having had a khahar khandegi, how will that person hope to enter Paradise? And a [female] person who has had a khahar khandegi and spends a lifetime with her [female] partner, then on the great day of Resurrection she will not be judged but rather will go directly to Paradise.[36]

This seventeenth-century author, an Islamic cleric, reflects the tolerance, support, and even encouragement that clergy of that era extended to women in terms of same-sex companionship.

Muslim Gays and Lesbians: Contemporary Activism

As discussed earlier, the treatment of and behavior toward homosexuals in contemporary Islam depends largely on the specific region where the "forbidden immoral act" takes place. Gays and lesbians residing under the Islamic Sharia face varying consequences. The severity of punishment that fatwas carry against homosexual behavior mirrors the extent of homophobia within a particular Islamic society. While many Islamic nations claim to be egalitarian and in line with human rights, the terms *egalitarian* and *human rights* tend to be defined selectively—and in strict alignment with national agendas.

Afsaneh Najmabadi points to a growing phenomenon, a shift in mentality which "demand[s] that national space be increasingly heterosocial."[37] While Najmabadi specifically addresses the issue of modernity in Iranian culture, this same point may be extended to other Islamic governments in the Middle East and elsewhere. In Indonesia, for example, which has traditionally demonstrated tolerance toward homosexuals, a new form of national identity with a distinctly "masculinist cast" is emerging. Tom Boellstorff notes that Muslim Indonesia is struggling with feelings of *malu,* a complex term that can be interpreted as "shame." In 1999, Muhammad Amir, secretary of the local Indonesian Muslim Clerics Council, declared that any open meeting by gays and lesbians would be "very embarrassing" (*sangat memallukan*).[38] Thus religiously driven conservatism coupled with a sense of national identity continues to create negative conditions for gays and lesbians in contemporary Indonesian society. To be patriotic increasingly implies that one must be heterosexual.

In fact, systematic campaigns against homosexuality have been instituted by numerous Islamic governments under the guise of protecting moral, cultural, and traditional values and safeguarding national identity. In the Islamic Republic of Iran, homosexuality is potentially punishable by death. Sharial Islam, adopted by the Islamic Republic of Iran as law, contains the following reference to lesbianism:

> Article 127: *musaheqeh* (lesbianism) is homosexuality of women by genitals.
>
> Article 128 states: the ways of proving lesbianism in court are the same by which the homosexuality (of men) is proved.
>
> Article 129: punishment for lesbianism is one hundred lashes for each party, Muslim or non-Muslim.
>
> Article 131: if the act of lesbianism is repeated three times and punishment is enforced each time, [the] death sentence will be issued the fourth time.
>
> Article 132: if a lesbian repents before the giving of testimony by the witnesses, the punishment will be quashed; if she does so after the giving of testimony, the punishment will not be quashed.
>
> Article 133: if the act of lesbianism is proved by the confession of the doer and she repents accordingly, the Sharia judge may request the leader to pardon her.
>
> Article 134: if two women not related by consanguinity stand naked under one cover without necessity, they will be punished by no less than a hundred lashes (*Ta'zir*). In case of its repetition as well as the repetition of punishment, a hundred lashes will be hit [delivered] the third time.[39]

To counter such virulent policies, many Muslim groups have created their own gay and lesbian support organizations, primarily outside their countries of origin. One such organization, HOMAN, was established in 1990 in Stockholm to defend the rights of Iranian gays and lesbians. As the first official Iranian gay and lesbian organization, HOMAN reports "all crimes against those sexual behaviors deemed 'perversion' in the Islamic Republic of Iran." According to HOMAN, its educational publication is the only one of its kind to provide uncensored information about HIV/AIDS in Persian.[40] HOMAN can be accessed on the Internet, providing links to the gay, lesbian, bisexual, and transgender communities.

Another Web site supporting Iranian lesbians is Khanaye Doost, a "site . . . dedicated to Iranian Lesbian, Bisexual, and Transgendered Women. A site for Iranian women who love women." The gay and lesbian Iranian community in diaspora also offers professional services and advice to those in need. For example, the Iranian Gay and Lesbian Healthcare Providers Association is a "professional organization with a mission to provide opportunities for gay/lesbian Iranian healthcare providers to network and unite, promote mental and physical health within the Iranian GLBT community, and challenge homophobia in the Iranian community." Members of this association are joining together to eradicate homophobia and other stereotyping of gays and lesbians.

Another nonprofit organization openly fighting for gay rights is the Lebanese-based Helem. Registered in Canada (Quebec) on February 11, 2004, Helem's "immediate concern is to empower the LGBT [Lesbians, Gays, Bisexuals, and Transgenders] community in Lebanon through civil rights and health awareness."[41] Under Lebanese law, "unnatural sexual intercourse" carries punishment of up to one year in jail. Although this punishment is mild in comparison to the punitive measures of neighboring Muslim nations, Helem's objective is to shield LGBT individuals from persecution and discrimination at any level and to engage in the systematic monitoring of human rights violations.

While the Internet has made it possible for Islamic homosexuals to connect, meet, and organize, Internet technology has also been responsible for the arrest and prosecution of countless individuals. According to Human Rights Watch in New York, hundreds of Egyptian gays have been arrested and tortured as a result of police agents snaring them through Internet gay personal ads. The Saudi government arrested more than one hundred gay men in Jeddah on March 10, 2005. Many received two-year jail terms and two hundred lashes. Sentencing took place behind closed doors and without access to legal counsel. When arrested for gay conduct in Saudi Arabia, it is not unusual for the accused to be sent immediately to a hospital for "reparative therapy," a euphemism for efforts to make gays straight.

However, in "Queer Sheik," an article published in the *New Republic* in March 2004, John Bradley writes: "Homosexuality used to be a death sentence in Saudi Arabia. But times are changing." Bradley suggests increasingly tolerant attitudes by religious authorities, including allowance of gay and lesbian bars, as well as the lifting of blocks from Internet Web sites and chat rooms. Bradley quotes *Okaz*, a Jeddah-based daily newspaper, as reporting that although "lesbianism was 'endemic' among schoolgirls," the head of the religious police insisted that he would not investigate schools for lesbian behavior. Bradley also calls attention to the book *Inside the Kingdom*, by Carmen bin Laden (sister-in-law of Osama bin Laden), in which homosexual affairs among the Kingdom's wealthy and idle women are openly discussed. Finally, Bradley's report quotes Mai Yamani, an anthropologist, who discloses that "all-female discos catering to rich Saudi women are often covers for lesbian get-togethers. Saudi princes, meanwhile, have frequented the Jeddah disco, where they openly interact with club-goers."[42]

In her 1996 book, *Unspoken Rules*, editor Rachel Rosenbloom includes brief summaries on the issue of homosexuality around the globe and, specifically, on the status of lesbians. Among thirty countries listed in the table of contents, three are officially Islamic nations (Jordan, Malaysia, and Turkey), and two others (India and Thailand) contain large populations of Muslims. The stories in each chapter point to systematic campaigns against homosexuality. For example, Rais Nur (a lesbian feminist who uses a pseudonym to protect her identity) insists that, while lesbianism is not outlawed in Malaysia, striking differences exist in the status of lesbians and gay men. Due to the AIDS epidemic, the gay organization Pink Triangle (PT) has been sanctioned by the Health Ministry of Malaysia to work with gay men. The Islamic government officially approves of PT, momentarily allowing its attention to lapse where the issue of gay morality is concerned. Nur indicates, "Such state recognition and opportunity for legitimacy, however, has not been extended to the lesbian population, which the government rarely acknowledges in any way." One of Nur's main concerns is the lack of support for Malay lesbians by ultraconservatives *and* by those groups that tend to be more open-minded and liberal; that is, none of the women's movement groups seem to be interested in the rights of lesbians. Nur adds that another problem lesbians face in Malaysia is the predominance of fear—of public backlash and possible humiliation if attempts are made to organize or become too outspoken. However, based on the slowdown of lesbians exiting Malaysia to overseas destinations (during the 1970s and 1980s), Nur remains optimistic that societal conditions will gradually improve.[43]

A study by Alison J. Murray regarding status and class differentiation among Jakarta lesbians reveals the existence of a "subcultural milieu, where lesbian sex is more common than . . . prescribed 'lesbian' signifiers" would indicate. In general, upper-class lesbians in Jakarta maintain a "straight" appearance at home and are more likely to be linked to the global lesbian and gay movement. The same elite Indonesian lesbians who carefully hide their gay identity in Jakarta will "come out" when traveling overseas to enjoy the international gay lifestyles of Amsterdam, San Francisco, or Sydney. Murray also notes that there is a world of difference between the gay and lesbian communities in Indonesia: "gay men are hypervisible and lesbians are invisible." She emphasizes that this form of invisibility varies greatly, depending on socioeconomic class. Lesbian women in the higher economic strata deliberately choose to "stay in"—hiding behind a wall of socially acceptable roles in order to retain power. Lower-class lesbians enjoy a much more dynamic subculture. According to Murray, it is the "lower-class [lesbian] women's relative powerlessness due to lack of money, education, and connections, ironically, [that] leaves them freer to create their own subcultures."[44]

In Jordan, the story is similar. While Akhadar Assfar reveals that there is no Jordanian law against the act of *suhak* (akin to the Arabic term *sahiqa*, lesbianism), she points out that "prejudice within the Jordanian society is more powerful than any legal prohibition." Due to the fabric of Jordanian society—composed of close-knit families and communities adhering to traditional religious and cultural mores—there is limited opportunity for lesbians to interact with each other. In Jordan, the family is one's *only* support system. However, in recent years Jordanian lesbians have begun to connect with two Arab-American organizations: the Gay and Lesbian Arabic Society and the Arab Lesbian and Bisexual Women's Network. Akhadar Assfar sums up the situation in Jordan by saying: "Lesbians in Jordan are without a mention, without recognition, very marginalized . . . YET WE EXIST."[45]

Turkey's first lesbian group, Venus'un Kizkardesleri (Sisters of Venus), was established in July 1994. Because Turkish lesbians cannot hope to achieve legal recognition or feel safe stepping into the public domain, this group remains isolated.[46] In general, it is almost impossible for a Turkish lesbian to "come out" to her family and friends. As in Jordan, there is no community support in place. In rural areas, forced marriages are arranged as a remedy to "fix" the lesbian problem. Generally speaking, arranged marriages are not forced on young lesbians in urban centers; however, many of these young women are sent to psychologists to be "cured of their illness." While membership in the Sisters of Venus is slowly growing, the fundamentalist movement in Turkey presents a real threat to the future success of this organization and to the wider acceptance of Turkish lesbians in general.

One North African lesbian Web site uses the word *sehakia*—akin to the Arabic term *sahiqa* (rubbing)—as an obvious metaphor. An article appearing on www.sehakia.org, written by "Julia" (no last name given), describes the daily struggles that Arab lesbians from the Meghreb (Morocco) face, whether living in exile or in their own homeland. The article uses the term *lesbophobia* in lieu of *homophobia,* and it promises that the Web site will be developed to include Arabic, French, English, *and* Berber languages. Inviting Arab lesbians (particularly those of North African descent) to join the *sehakia* organization, this site is representative of grassroots efforts to create a semblance of legitimacy around lesbian interaction.

From a Palestinian perspective, Gila Svirsky has translated an article that deals with the realities of being an Arab lesbian. This article is written by Mansiya (a pseudonym meaning "the forgotten one" in Arabic), a young Palestinian woman living in Israel who describes her lesbian identity in terms of being an outcast. Mansiya states, "In Arab society, we do not yet have awareness of or openness to the subject [lesbianism], and I cannot fight an entire society by myself. In Arab society, being a lesbian is like being a prostitute, and a prostitute is ostracized and, in the worst case, murdered."[47] She underscores the difficulty of being a lesbian in a culture that dishonors any form of deviation from heterosexuality. She admits to living a double life and to the suffering inherent in that reality.

Throughout the Muslim world, then, women with lesbian proclivities— in fact, all nonheterosexual individuals—face the constant threat of exposure and ostracism. It is noteworthy to mention that, out of this climate of fear, an increasingly popular phenomenon is emerging: surgical gender change. In the Islamic Republic of Iran, where homosexual behaviors carry the death penalty, "hundreds of people are having their gender changed legally, bolstered by the blessing of members of the ruling Shiite clergy."[48] An

April 3, 2006, Reuters news report describes the predicament of five Saudi women who opted for gender change surgery:

> Riyadh: Five women traveled abroad from Saudi Arabia to have sex-change surgery after developing a "psychological complex" because of male domination. Women in Saudi Arabia are not allowed to drive or go to public places without a male relative. The Government said that people who had the surgery were never arrested, although their cases were examined by religious authorities.

Approving of gender changes is not approving homosexuality, stated Mohammed Mahdi Karminia, a cleric in the holy city of Qom. According to a January 25, 2005, *Los Angeles Times* article, Karminia is a leading proponent for using hormones and surgery to change one's gender. In Karminia's own words, "We have said that if homosexuals want to change their gender, this way is open to them. As a matter of fact, there is no reason why a gender reassignment surgery should not take place.[49] Dr. Bahram Majlali, a Paris-trained surgeon in Tehran, has been a major influence in terms of educating the Iranian clerics concerning transsexuality. According to Majlali, transsexuality is not a choice; rather, it is a condition created by God which can be physically "repaired." Majlali and a small group of colleagues have been instrumental in changing the clerics' attitudes toward transsexuality. As a result, thousands of Iranian transsexuals have been able to receive sex-change surgery legally, with each procedure being partially financed by the Islamic Republic of Iran.[50]

Ayatollah Khomeini gave his blessing to this type of surgery and issued a 1976 fatwa endorsing it. Khomeini believed that if men or women felt trapped in the wrong body, they should be permitted to experience relief from their misery.

Khomeini's ruling on the validity of sex change went largely unquestioned because of the *absence* of such topics in the Qur'an. Since sex change is not mentioned in the Qur'an, there are no grounds on which to justify its prohibition. This "vacuum" phenomenon also plays a significant role regarding consequences for lesbian behavior. Even though (and perhaps because) lesbianism is not addressed in the Qur'an, Muslim jurists have been able to categorize it as a punishable offense.

Viewing homosexuality as a misery or disorder not only wreaks psychological havoc, shame, and confusion on nonheterosexuals but also supports fundamentalist Islamic dogma vilifying the West. In religious discussions and sermons, imams target the United States—and Israel to a lesser degree—as culpable for corrupting Muslims and undermining the faithful. Public proclamations such as the following made by Imam Khalil El Moumni in 2001 in the Netherlands further the idea of same-sex behavior as a disorder: "Homosexuality [is] a disease, a sin, and a threat to social fabric, sending far-reaching ripples throughout Dutch society."[51]

In nations such as Iran with an Islamic constitution, legal pronouncements (including punishment for lesbian behaviors) are determined through interpretation of Sharia. From one Islamic society to the next, interpretation of Sharia varies according to region, culture, community, and jurist. It is precisely this arbitrary quality that creates unending possibility for exploitation, where women live habitually under the influence of male power and jurisprudence.

Homosexuality, Fatwas, and the Internet

The act of *sihaq* (lesbianism) in *fiqh* (Islamic jurisprudence) was addressed at the close of the twentieth century by Islamic scholars such as Abd al-Kareem Zaydaan, a former professor in the Colleges of Law, Arts, and Islamic Studies at the University of Baghdad in Iraq. His publications examine law in various schools of Islamic Sharias. In Zaydaan's collection of religious rules and regulations concerning women, he emphasizes that the act of sihaq is an illicit and shameful sexual relationship and must be punished.[52] Publications such as those of Zaydaan have set the precedent for issuance of fatwas against lesbians, both on the Internet and in the public sphere.

To say that the world of Internet technology has penetrated religious circles and has opened up additional gates to salvation may be an understatement. It is now possible for the concerned believer to visit various Islamic affiliated Internet sites, explore the bank of fatwas, search by key words, and match any specific fatwa to one individual or group of ulamas. Religious chat rooms have become popular destinations for exchanging information with other Muslim brothers and sisters. The problem then becomes one of authenticity; if the Web address is not linked to a credible religious institution or religious scholar, then any individual can create a site and "package" a personal and culturally tinted version of religious guidelines.

One conservative Islamic Web site, w, claims that the testimony of a lesbian is unacceptable because she is considered to be an "evildoer." Text from this site reads: "If two women masturbate one another, then they are cursed fornicators."[53] On this same site, warnings are issued to Muslim women who may come into casual contact with lesbians:

Some scholars, like Al-'Izz Ibn 'Abd As-Salam, say that a lesbian is not permitted to look at a Muslim woman, and that a Muslim woman is not permitted to uncover (take off her hijab) in front of a lesbian, because she is an evildoer who cannot be trusted not to describe her attitude towards others.

Another statement regarding lesbian behavior on this same Web site claims to reference hadith, pronouncements of the prophet Muhammad himself:

As for lesbians, the Prophet, peace and blessings be upon him, said about them: *"If a woman comes upon a woman, they are both Adulteresses."*[54]

A fundamental problem exists in this statement: the reader is not able to see the source of hadith on this site in order to establish its authenticity. Additionally, as stated earlier, there are no Qur'anic references to lesbian behavior. These muftis have not only put words in the Prophet's mouth but have also arbitrarily linked lesbian behavior to adultery.[55] The consequence for adultery in Islam—that is, engaging in sexual relationship outside of marriage—is harsh, to say the least. Stoning to death, imprisonment, and/or lashing are punishments meted out by different Islamic countries.[56]

This same Web site also offers a question-and-answer format, in addition to publishing articles on various religious and social issues. The following question on the issue of tolerance and homosexuality receives an uncompromising fatwa, particularly in regard to lesbianism:

Title of Fatwa: Homosexuality and Lesbianism, Sexual Perversions
Date of Reply: 17/May/2004
Topic of Fatwa: Sexual perversity

Question of Fatwa: In a recent TV show, some lesbians and gays appeared and the announcer said that we should show some more respect to the feelings and behavior of others. He further commented that we should know how to live together and accept others. Myself, I was stunned by such words and could not utter a word. Please enlighten me on Islam's stance and reply to such deviation.

Content of Reply in the Name of Allah, Most Gracious, Most Merciful: As for lesbianism, it is also no more than a perversion and an attack against the natural relation between a man and a woman. There is no certain punishment for lesbianism. Still, disciplinary punishment is there for any perverted person who commits it. *The Kuwaiti Encyclopedia of Islamic Jurisprudence* states: "Muslim jurists agree that there is no certain *hadd* (punishment) for lesbianism. However, they agree that disciplinary punishment should be administered, since it is a sin." Such an act spoils the doer's character and makes her testimony unacceptable, as stated in the above named encyclopedia: "Muslim Jurists agree that a witness should be morally sound. A pervert cannot be taken as a witness. Since lesbianism is an act of perversion, a lesbian cannot be a witness. Even with the jurists not declaring this openly, it can still be understood from their words and conditions."

As evidenced by this statement, these muftis (whose names are not provided) are quick to throw tolerance out the door. While they refrain from suggesting specific punishments for the "crime" of lesbianism, they clearly agree that some form of disciplinary action should be taken.

In addition to issuing fatwas, a number of Internet Islamic sites include comments by people posing as religious scholars. The Islamic Society of North America (ISNA) posted the following statement on its Web site on the issue of homosexuality by a Dr. Muzammil Siddiqi (since no professional credentials are listed for Dr. Siddiqi, it is impossible to know if this individual is a licensed physician, religious jurist, or neither):

Statement by the Islamic Society of North America
Dr. Muzammil Siddiqi of the Islamic Society of North America (ISNA) has written:

Homosexuality is a moral disorder. It is a moral disease, a sin and corruption. . . . No person is born homosexual, just like no one is born a thief, a liar, or murderer. People acquire these evil habits due to a lack of proper guidance and education. . . . There are many reasons why it is forbidden in Islam. Homosexuality is dangerous for the health of the individuals and for the society. It is a main cause of one of the most harmful and fatal diseases. It is disgraceful for both men and women. It degrades a person. Islam teaches that men should be men and women should be women. Homosexuality deprives a man of his manhood and a woman of her womanhood. It is the most unnatural way of life. Homosexuality leads to the destruction of family life.

This statement was eventually removed from the ISNA site. Perhaps Dr. Siddiqi realized that his attack on homosexuality as "dangerous for the health of the individuals and for the society" and being "a main cause of the most harmful and fatal diseases" lacked any scientific or medical justification.

Ontario Consultants on Religious Tolerance operates a Canadian-based Web site. Opinions regarding homosexuality have been posted on this site by two Muslim groups, Ahmadi Muslim Jama'at and Mission Islam. The reader should note that the Ahmadi group does not belong to any mainstream Muslim community and is considered illegal in Pakistan.[57]

Ahmadi Muslim Jama'at [a Canadian Muslim group] . . . published an essay "Homosexuality & Islam" which views homosexual behavior as a symptom of the decadence of society. "*As this process continues, people find and invent even more bizarre and perverted means to satisfy natural urges, and trends like child and adult pornography, bisexuality, homosexuality, and bestiality appear.*"

Ahmadi Muslim Jama'at makes a number of points: . . . either the sexual license will cure itself through its own excesses (as it is doing now in the shape of numerous venereal diseases) or the wrath of God will fall in shape of multitudes of Sodoms, Gomorrahs, and Ubars.

Homosexuality has been considered deviant behavior throughout human history. Homosexuals have redefined sexual abuse of children as "natural and acceptable." Homosexuality cannot be caused by genes because there are essentially no gays and lesbians in Russia, China, and many other countries. If there is a "gay gene" it would cause homosexuality to die out quickly because homosexuals typically do not have children. Homosexuality "*is utterly contrary to every natural law of human and animal life, and counter to the morals, purposes, and institutions of a procreative society.*"

We as Muslims need to state unequivocally and unambiguously that homosexuality is a deviant behavior and that there is not even an iota of doubt that Islam condemns the behavior.

. . . homosexuality is clearly and explicitly condemned by the Qur'an (7:80–83, 11:77–79), the Prophet, and his progeny. When we have a conflict with the Qur'an, which is the word of God verbatim, we do not ask where the Qur'an went wrong but rather why are we, limited beings, in conflict with the wisdom of the absolute, God Almighty. As Muslims we do not make up our religion, but we receive it and we obey it. Thus stated, we need to clarify that it does not mean that we hate the homosexual person but rather that we find the behavior abhorable. We want to help with sensitivity and care whoever has these tendencies or practices such behavior.[58]

Both of these opinions are markedly flawed and fail to persuade the reader. First of all, consider Ahmadi's claim that "there are essentially no gays and lesbians in Russia, China, and many other countries" and that "if there is a 'gay gene' it would cause homosexuality to die out quickly because homosexuals typically do not have children." Statements of such gross inaccuracy hardly help to establish the group's credibility. Also, equating homosexuality with pederasty is not only far-fetched but also an invalid and harmful argument. As for Mission Islam, this group attempts to hide its vituperative nature behind a seemingly compassionate mask, offering help and assistance to homosexuals.

Fatwas are issued not only against lesbians and gays but also against the nonprofit organizations that support them. A fatwa was issued on July 16, 2001, by the British Muslim group Al-Muhajiroun against the international Muslim grassroots organization Al-Fatiha, a foundation supporting lesbian, gay, bisexual, and transgender individuals, as well as all others who question their sexual orientation and gender identity.[59] Al-Fatiha promotes "Islamic notions of social justice, peace, and tolerance to bring all closer to a world that is free from prejudice, injustice, and discrimination." The following is the fatwa issued by Sheikh Omar Bakri Mohammed of Al-Muhajiroun against the Al-Fatiha group:

The very existence of Al-Fatiha is illegitimate and the members of this organization are apostates. Never will such an organization be tolerated in Islam, and never will the disease that it calls for be affiliated with a true Islamic society or individual. The Islamic ruling for such acts is death. It is a duty of all Muslims to prevent such evil conceptions from being voiced in the public or private arena.[60]

It is crucial to note the harsh language of this fatwa: "The Islamic ruling for such acts is death." As previously noted, many individuals who post "fatwas" on various "religious" Web sites do so without any real religious authority.

One of the most controversial fatwas against homosexuality and lesbianism is attributed to the Grand Ayatollah of Iraq, Ali al-Sistani. On March 16, 2006, Ayatollah Sistani issued this fatwa on the Arabic version of his Web site, proclaiming that homosexuality was forbidden and that gays "should be killed in the worst manner possible." He added that he was spiritual leader of all Iraqi Shiites, including the Supreme Council of Islamic Revolution in Iraq and its Badr Corps. On his English-language site, he made no fatwa, although he did mention the crime of sodomy between men and boys.

Responses to Sistani's fatwa included the following online article two days later:

"Sistani's murderous homophobic incitement has given a green light to Shia Muslims to hunt and kill lesbians and gay men," says exiled gay Iraqi Ali Hili of the London-based gay human rights group OutRage. Hili also heads up the new Iraqi LGBT–UK Abu Nawas group, which consists of exiled gay Iraqis and has close links with clandestine gay activists inside Iraq. "We hold Sistani personally responsible for the murder of lesbian, gay, bisexual, and transgender Iraqis. He gives the killers theological sanction and encouragement." Hili accused the West of allowing Sistani and the Badr Corps to go on a witch hunt of lesbian and gay Iraqis. "Despite Badr's murderous record, the UK allows its political arm, SCIRI, to have offices and fundraise in the UK. Badr is the terrorist wing of SCIRI. Badr should be proscribed as a terrorist organization," said Hili. He also alleged that Badr militants are entrapping gay men via Internet chat rooms. "They arrange a date, and then beat and kill the victim," Hili said.[61]

Debate continues regarding the interpretation of Sistani's fatwa, as evidenced in this response by Juan Cole, professor of modern Middle East and South Asian history at the University of Michigan:

UPDATE (03/19/06): Writing for *Indybay*
Juan Cole says much of the Sistani report is untrue: the charge leveled by some, and mentioned at Pandagon, that Sistani has called for the killing of Sunnis, is completely untrue. The implication given by exiled gay Iraqi Ali Hili of the London-based gay human rights group OutRage that Sistani has called for vigilante killings of gays is untrue, though it is accurate that Sistani advises that the state make homosexual activity a capital crime; it is also accurate to call this "sick."

Fortunately, in this climate of fear, fatwas, and propaganda, a growing number of highly educated and fearless individuals—many of whom are women—are making their voices heard. One is Irshad Manji, a progressive Muslim born in Uganda and author of *The Trouble with Islam: A Wake-up Call for Honesty and Change*. In an October 28, 2002, interview with Bangladeshi physician Taslima Nasrin, Manji describes herself as an advocate for secular humanism:

> The real conflict is not between the West and Islam, or even Christianity and Islam. It's [between] secularism and fundamentalism, irrational blind faith, and a rational, logical approach, between innovation and tradition, between past and future, between those who value freedom and those who do not.

Her book calls for major reform, which begins with questioning the divinity of the Qu'ran. *San Francisco Chronicle* reporter Matthew Kalman writes, "Manji argues that crimes are being perpetrated under the banner of a religion, which claims more than a billion adherents who have lost the ability to question their leaders." Needless to say, Manji has become a popular target for Islamic fundamentalists:

> There is talk of a fatwa. She receives hate mail and death threats by the megabyte and glories in posting them on her Web site, www.muslim-refusenik.com. She is accompanied by bodyguards at public appearances and has been denounced by her coreligionists for "poor scholarship" and "Muslim bashing." Critics have denounced her reading of Middle East politics.

In 1998 in Canada, Manji hosted and produced *QueerTV*, a commercial television program exploring the lives of gays and lesbians:

It was syndicated through the San Francisco–based Web portal Planetout. com and became one of the few programs anywhere to be streamed entirely on the Internet, circumventing state-sanctioned censorship and rapidly reaching a global audience.[62]

Increasingly, the Internet is proving to be an effective tool in terms of working outside traditional modes of censorship. The only exception to this rule is, of course, those nations (such as Iran, North Korea, Saudi Arabia, and China, to name a few) that prevent their citizens from viewing sites not in alignment with their political agendas.

Queering the Qur'an

In contemporary societies, whether Muslim or non-Muslim, the environments in which many nonheterosexuals live can best be described as oppressive. Unable to practice their sexuality for fear of scandal and—in some cases—under threat of severe punitive measures, many choose to remain "in the closet," leading double lives and suffering from a type of isolation that heterosexuals can only imagine.

Researching contemporary theories of sexuality, power, and oppression, one finds Suzanne Pharr's definition and application of oppression theory to be particularly useful in explaining rejection of the nonheterosexual populace.[63] Pharr's theory focuses on how and why oppression happens; that is, how a community oppresses a group or individual and who benefits from such oppression. The primary benefit to a community seems to be maintenance of the established status quo. Those individuals holding the reins of power within the community remain secure. Once usurpation of power is complete, it never has to be redefined or relinquished. This paradigm is especially attractive to those individuals operating under religious banners. As authority figures, they never need to bend in their strict interpretation of religious doctrine. History informs us that once religious ideologies take root within a given society, those roots gradually (and often insidiously) embed themselves in all aspects of public and private life. In this way, religious dogma is constantly interpreted and manipulated to fit the needs of those in power—whether from a political, societal, or economic standpoint.

The emotional toll on individuals forced to the edge of "acceptance" by a community and its existing power structure is enormous. Their quality of life is proscribed by the constant fear of being exposed. A community's disapproval of its homosexual citizens stirs feelings of guilt, shame, and internal anger: guilt in the face of religious precepts, shame against the backdrop of family expectations, and anger at society's label of having been born "abnormal." This ongoing sense of disapproval often leads to depression and, in extreme cases, suicidal behavior.

In his study of Muslim homosexual South Asians in England, Andrew K. T. Yip identified similarities in discourses between Christians and Muslim gay communities in the West. According to Yip, both communities "construct sexuality-affirming hermeneutics, involving not just the [religious] texts, but also the interpretive authority of such texts."[64] In other words, Christians and Muslims both use various strategies to transgress traditional discourse and construct their own identity. Yip cites the younger generation of British Muslims as being increasingly more tolerant than their elders, in part because of their exposure to Western values and in part because they have developed a broader interpretation of the Islamic texts.

In Yip's study, "coming out" to family members led to various responses. Although there were isolated cases leading to extremely negative responses—such as physical assault and forced marriages—most family members responded with cautious tolerance. Not surprisingly, parents pressured their children to marry in hopes of guiding their offspring to a heteronormative life. Ironically, when many of these individuals gave in to marriage, they felt relieved from the parental "gaze" and found that it was easier to explore their sexuality discreetly. Yip reported that, in some cases, a tacit agreement was made with spouses or even with parents, allowing continuation of desired sexual activities as long as the individual remained married. According to Yip, "Invariably, this kind of double life exacted enormous emotional and social costs on the participants. Some consequently resorted to divorce, which often complicated familial relationships, since it tarnished family honor." Yip's study led to another revealing conclusion: "A small number of participants opted for marriage because they themselves believed that it would 'cure' their homosexuality. This reflects 'internalized homophobia,' underpinned by a sociocultural environment that offers little or no space for any alternative to heteronormativity." Yip described another strategy used by LGBT Muslim groups as "queering the Qur'an":

LGB Muslims recognized that religious texts constitute the primary—though not exclusive—basis of religious censure of homosexuality. Even a theologically uninformed person would often use religious texts to buttress her/his censure of homosexuality, no matter how unsophisticated the argument is. The strategy of "queering" religious texts (in the case of LGB Muslims, the Qur'an, the Shari'ah, and the Hadith are key material) takes several approaches. The most common of these is the critique of traditional interpretation of religious texts that seemingly censures homosexuality, by highlighting its inaccuracy and sociocultural specificity.[65]

As noted in this chapter, the lives of Muslim homosexuals, and lesbians in particular, are anything but "gay." Multiple social, cultural, family, religious, and emotional challenges have to be dealt with on a daily basis. The younger generation of Muslims—both in their indigenous countries and in diaspora—are developing strategies that question traditional interpretations of religious texts and therefore question the authority of the older generation. However, many still face the unhappy alternative of choosing between their sexuality and their families, of embracing freedom of expression or succumbing to the powerful influence of community and religion. Where gays and lesbians are concerned, particularly those living under Islamic dictates, the prevalence of sham marriages and suicidal attempts reflects all too clearly the tragic effects of an incarcerated mind and spirit.

SIX

Bodies Confined,
Spirits Cleansed

Throughout the history of Islam, women have often been physically segregated and purposefully excluded from the public sphere. To maintain authority, the established patriarchy has relegated women to narrowly circumscribed spaces, significantly restricting their mobility and participation in the wider world. Within this paradigm of invisibility, women have had to develop creative strategies in order to survive emotionally and psychologically—strategies that include the creation of cultural rituals to defy the system without offending it. Moreover, these rituals and practices have ensured women crucial access to each other, turning the tables, so to speak, by deliberately excluding men from female-only environments. Thus in some public and private spaces, women have established traditions to keep each other's company and, equally important, to sustain their ability to render each other comfort and support. These all-female circles, or communions of spirit, include sharing ritual preparation and enjoyment of foods, honoring saints, visiting shrines, and reading the Qur'an or various books of Du'a (prayers to imams). Whether sharing love offerings of food, praying, dancing, or weeping together, women have found ways to thrive within restricted environments.

In exploring the phenomenon of spatial segregation, one finds religious and cultural influences working together to produce the numerous constraints still facing women in Islamic societies. However, in her discussion of the term *Islamic feminist,* Miriam Cooke points out the following:

To call oneself an Islamic feminist is *not to describe a fixed identity but to create a new, contingent subject position.* This location confirms belonging in a religious community while allowing for activism on behalf of and with other women. This linking of apparently mutually exclusive identities can become a radical act of subversion.[1]

Increasingly, these women are acknowledging the diverse ways their bodies are manipulated, especially in the "struggle over control of public space." To reclaim their rightful spaces in society, Islamic feminists are engaging in global networking, a relatively new strategy of coalition building that promises to support their objectives. In fact, Cooke asserts that Islamic feminists often enter into "alliances others might reject [because] . . . religion gives observant women the tools to construct alliances that secular women may not trust."[2]

It should be noted that other scholars, such as Azza M. Karam, in describing feminist thought and praxis in Egypt, relies on three categories: secular feminism, Muslim feminism, and Islamist feminism. According to her classification, secular and Muslim feminists tend to appropriate human rights arguments whereas Islamist feminists counter with arguments based on religious fundamental values.

No matter which label one chooses to describe this newly emerging activism, it is clear that women are refusing to remain within the narrow boundaries assigned to them. Against a backdrop of centuries-old patriarchal domination, the extent of courage and determination that Muslim women continue to demonstrate becomes ever more apparent. Theirs is an indefatigable will.

Spatial Segregation:
Religious vs. Cultural Influences

According to Fatima Mernissi, from the very beginning of Islam's history, conflict has existed around the issue of menstruation. Women have been labeled as unclean and therefore have been prohibited from entering mosques, participating in prayers and religious rituals, or touching the Qur'an while menstruating.[3]

Mernissi questions, "Are periods the source of sullying?" A'isha and other wives of the Prophet never lost an opportunity to ensure that the Prophet did not adopt phobic attitudes typical of pre-Islamic Arabia on that subject. According to testimony from Maymuna, one of the Prophet's wives, "It happened that the Prophet recited the Koran with his head on the knee of one of us while she was having her period. It also happened that one of us brought his prayer rug to the mosque and laid it down while she was having her period."[4]

Based on testimonies of Maymuna and A'isha, the prophet Muhammad maintained a phobia-free attitude toward menstruating women. Why then does religious doctrine dictate that a woman in her monthly cycle is religiously impure and must be avoided? Mernissi posits that this misogynistic behavior prevailed in Arabia before the Prophet's time and reasserted itself among the *fughaha* (religious scholars) soon after his death.

To further understand the marginalization of Muslim women, one turns to the sacred text of the Qur'an, Sura 2:222, *Al Baqara* (The Cow):

> They ask thee
> Concerning women's courses.
> Say: They are
> A hurt and a pollution
> So keep away from women
> In their courses, and do not
> Approach them until
> They are clean.[5]

According to the ahadith of both al-Bukhari and al-Muslim, this verse deals only with the issue of sexual intercourse and suggests that a man and his wife should abstain from sex during menstruation. Not one verse in the Qur'an refers to segregating women physically from public spaces during menstruation or infers that women must move separately from men during their monthly cycle. How then has the patriarchy managed to devalue women based on the natural life cycle?

Rose Weitz addresses the long tradition of marginalizing women in Middle Eastern cultures:

> Historically and cross-culturally, menstrual blood has been considered both magical and poisonous, and menstrual taboos have structured and restricted women's lives. The opinion of women's bodies in many cultural perceptions as corrupting, contaminating, unclean, and most of all sinful is a common theme which most religions have discussed and treated as something abnormal.[6]

While menstruation is the most normal aspect of being a female and signals the likelihood of a fertile female, the idea of considering menstruation as a sickness and an abnormality seems entirely illogical. Across a wide spectrum of cultures, however, this negative response to women's menstruation remains deeply internalized in the collective psyche.

Al-Muslim's hadith in *kitab al-haid* (Book of menstruation) states the following:

> (577) A'isha reported: When anyone amongst us (amongst the wives of the Holy Prophet) menstruated, the Messenger of Allah (may peace be upon him) asked her to tie a waist-wrapper over her (body) and then embraced her.[7]

The footnote affixed to this commentary offers further explanation:

> This tradition has been the target of worst criticism by the hostile critics of the Hadith. They assert that it contravenes the teaching of the Qur'an (ii:222) in which it has been commanded to keep aloof from women during the menstrual period. But these critics little realize that it is [only] sexual intercourse with the menstruating women which is prohibited. The hadith gives no indication that the Holy Prophet acted against this injunction of the Qur'an. The very wording that he ordered her to tie a waist-wrapper on the lower part of her body gives a clear indication that the Holy Prophet did not have sexual intercourse with his wives during this period of menstrual discharge; he simply embraced them. The verb *yubashira* does not necessarily mean sexual intercourse. It denotes to have a contact, to touch.

The author asserts that menstrual discharge is looked upon as "pollution" in a number of cultures and religions, resulting in the segregation of women during their periods. According to Yusuf Ali, a commentator on the Qur'an, the case is different with Islam. While menses is regarded as an impurity, Islam does not in any way perceive the whole body of the woman as "polluted." Although sexual intercourse is forbidden during menstruation, lying with one's wife, embracing, kissing, dining, and keeping company with her is sanctioned. Al-Muslim emphasized, "There is no idea of segregation on this account in Islam." The hadith of al-Muslim continues: "The menstruating woman is permitted to wash the head of her husband, comb his hair, and her left-over [food and drink] is clean, and one is permitted to recline in her lap and recite the Qur'an."[8] Another interesting point raised by al-Muslim centers on permission for menstruating women to enter the mosques:

(587) A'isha reported: The Messenger of Allah (may peace be upon him) said to me: Get me the mat from the mosque. I said: I am menstruating. Upon this he remarked: Your menstruation is not in your hand.[9]

In the publication *Sahih al-Bukhari* (the authentic ahadith of al-Bukhari),[10] an informative account is provided concerning holy sites and the menstruating woman.

Volume 1, Book 6, Number 293:
Narrated al-Qasim:

A'isha said, "We set out with the sole intention of performing Hajj and when we reached Sarif (a place six miles from Mecca) I got my menses. Allah's Apostle came to me while I was weeping. He said, 'What is the matter with you? Have you got your menses?' I replied, 'Yes.' He said, 'This is a thing which Allah has ordained for the daughters of Adam. So do what all the pilgrims do with the exception of the Taw-af (Circumambulation) round the Ka'ba." A'isha added, "Allah's Apostle sacrificed cows on behalf of his wives."

This passage clearly alludes to the presence of menstruating women in the holiest site in Islam, the cube-shaped structure called Ka'bah, the foundation of which was supposedly constructed by the prophets Abraham and Ishmael.[11] Located in Mecca, the Ka'bah is the *qibla*, or direction in which the believer orients her/himself for daily prayer.

In the time of the Prophet, then, women were not restricted from entering holy sites simply because they had their periods. In another footnote, al-Muslim describes the word *mohid* (being in the phase of *haid*, or menstruation) as a noun of place, referencing the female organ, which secretes the blood of menstruation. Thus the distinction is made that the blood itself is the source of "pollution" and not the woman. He further explains that if a woman is not permitted to enter the mosque during menstruation, it is because she may be leaking drops of blood, which may fall in the sacred place.[12] This commentator of the hadith, in attempting to justify why a menstruating woman is barred from entering holy sites, does not elaborate further. No justification is provided to explain why a woman *not* leaking blood would be forbidden entry, as Sunni Muslim women are commonly not allowed to enter mosques. Only one side of the issue is considered; the commentator clearly avoids discussing the broader ramifications.

Islamic fundamentalists have applied the most rigid interpretation to ahadith and to readings of the Qurʾan. Close examination of Qurʾanic text coupled with testimonial evidence from the Prophet's own life fail to support their assertions. Rather, the segregation of women, especially within the religious spaces of mosques, shrines, and other holy sites, appears to be rooted in long-standing cultural traditions perpetrated by patriarchal-based systems.

The Veil in Qurʾan and Hadith

One of the most debated contemporary issues around Muslim women's rights is that of the veil. The Arabic word *hijab* (veil) also means "screen" or "curtain," and not only refers to the physical veiling of a woman's hair and body but also implies specific rules and regulations. From a physical aspect, hijab refers to items of clothing that a woman wears out of modesty, or it refers to a physical barrier that provides spatial segregation. The psychological/ethical aspect of hijab relates to a less tangible domain and often suggests self-restraint. For example, among the Muslims of South Asia, a woman mourns the loss of her husband by remaining indoors, secluded from public view. This observance is a type of hijab, referred to in Urdu as *purdah neshini*.[13] To Muslim Sufis, hijab is viewed in quite a different way—as part of the process for attaining enlightenment.[14] To be trapped in earthly reality is referred to as *mahjub* (veiled). As long as an individual is mahjub, he or she remains distanced from the Divine.

Within its folds, then, the veil carries semantic versatility, meaning different things to different people in different times and places. "The various connotations it has, the many emotions it arouses, testify to its continuing, perhaps even growing, significance in the modern world."[15] Wearing of the veil continues to be debated from multiple perspectives. In the West, Muslim women take up the hijab to outwardly announce that they belong to the religion of Islam. Although many Muslim women throughout the world wear this "badge" of identity willingly and proudly, millions of others would drop it instantly if the choice were theirs. While some women claim that their freedom and emancipation come from being *muhajjabeh*, or veiled women, numerous others find wearing the veil to be onerous and unnecessary.

From an early age, most Muslim women are instructed that wearing the veil fulfills a religious duty, or *fard*. They assume that the Qur'an sanctions this practice and, quite naturally, are eager to obey Allah's command. But what exactly does the Qur'an say about veiling? In fact, the Qur'an does not specify how much of a woman's body must be covered, nor does it elaborate on the manner of veiling or the color and style. While Muslims agree that women should clothe themselves modestly, especially in public, many point to the fact that no specific mention is made in Qur'anic text regarding covering a woman's hair. The following verses are commonly used to justify the wearing of hijab:

> Al Ahzab (The Confederates)
> And when ye
> Ask (his ladies)
> For anything you want,
> Ask them from before
> A screen: that makes
> For greater purity for
> Your hearts and for theirs (33:53)[16]

> Prophet! Tell
> Thy wives and daughters
> And the believing women
> That they should cast
> Their outer garments over
> Their persons (when abroad):
> That is most convenient,
> That they should be known
> (As such) and not molested
> And God is oft-forgiving,
> Most Merciful. (33:59)[17]

Yusuf Ali's commentary on *Al Ahzab*, Sura 33, verse 53, states:

The actual manner of showing respect to ladies may differ in different circumstances. But it is an essential principle of good society to show the greatest deference to them. To the "Mothers of the Believers," this respect was due in an exceptional degree.[18]

This commentary makes it clear that the primary reason for segregation (in this case, with a screen) is to show women respect, not to exclude them. Furthermore, Muslim feminists such as Fatima Mernissi emphasize that when ulama use verse 53 to justify public segregation of women, such interpretation is misogynistic. Mernissi claims, quite convincingly, that the Prophet himself placed a hijab, or curtain, between himself and another man, Anas Ibn Malik, one of his companions who stood at the entrance of the Prophet's nuptial chamber. The Prophet had just married and was impatient to be left in privacy with his new wife, Zaynab. Mernissi, drawing primarily on Al-Tabari's commentary, strongly suggests that this verse has been misinterpreted for patriarchal self-serving purposes.[19]

As for verse 59 ("women . . . should cast their outer garments over their persons [when abroad])," Yusuf Ali emphasizes that the garment (*jilbab*) referred to is simply a modest form of clothing. The Qur'anic text does not provide any details as to color, material, or embellishments. The text does not point to the necessity of covering the hair or face, nor does it indicate how long the garment should be (i.e., ankle length, below the knee, etc.). Another revelatory line in Yusuf Ali's note 3764 reads: "It was never contemplated that they [ladies] should be confined to their houses like prisoners."[20]

The following excerpt from the hadith of al-Bukhari describes Muhammad's wedding night and directly relates to the revelation of Qur'anic verse 33:53. Note how Anas b. Malik recalls the incident of the curtain (hijab):

Al-Bukhari, Book 008, Number 3333

Anas b. Malik (Allah be pleased with him) reported: When Allah's apostle (May peace be upon him) married Zainab bint Jahsh, he invited people (to the wedding feast) and they ate food. They then sat there and entered into conversation. He (the Holy Prophet) made a stir as if he was preparing to stand up, but (the persons busy in talking) did not stand up. When he (the Holy Prophet) saw it, he stood up and when he did so, some other persons stood up. 'Asim and Abd al-A'la in their narrations made this addition: Three (persons) sat there, and Allah's Apostle (may peace be upon him) came there to enter (the apartment) but he found the people sitting there. Then they stood up and went away. He said: Then I came and informed Allah's Apostle (may peace be upon him) that they had gone away. He (the Holy Prophet) then came there until he entered (the apartment). I also went and was about to enter, when he hung a curtain between me and him (and it was on this occasion that) Allah, the Exalted and Majestic, revealed this verse: "O you who believe, enter not the houses of the Prophet unless permission is given to you for a meal, not waiting for its cooking being finished." Surely this is serious in the sight of Allah.

Imam Qurtubi, thirteenth-century orthodox theologian and author of "*al-Jami'li ahkan al-Qur'an*" (Compendium of legal rulings of the Qur'an), offers the following interpretation of hijab (talking behind a screen or curtain):

This verse [33:53] provides the permission to ask, from behind a screen (hijab), the Wives of the Prophet for any necessary thing, including any matters of religion. And all Muslim women would be bound by the same rule. Besides this verse, other principles of the Islamic doctrine also tell us that a woman (for her honour) deserves to be hidden—her body as well as her voice.[21]

Qurtubi adds one more dimension to hijab—the sound of a woman's voice. Indeed, her voice also needs to be hidden or, better yet, silenced. Thus, according to this imam's interpretation, women would do well to remain invisible and voiceless.

Feminists take a markedly different viewpoint of hijab, as it is used in verse 33:53. Fatima Mernissi argues that Allah's command was to create a barrier or space divider between two (or more) men, *not* between a man and a woman. Placed in historical perspective, the revelation mentioned in verse 33:53 occurred during 627 and possibly mirrors that year's events. Indeed, 627 was a disastrous year for the Prophet's military campaign, a year in which trench construction (literally establishing dividing barriers) was particularly necessary. Mernissi states, "The verse of the hijab is part of verse 33, *Al Ahzab* (The Clans). This verse describes among other things the siege of Medina, known as the Battle of the Khandaq, the Battle of the Trench, for Muhammad ordered his forces to dig a trench around the city to protect it."[22]

Toward the end of *Al Ahzab*, an interesting verse appears pertaining to moral codes. Specifically, the verse forbids wives of the Prophet to remarry after his death. Mernissi posits that given the historical context and prevailing cultural mores, the verse of the hijab was intended to guide men in proper social conduct toward women—instructing them to behave respectfully, resist temptation, and exercise restraint. Mernissi emphasizes the greater significance of hijab, which goes beyond a physical piece of cloth or curtain to embrace ethical behaviors. The essence of hijab would imply the unacceptability of gazing or staring excessively at a woman in public. The ethical aspect of hijab would protect women and keep them safe from prying, aggressive behavior. Perhaps the veiling of women (the imposition of physical hijab) evolved to compensate for men's general inability or unwillingness to exercise restraint—that is, for their failure to follow those ethical behaviors set forth by the Prophet.

Spatial Segregation and Contemporary Fundamentalism

Women's empowerment implies the right of every woman to exercise autonomy physically, mentally, emotionally, and spiritually. An empowered woman is not a victim and does not live under the influence of authority figures, be they fathers, brothers, or husbands. A woman's basic right to control her sexuality—and by extension, her body—has always been an irresistible target for fundamentalists, regardless of the specific religious genre. Clashes intensify between the forces of fundamentalism and those who defend women's rights when a third element, patriarchal power, is added to the quotient. In today's world, these opposing forces impact women everywhere, creating fewer opportunities for gainful employment and economic security. For Muslim women, this goes hand in hand with restricted mobility and access to public spaces. With the expansion of radical Islam, voices of secular women become further marginalized in both the political and social realms. Leila Ahmed eloquently addresses this phenomenon, citing "the growing strength of Islamist movements today, which urge the reinstitution of the laws and practices set forth in the core Islamic discourses."[23]

Many scholars believe that feminism as practiced in the West can never be implemented in the same way in Muslim societies. However, Ziba Mir-Hosseini argues that feminism is simply the "possibility to make dignified choices in life," insisting that the religion of Islam must accommodate gender equality. She responds to the oppressive construct of gender relations in

Islamic law by stating that "religious intellectuals must realize that their vision of Islam cannot be realized without addressing core problems of power relations; one of these is gender inequality. They must understand that as long as the inequality within the family as constructed by fiqh is left unchallenged, Islam cannot be reconciled with democracy and pluralism. Gender inequality not only embodies but also reproduces other kinds of inequality. This is the core issue that needs to be debated in the process of reconciling Islam with modernity and creating a civil society."[24]

Religious text—including Qur'anic verses and ahadith of the Prophet—continues to be rigidly interpreted in an ongoing effort to push women back to a subservient past, holding them hostage in narrow domestic environments. Indeed, religious scholarship proves to be a form of manipulation. Add to this a hefty dose of patriarchal authority, and the result is a lethal formula of domination that is all too familiar to many women living in contemporary Islam.

The believer will ask: which scholarship should guide the community as to the proper place for women? Can one rely on esteemed scholars of the past, such as the twelfth-century scholar al-Jawzi, whose work is still considered a guiding light by fundamentalists today?

Born in Baghdad in 1126, 'Abd ar-Rahman ibn 'Ali ibn Muhammad Abu al-Farash ibn al-Jawzi was a conservative jurist who wrote *Kitab ahkam al-nisa* (Book of Rules for Women). Perusing the manuscript, one finds chapter 26 entitled "Advice for Women against Going Out" and related chapter titles, such as "The Benefits for the Woman Who Opts for the Household" and "Evidence Proving That It Is Better for a Woman Not to See Men."

As a noted Sunni theologian, al-Jawzi spouted conservative viewpoints supporting the policies of Baghdad's ruling establishment. Reminiscent of today's revolutionary commando figures, al-Jawzi mounted rabid attacks, persecuting anyone who dared oppose his strict traditionalist interpretations. Particularly critical of Sufis and of theologians who practiced Shi'a Islam, al-Jawzi exploited his excellent relations with successive caliphs and their advisers. History records that in return for his loyalty, al-Jawzi received a plethora of financial and social favors; the caliphs made him master of five colleges and the leading Hanbali spokesman.[25]

As to women's issues, al-Jawzi's bias and misogyny are unmistakable. When asked to offer his ruling on the rows of prayers inside the mosque, he replied, "The prayers of men who are seated behind women are worthless." This ruling signaled a move toward banning women from mosque attendance and transforming sacred public places into male-only domains. In one of his writings, al-Jawzi posed the following question, which in itself contains a betrayal of the religious texts: "Is it permitted for women to go to the mosque?" He replied to his own question with this admonition: "If she fears disturbing men's minds, it is better for her to pray at home." Curiously, in his argument he cites al-Bukhari's hadith in which the Prophet said the mosques of Allah are not closed to women. In the same breath, however, al-Jawzi proclaims that Friday prayer in the mosque is not a woman's duty and that women should avoid leaving their homes as much as possible.[26]

For today's Islamic fundamentalist who would prefer life to revert to the twelfth century, yet another figure emerges to fan the medieval flames of understanding. Her name is Halah Bint Abdullah, and her advice guides for Muslim women today are penned under the watchful eyes of various religious leaders and male sheiks. Halah Bint Abdullah has developed a list of fifteen "disadvantages" for unveiling. Her list includes the following:

Sixth: Making the woman equal to man as to treatment and rights, especially in some Islamic and Arab countries.

Tenth: Unveiled women would become the protectors and maintainers of men.

Fourteenth: Degrading and humiliating the unveiled woman in the common service and job sites which are supposed to be allocated to men only.[27]

This Muslim author may be more clever and self-aware than she appears at first glance. By ingratiating herself with the conservative religious authorities, she follows in al-Jawzi's footsteps, securing a fairly comfortable niche in a hierarchical system that prefers to exclude women from the public sphere. Her insistence that women should be "separate from and unequal to men" is merely a reflection, a mantra of the culture into which she was born. Any child and/or young woman bombarded with negative messages about her gender will likely become an adult with similarly limited perspectives. These women will feel secure only when supervised and managed by men. The notion of independent thinking will always remain foreign to them, and they will prefer to do as they are told. The tragedy of Halah bint Abudullah is that she represents thousands of other women, caught unaware in a sisterhood of complacency.

In his book *Simaye Zan Dar Kalame Imam Khomeini* (Images of Women in Imam Khomeini's Speeches), Ayatollah Khomeini stated his opinion on the subject of unveiling and the emancipation of Iranian women:

> As you experienced it, for the past twenty years or so, we had this undig-nified unveiling of women in our country. Has anyone realized what has happened? They [the shah's government] forced women to go out to seek employment in various offices. Have you realized that in any office they entered they have paralyzed the work force and ruined the work itself? Right now . . . our ulama's advice is not to encourage it. Do not encourage small town women to get employment, because any time any woman starts to work she will spoil the job. Do you want to have your freedom ruled by women?[28]

This is the same Khomeini who gave his blessing for women to be edu-cated at the legendary Feyziyeh Seminary in the holy city of Qom. Ayatollah Khomeini studied at this centuries-old training site for male religious schol-ars, as did Iraq's Grand Ayatollah Ali al-Sistani. After the 1979 revolution, the Qom seminary admitted over four hundred women. A board of seven ayatollahs and scholars approved by Khomeini founded an extensive cen-ter for women's education, Jame'at al-Zahra (University of al-Zahra). In fact, many Islamic seminaries have been established in Qom exclusively for women.

However, it should be noted that none of these female scholars will be allowed to teach men or deliver sermons. The educational facilities in which they study are wholly segregated, yet their instructors must be male. These male instructors conduct their lectures from behind a partition. If a stu-dent has a question, she must write it on a piece of paper. All questions are collected and presented to the instructor, who reads each question, then answers it aloud. The women are not allowed to speak, nor can they move beyond the partition placed between them and their instructor. This par-ticular form of hijab is in response to a woman's voice. If heard by strange men (outside the family circle), the feminine voice might create chaos or *fitna*, causing men to go astray. Thus this "spatial hijab" is observed in the classrooms of Qom seminary at all times.

Sharia Misused: An Excuse for Gender Discrimination

Among Middle Eastern nations enforcing hijab, the Sharia-based governments of Iran and Saudi Arabia have set particularly rigid guidelines. In August 2007, the *Wall Street Journal* reported that General Ismail Muqaddam, commander of the Iranian Islamic Police, claimed that almost a million men and women had been arrested for violating Islamic dress codes, and of these, over 20,000 individuals were being held in Iranian prisons.[29] One must assume that most of these detainees were young women. A year prior to this mass arrest, in response to illegal discrimination against women in Iranian law, the "One Million Signatures Campaign" was launched by Iranian activists. Their objective was to gather signatures online from the international community. At a peaceful 2006 women's rally held in Tehran to support this campaign, numerous men and women were arrested. For example, Delaram Ali, a student and women's rights activist participating in the rally, was sentenced to almost three years in prison and ten lashes.[30] The brutal treatment of this young woman demonstrates the abusive potential of Sharia law. No historic evidence exists that women were lashed during the Prophet's time for any reason. So why should it be a commonplace, accepted practice today?

Punitive measures against women do not always take the form of physical brutality. Equally damaging are policies that keep women figuratively leashed and under male domination. One such example is the story of Nadia Bakhurji, a Saudi architect. In her initial efforts (2005) to be elected to the ten-member Board of the Council of Saudi Engineers, Bakhurji put forth an activist agenda: to help female engineers professionally; to seek job opportunities for women through training programs; to help them overcome obstacles in the field; and to promote the council's agenda.[31] She was the only woman campaigning, along with seventy-two men. Unfortunately, Bakhurji was prohibited from remaining a candidate. She told the BBC that because there were no polling stations for women and women were not trained to oversee the polling stations, the Saudi Arabian government had declared that women could not run for elected office.[32] Bakhurji's persistence finally paid off. Claiming that she was within her rights as a citizen, both religiously and legally, she refused to be discouraged and won a seat in 2006. To make her victory even sweeter, Bakhurji received the following praise from the chairman of the Kingdom Holding Company, Prince Alwaleed bin Talal bin Abdulaziz Alsaud: "Saudi women are able to do any job a man can do, if not better."

Gender discrimination is not unique to the Middle East. In the Central Asian nation of Afghanistan, this particular issue reached critical proportions during the Taliban's rule. Although the Afghan government is no longer Sharia-based, women still face huge obstacles. In 2001, the United States invaded Afghanistan to eliminate the Taliban and, in part, to put an end to the Taliban's brutal treatment of Afghan women. The Taliban's rigid Qur'anic interpretations, tinged with nomadic tribal and patriarchal practices, set new records for the denigration of women. For example, even if a woman were covered completely by her *chaderi* (the Afghan hijab, a full-length veil that conceals the entire body except for an open slot at eye level), she could be harassed by the Taliban for wearing white socks, which were deemed to be sexy and eye-catching. According to Martha Burk:

> Four years after the U.S.-led war to remove the Taliban, the group is on the rise again in Afghanistan, under the nose of the U.S.-backed government. Women who criticize local rulers or who are merely active in public life as political candidates, journalists, teachers, or NGO workers face increasing threats and violence. Many women are still in the *burqa*, afraid to take it off because of the returning Taliban and the lack of security. Violence against women and girls remains rampant, and according to the Afghan Independent Human Rights Commission, over three hundred girls' schools have been burned or bombed.[33]

Once the United States installed Hamid Karzai as president of Afghanistan, essentially naming him protector of democracy, a collective sigh of relief was audible throughout the free world. But how is it possible for high-ranking Afghan officials to attack a female Member of Parliament (MP) whose only "indiscretion" is an insistence on democratic practices?

> Bottles were thrown, insults traded, and chairs knocked over in the bedlam. This was no bar room brawl, however. It was the scene in the Afghan parliament on Sunday when a woman MP dared to stand up to a male colleague . . .

Malalai Joya, 28, interrupted a former warlord as he praised the holy warriors—or Mujahidin—of Afghanistan during a debate to mark the anniversary of their defeat of communism. She declared that there were "two types of Mujahidin—one who were really Mujahidin, the second who killed tens of thousands of innocent people and who are criminals."

Angry members of the assembly, which is dominated by former faction members, threw a plastic bottle and swore at the woman MP. Moderate MPs had to form a protective ring around Mrs. Joya as she was hurried from the chamber. "My supporters heard one MP tell someone to wait by the door and knife me as I walked out," she said.

Mrs. Joya caused a similar outburst at a Loya Jirga—a traditional gathering—in 2003 by insisting that former warlords guilty of atrocities deserved punishment.[34]

In Bangladesh, women suffer repression under a Sharia-driven government. Because illiteracy is rampant among women in Bangladesh, they have little access to credit and few rights to inheritance under the law. "Most women in the rural areas are forced to sell their goods through a male wholesaler or with the help of their husbands or sons, because women are not allowed to buy or sell goods in the *haats* [small temporary shacks] and bazaars."[35] This limited access to public spaces necessarily curbs their economic prosperity, resulting in lowered social status and opportunity.

The cycle is a familiar one. Clearly, fundamentalism breeds gender-biased norms. When women are not recognized as equal citizens, the obstacles they face are "compounded by localized Sharia interpretations of Islam, where family laws frequently require women to obtain a male relative's permission to undertake activities that should be theirs by right. This increases the dependency women have on their male family members in economic, social, and legal matters." Eliza Griswold spoke with Mufti Fazlul Haque Amini, a member of Parliament in Bangladesh since 2003. This religious leader stated that "secular law has failed Bangladesh and . . . it's time to implement Sharia, the legal code of Islam." The potential for fundamentalist ideology to exercise detrimental effects on women—to exclude and marginalize them socially and economically—is undeniable.[36]

In Indonesia, conservatives are trying to introduce elements of Islamic law into the Indonesian constitution. Several regencies, or local governments, have already introduced similar bylaws. The possibility of instituting an Islamic dress code for women, as well as restricting their presence in public spaces, has created an anxious atmosphere for women used to wearing what they want and going where they please. "Under a draft anti-pornography bill being considered by Indonesian lawmakers, women who wear clothes deemed to be revealing may be jailed or fined as much as $111,000. Couples who kiss in public may face a five-year sentence or a $55,000 fine."[37] Under new bylaws, women found alone in the streets after 7 p.m. must prove they aren't prostitutes. While Indonesia has yet to incorporate Sharia into federal law, the province of Aceh (at the tip of Sumatra) has already made the shift to a Sharia-based legal system.

Next door to Indonesia, Malaysia also boasts a growing conservative Islamic party. In 2006 Prime Minister Abdullah agreed to police morality through the Department of Islamic Advancement. "Director-General Mustafa Abdul Rahman said that his office, known as Jakim, is "directly in charge of taking care of the moral standard and behavior of the masses, particularly Muslims."[38] This cryptic warning promises to set limits on women's mobility and visibility as soon as Sharia is implemented.

Although approximately 60 percent of Malaysia's population is Muslim, one would assume consideration for the rights of the remaining 40 percent. However, in March 2006, Prime Minister Abdullah backed a police decision to force policewomen to wear Muslim headscarves, or *tudung*, during official parades. Many Muslims are justifiably concerned. After all, if non-Muslims can be forced to wear tudung, what about Muslims who choose not to wear tudung? As reported on Bloomberg.com, "Islamic conservatism, with a strong emphasis on moral values, is becoming more appealing. . . . Ambitious politicians and bureaucrats are trying to advance their careers by adopting a more Islamic stance in public."[39]

The art of "interpretation" (i.e., the interpretation of key Islamic texts) relates directly to the current global expansion of Islamic fundamentalism. As the author Katajun Amirpur points out:

The fact that the Qur'anic interpretations of scholars such as Tabarsi, Razi, Tabataba'i, and Qutb differ so substantially from each other is . . . proof that all exegesis can be classified as *tafsir bi-ray*, i.e., interpretation according to personal opinion and enthusiasm.[40]

In terms of women's issues—specifically, the segregation, exclusion, and marginalization of Muslim women—certain danger lies in Islamic fundamentalist interpretation drowning out and ultimately silencing voices of moderation.

In Malaysia, a small but effective group of Muslim women are using their knowledge of the Qur'an to push forward moderate reforms. They have created Sisters in Islam, an organization dedicated to restoring women's rights and dignity:

> Dignity is important and that is why the "sisters" are well-known opponents of the exclusively male group of Sharia judges. After all, in Malaysia's rapidly modernized society, women often enjoy more dignity at work and in public life than they do in private, where Islamic law rules supreme on family-related matters. [Members of the Sisters in Islam] are self-confident, knowledgeable, rhetorically agile, modestly dressed women without headscarves [who] speak fluent English. They meet with Malaysian and foreign Koran scholars for study sessions, write columns for the press, train lawyers . . . and offer legal assistance. Their brochures have provocative titles like "Are Muslim men allowed to beat their wives?" In accordance with a free interpretation of [Qur'an] Chapter 13:11, they advise victims of marital abuse to help themselves: if you don't do something to change your condition, God will not help you either. . . .
>
> Their most ambitious project for the future is to obtain a complete revision of Islamic family law.[41]

Reclaiming Sacred Spaces: Women in the Mosque

A majority of Muslims follow Sunni doctrine, generally prohibiting women from attending the same mosque as men. The Shi'i tradition differs somewhat, in that segregated spaces within the same mosque are allocated to women.

Neither the Qur'an nor the Sunna (traditions of the Prophet) prevent women from entering mosques. In fact, in *Kitab al-Jum'a* (Book of Friday)—written two centuries after the death of the Prophet—Imam Bukhari quotes the following hadith: "Do not forbid the mosques of Allah to the women of Allah." Throughout Muslim history, however, men have not welcomed women into the mosques. This tradition emerged in alignment with patriarchal rule, *not* according to the rule of Islam. During the Prophet's lifetime, mosques were not only places of worship but also centers for education, political discussion, and social interaction. The mosque was a place where everyone in the community was welcome, including women.

Adhering to the prophet Muhammad's example is Shamima Sheikh, a South African Muslim, who participated in a March 2006 conference at the University of Witwatersrand (WITS) in Johannesburg. At the conference, young Muslim architectural students submitted proposals for a mosque to be built on university grounds. Some of these proposals designated segregated spaces for women, insisting that any other *bid'ah* (innovation) would go against the doctrine of Islam. One young student defended his architectural plan, stating that the practice of "women and men reading [Qur'an and praying] alongside [was] unacceptable; they [have] to be completely separated." He supported this assertion by insisting that men at WITS could not control their libidos.[42] The following is Shamima Sheikh's solution to this conundrum:

Therapy for Male "Sexuality"

For those men and women who view each other only as sexual beings, the mosque precinct—a holy precinct—can be therapeutic. On seeing women in the holy precinct, the depraved soul has to recognize that women are not just sexy beings but spiritual beings, members of the *ummah* [Muslim community], their sisters in faith. If women are invisible in this holy precinct, his perception of women as just sexy beings will not be challenged, and he will never be able to reclaim his full humanity, his Islam. May Allah guide us and help us respect each other.[43]

Because Muslim women have traditionally been barred from praying together with men, they have resorted to prayer at home or in segregated mosque spaces allocated for their use. While *salat* (the act of praying) can be performed anywhere, it is considered more meritorious when performed inside the mosque, in unison with others.

Muslim women in India mostly pray in buildings adjoining mosques. However, women in Pudukkottai, Tamil Nadu (a small town in southern India), are struggling to start a mosque of their own. When interviewed on this topic, women described the need for a community space in which to discuss crucial issues affecting their personal lives—such as dowry, divorce, and child custody—without the interference of male *jamaat* (community elders) who adjudicate on family matters at the mosques. Women have always been excluded from these decision-making sessions. Furthermore, when decisions concerning their welfare are made by the all-male jamaat, outcomes rarely rest in their favor. The idea of a mosque for women began as a result of numerous complaints by local Muslim women about these partisan rulings. One woman stated: "Women are oppressed. The jamaat does rule against them most of the time."[44]

A BBC online report describes the obstacles these women face in creating a mosque of their own. For example, although the women's fund-raising efforts have been largely successful, they face heavy opposition:

> Aneesur Rahman Azami is the director of the Islamic Research and Guidance Centre. He says the women's demand for their own mosque is against Islam. "Islam doesn't allow women to build their own mosque. And if they do, it throws up many questions. Will they have a woman imam? If yes, then there's the issue of purity—a woman can't lead the prayer when she's menstruating."

Daud Sharifa, who directs the women's efforts, remains sanguine about the mosque project. Yet Ms. Sharifa readily admits to the challenges, including having received several death threats. "It's Allah who knows when I'm going to die. So I don't bother about it. I don't bother about this life. I'll do this till the end of my life."[45]

In China's Ningxia Autonomous Region, a large number of Hui people reside, all of whom are Muslims. An online article discussing Chinese Muslims explains their history:

> The 9 million Hui are descended from Middle Eastern traders and their converts, who came to China around the fourteenth century. The Hui speak Mandarin, mostly look like Han Chinese, and, except for their refusal to eat pork, follow Han customs.[46]

According to Hui Islamic tradition, a woman can be appointed to the position of *ahong* (imam) in a mosque.[47] This unorthodox Islamic practice is likely due to centuries of isolation from other Muslim countries, as well as contact with Confucianism and its teaching of secular virtue: "Most strikingly, in the past 150 years women-only mosques or *nusi* [from Arabic *al nisa,* women] and female imams have emerged—unique in the Islamic world, where elsewhere women worship in the same mosque as men, but in a separate curtained or partitioned space, and hear the same male preacher." Today, ahongs receive training in Arabic and Qur'anic recitation and study important religious texts. Many of them travel to Malaysia, Indonesia, or the Middle East for training. These women lead prayers, deliver Friday sermons to women, and instruct students—both male and female—in religion. Ahongs are much preferred by Hui women, who stress the convenience of women having their own place to pray, given the requirements of ritual ablutions beforehand and the shyness of men teaching women.[48]

Persistent efforts by Arab Salafi and Wahhabis to persuade Huis to follow more purist Islamist practices have thus far failed. If fundamental Islam eventually succeeds in penetrating the Hui community, this unusual tradition of female imams will likely be eradicated.

In Morocco, the government has taken a surprising stance toward women, empowering them as religious preachers. This decree was issued in response to preaching by radicals, whom many held responsible for the 2003 suicide bombings that took the lives of forty-five people in Casablanca. An April 5, 2005, article from the *Morocco Times* reported the graduation of fifty women as *morshidat* (female guides). Morshidat will not be leading prayers in mosques, but will be dispatched around the country to teach women—and, on occasion, men—about Islam and its practice.[49] "The Morshidat will be in charge of leading religious discussions, give lessons in Islam, give moral support to people in difficulty, and guide the faithful towards a tolerant Islam, one of the graduates told Al-Jazeera TV channel."[50]

Other duties will include assisting with literacy programs and providing legal advice regarding the recently reformed family law, the *Moudawwana*. Two of the first morshidat were Samira Marzouk and Fouzia Assouli. Marzouk, who is married, emphasized the importance of furthering Islamic principles of tolerance and acceptance. Assouli, president of the Democratic League for the Rights of Women at the time of her appointment as morshidat, hailed the morshidat initiative as an integral step toward women's liberation.[51] The Moroccan monarch, Mohammed VI, applauded the initiative by emphasizing that Islam carries a message of renewal and reform, which includes the equality of men and women. According to the king, "It is true that a bird needs two wings to fly."[52]

Other Moroccan newspapers have suggested that the women preachers might be allowed to lead prayers. However, a May 27, 2006, Reuters report from Rabat reported the following by Moroccan scholars against women leading prayers:

> Morocco's highest religious authority decreed that women should not lead prayers, marking out the limits of recent liberal reforms designed to promote a tolerant Islam in the country. Earlier this month, the government appointed fifty women as state preachers, who will give basic religious instruction in mosques while providing support to people in prisons, hospitals, and schools across the country. But they will not have the right to lead Friday prayers, which remains solely a male preserve. "It has never been proved, be it in the history of Morocco or among the Ulamas (clerics), that a woman has led in the mosque the prayers of men or women," stated the fatwa.... "This is a tradition perpetuated by the inhabitants of this peaceful country and consecrated down through time."

A new era of participation by women in the religious sphere is also unfolding in Turkey. Sule Yuksel Uysal, a Turkish woman appointed by Turkey's directorate of religious affairs (Diyanet), is one of two hundred state-paid *vaizes*, or female preachers, whose very existence breaks with centuries of Muslim tradition. Ali Bardakoglu, head of Diyanet, stated, "Anyway, the Koran has taught the equality of men and women for 1,400 years." The Turkish vaizes make no claims to be religious leaders, leaving Turkey's mosques in the hands of men. According to Mrs. Uysal, their fundamental role is to provide women with a woman's perspective on Islam. Not all Turkish men are enthusiastic about this new educational opportunity for women. Meryem Uzun, a Turkish woman from the city of Mardin explains: "One of the first sermons I heard was about women's marital rights.... When I told my husband what I had heard, he got angry and tried to prevent me [from] going to the mosque again."[53]

Turkish women now have the right to lead groups on the annual pilgrimage to Mecca; however, a male *mahram* must be present alongside the female guide.[54] Also, in fifteen Turkish provinces, women serve as deputy muftis. Their responsibility as specialists in religious law is to monitor the work of imams in mosques. In recent years, Turkish women have benefited from a host of progressive efforts to legitimize their place in the religious order.

As mentioned earlier in this book, Dr. Amina Wadud made history in March 2005 when she became the first Muslim woman in 1,400 years to deliver a sermon and lead a mixed-gender congregation. No mosque agreed to host this historical event; therefore, the ceremony was held in a New York City art gallery. As would be expected, this event stirred controversy and opposition in the Muslim world. In October 2005, Dr. Wadud led another mixed-gender Friday prayer, this time in Barcelona:

> One of the world's leading experts on the Qur'an and its discourse on gender led a mixed-gender congregation in a Friday communal prayer in Barcelona, Spain, yesterday [October 28]. The impromptu prayer came after Wadud, professor of Islamic Studies at Virginia Commonwealth University, was invited to lead a congregation by several Muslim women during a question-and-answer period following a talk by Wadud at the International Congress on Islamic Feminism. After answering a slew of questions on the historic mixed-gender prayer she led earlier this year in New York City, members of Spain's Muslim community quickly organized a makeshift prayer in a conference room at the Alimera Hotel in Barcelona, where the Congress was being held.

> About thirty worshippers participated in the prayer. Before the prayer, a minor controversy erupted about whether Spanish television cameras could record the event, with several congregants refusing to be filmed. Soon the TV cameras were removed, and the prayer began with the call to prayer, followed by a short sermon by Wadud.[55]

With courage, enormous self-respect, and dignity, Amina Wadud risked her physical safety to step into this leadership role. Saudi Arabia's top cleric, Sheik Abdul Aziz-Seikh, described her as "an enemy of Islam" who had "violated God's law." She received letters filled with obscenities and death threats. However, other women are following in her footsteps, slowly reclaiming their rightful place in the religious sphere. Pamela Taylor's 2006 article about the progressive views of Grand Mufti Ben Cheikh of Marseilles is particularly telling:

> It's not often that one is asked to lead a grand mufti in prayer.[56] Especially if one is a woman. Indeed, until this February, no Muslim woman had ever been asked to lead a grand mufti in prayer. So it was, understandably, with an edgy mix of trepidation and elation that I recently agreed to lead prayers for a congregation that included, upon his request, the former Grand Mufti of Marseilles, Sohaib Ben Cheikh. My excitement and anxi-

ety were only heightened by the importance of what I was about to do. For a woman to lead a mufti, even a mufti known for his liberal views, was not just ground-breaking; it could be the lynchpin in the effort to legitimize women imams. . . .

That he decided to go beyond simply issuing a ruling, and chose to participate in a women-led prayer himself, sends an unequivocal message. A message that cannot be ignored by his fellow al-Azhar alumnae, who are among the most respected scholars in the Islamic world. A message that I dearly hope will help assuage the doubts of those who are sitting on the fence, undecided as to whether Islam bars women from religious leadership or not. A message that I dare to believe will eventually change the face of Islam as we know it today, restoring the community's commitment to justice and equality.

Grand Mufti Sohaib Ben Cheikh stands steadfast in his conviction that equality must be accorded to *all* Muslims. "We challenge not the religion, but the patriarchal practices that have infiltrated Islamic practice and Muslim society." The first religious scholar of his status to endorse female imams, the Grand Mufti asserted the following:

> Women's leadership as imams cuts at the root of so many evils currently plaguing Muslim societies. It challenges popular notions of sexuality that cast women as temptresses and men as weak and dominated by sexual urges. It belies the idea that women are emotional rather than intellectual, and in need of a firm male hand to keep them in balance. It shatters a social order in which men must go out to work and women must stay home to raise babies and care for the house. And it defies the convention that good women are silent, submissive, and serene.[57]

The idea of accepting women into mosques is beginning to take root. In Qom, Iran, for example, as holy a site to Shia Muslims as the Vatican is to Catholics, lives Yusef Saanei. He happens to be one of fifteen grand ayatollahs in Iran and, at age eighty, espouses a markedly reformist version of Islam. Advocating absolute equality between the sexes, Grand Ayatollah Saanei has been quoted as saying:

> I believe that a woman can lead prayers in the mosque. A woman can become the Supreme Leader, let alone the president. Islam knows no

discrimination between its followers, whether on grounds of nationality or race or gender.[58]

In 2005, the Council on American-Islamic Relations (CAIR) announced distribution of a "Women-Friendly Mosques" brochure. This document stands as perhaps the most enlightened statement CAIR has issued in its eleven-year history.[59] According to CAIR's Web site,

> An important challenge facing Muslims today is the need to revitalize the *masjid* [mosque] as a center of the community. In the time of prophet Muhammad, peace be upon him, the masjid was a place where all were welcome, all participated, and all contributed regardless of their age, gender, ethnicity, and status. . . . In short, it was the place where community life happened.

The Web site document traces Qur'anic verse and cites various ahadith, demonstrating that women were not barred from houses of worship in the Prophet's time and furthermore that, as Muslims, women have the right to circulate in public places. Another interesting aspect of this document counters the argument against women sharing the main prayer hall. This argument is

> based on the principle of guarding against corruption (*dar' al-mafasid*). The principle states that "whatever leads to haram is haram." The principle, though not widely accepted by Islamic jurists, has been extensively used to limit Muslim actions that are otherwise lawful under Shari'ah. It was invoked by some jurists to reject the use of radio, TV, the press, and other inventions because these have also been used to promote corrupt practices. Indeed many good practices and devices could be declared unlawful, including the use of Internet and democratic governments.[60]

It comes as no surprise that milestone events affecting women's rights (vis-à-vis the mosque) have occurred outside the Middle East in Muslim diasporas, far from strongholds of traditional patriarchy. New possibilities, newly emerging traditions, and the transformation of cultural attitudes continue to develop and thrive beyond the motherlands of Islam. How soon these practices will become accepted and adopted by Muslims in the Middle East, India, and Asia is another question. Khaled Abou El Fadl, a UCLA law professor, addressed the issue of women-led prayer in mosques in a June 2005 keynote speech in Los Angeles. He pinpointed two basic issues "that questioned women's intellectual capacity to lead prayer, and . . . argued that women-led prayer would create *fitna* [chaos] due to the potential to sexually excite men." As to the intellectual capacity of women, Sarah Eltantawi and Zuriani Zonneveld reported, "Abou El Fadl concluded that Um Salama, a woman of the Prophet's time, enjoyed a very high degree of religious authority, as did A'isha, the Prophet's wife."

> In fact, according to El Fadl, "About 30 percent (if not more) of Islamic jurisprudence was created by these two women." When jurists later wrote about these two women, many "exceptionalized" them in order to get around the potential legal implications of the fact that these two women were certainly of the highest intellectual capacity at the time of the Prophet. Jurists later argued that the status of A'isha and Um Salama could not be instructive for laws regarding women, since these women were close to the Prophet, and it is therefore impossible to find any women of comparable intellectual ability in any other period.

On the second issue relating to fitna, El Fadl emphasized the "sexual anthropology" of that particular historical period, noting the radical shift in sexual mores over time. He also cited the renowned Muslim historian and scholar al-Tabari (839–923), who spent most of his life in Baghdad writing commentaries on the Qur'an and believed that woman-led prayer was acceptable at all times. Other jurists who agreed with al-Tabari established powerful followings during the tenth through twelfth centuries in Iraq, Syria, and Egypt. However, these schools of thought eventually fell into decline and disappeared.[61]

Thus according to Professor El Fadl, the practice of women leading prayers is not new to Islam. The primary obstacle to women stepping into the mosque and into leadership roles is not religious doctrine but the oppressive mix of politics and patriarchy.

Resistance through Ritual

Religion and morality cannot be dictated by force. One is unlikely to persuade people to follow paths of "righteousness" by preaching exclusion, aggression, and fanaticism. What matters in the end is the ability to engender trust, by setting behavioral examples of compassion and tolerance. When gender-based issues are politicized to gain power and authority, the resulting political agendas ultimately meet with resistance. Fundamentalist Islam, with its long tradition of segregating and marginalizing women, faces this very dilemma.

Women are increasingly realizing the importance of joining in cooperative efforts, despite differences in nationality or language. Only by standing united in the struggle against social, religious, and cultural oppression can they hope to achieve established objectives.

Across the globe, countless Muslim women face the same threat: the expansion of Islamic radicalism. In their struggle to transcend Islamist restrictions, Muslim women have had to develop strategies that demand patience, resilience, and creativity. Some who are literate and gifted educate their "sisters" through the written word. Others with leadership capabilities engage in networking, organizing grassroots efforts, and disseminating information.

Many women find refuge in ritual experiences that cleanse the spirit, either privately or in community with other women. Performance of religious ritual brings women together in a shared experience of solidarity. These women-only rituals are most often viewed as events where "women say, mean, and do things about themselves as women . . . [uniting] women through a ritual focus on specifically female roles and value."[62] Cornelia Sorabji emphasizes the fact that religious rituals, such as *mevluds,* allow Muslim women "time off" to be with other women. Unlike *muluds* in the Middle East, where festivities are mixed gender and center around the birth of the prophet Muhammad, mevluds in Bosnia, for example, invite women to identify with the mother of the Prophet. Even if the women attending these female-only mevluds are not particularly religious, the ritual's comforting and peaceful quality gives them an opportunity to renew their spirits. Such gatherings also allow women to socialize.

The mevlud ritual functions similarly to the *sofreh* (religious banquet hosted by Shi'i women in Iran) mentioned in chapter 2. At the sofreh, held in a private home and for women only, participants eat specific foods, recite the Qur'an or other prayers honoring a particular Shi'i imam, and receive psychological and emotional support from each other.

Sofrehs are event-specific. For example, they may be held in response to emergencies and crises (Sofreh Bibi Zaynab), to attain peace of mind or regain health (Sofreh Fatima al-Zahra), or to honor and ask protection from the holy women related to the Prophet (Sofreh Zanan-e Moghadas).[63] While food has a strong association with potency and magic and can serve for healing or medicinal purposes, it can also serve as a metaphor for religious purposes, creating a sacred connection or bond between humans and God or holy spirits and saints. The sofreh is a communal expression of faith and thanksgiving for *barakat*, or God's blessings. Using the preparation and ritual presentation of food as a centerpiece, the sofreh invariably provides women with spiritual nourishment as well.

6.1. Women taking turns stirring a votive sweet dish called *sholeh zard*, one of the food items required for a specific *sofreh nazri*. This dish is similar to rice pudding, with the addition of almonds, pistachios, and saffron. Each of the participants has donated ingredients as well as time to prepare this dish. In this way, they will share the *baraka* (blessing) obtained from such a col-laborative effort. The author participated in this particular event.

Bodies Confined, Spirits Cleansed

6.2. *Sholeh zard* ready for distribution after cooling. Each dish is decorated with cinnamon powder and ground pistachios. The names of Imams Hossain and Ali and Fatima Al Zahra are inscribed with cinnamon powder on the cooled surfaces of some of the dishes. This votive sweet dish is prepared to commemorate the martyrdom of Hossain in *ashura* during the month of Mahram.

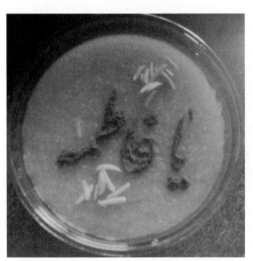

6.3. This prepared *sholeh zard* is ready for distribution. It is inscribed with "Ya Fatima" (Oh you Fatima), recalling the daughter of the prophet Muhammad, the first lady for Shi'i followers.

Dr. Noor Kassamali, in her study of healing rituals, explains the underlying significance of such ritual gatherings by women:

> These gatherings . . . subvert [women's] usually subservient social position in the normally male-dominant religious and cultural hierarchy. At these rituals, the women are in control not only of the rituals themselves but, symbolically, of the well-being of their families and communities. These rituals also serve to remind us that, despite the protestations of male-dominant orthodoxy, Muslim women, like women of other faiths, have their own parallel expressions of religiosity.[64]

Muslim women also visit the shrines of saints, whether the shrine of Sayyidna Zainab in Cairo or the Qadamghah shrine in Shiraz. This is a cultural practice that, like the sofreh, eschews the company of men, although men are at liberty to visit the shrines whenever they please. While orthodox Islam disapproves of these pilgrimages as being akin to ancestor (or idol) worship, shrines and tombs of saints continue to be popular destinations. Shi'i women especially frequent the shrines of the prophet Muhammad's descendants—shrines that are established in Iraq, Iran, Syria, and Egypt. In fact, almost every town throughout the Middle East has its own local saints so that, generally speaking, women do not have to travel far. The shrines also serve as meeting places for women with common interests and concerns. The shrine environment allows them to socialize, temporarily beyond the control of husbands, fathers, or brothers. As might be expected, women prefer the shrines of holy women, where they frequently ask for guidance and blessings in matters of marital discord or infertility.

For centuries, Muslim women have depended on each other for sustenance and healing, whether the healing in question addresses the mind, body, or spirit. Herbal cures have been used for generations. From Iran to India, from Tanzania to Uzbekistan, Muslim women seeking relief from ailment or crisis will turn to a respected herbalist or medicine woman for healing. Often these women are masters in the art of consolation as well as cure—whether the patient is hoping to increase libido, induce abortion, or mend a broken heart.

In her essay concerning the Tuareg, a seminomadic Muslim people of Niger and Mali, Susan Rasmussen discusses the important role that women play as social mediators and medico-ritual healers:

Herbal medicine women practice healing using a combination of plants, verbal incantations, ritual motions, massage, and psycho-social counseling. Medicine women trace their profession back to founding matrilineal ancestresses, apprentice with older kinspersons, and treat predominantly, though not exclusively, women and children.[65]

For generations, Muslim women have relied on each other to obtain religious and herbal cures. Across the Middle East, women frequent herbalist storefronts, shopping for ingredients and exchanging recipes. The following recipe for increasing a woman's libido was given to me by an herbalist in the city of Shiraz in 2004:

In a medium-sized pot, mix cumin seeds, fennel seeds, and linseeds in equal amounts. Add water, bring to boil, and brew the seeds for half an hour. Drink as a tea. Repeat this procedure at least twice a day.

In Arabic, the word *hakim* may refer to a "medicine man," a devout Muslim knowledgeable in the ways of traditional healing. The *hakima* is his female counterpart, also acknowledged and respected for her mastery of herbal medicine. Women generally find the hakima by word of mouth, since her practice is likely to depend on discretion and mutual trust.

In more rural settings, particularly among the Muslims of Central Asia, women perform healing roles in much the same way as men. A study of shamanic practices in northern Afghanistan found both males and females participating as *baxli,* or healers. Female baxli, often skilled in obstetrics, attract a middle-class clientele—wives of "generally prosperous artisans, urban merchants, and suburban owners of orchards." A female baxli's "popularity is associated with the fact that, in a society culturally dominated by males, women have no social life outside the company of kinswomen and no access to the economic life of the marketplace." More often than not, women visit the baxli without their husband's approval or knowledge.[66]

The tradition of women serving each other in a healing capacity enjoys a long history. The pre-Islamic *jahilia* women of Arabia "were priests, soothsayers, prophets, participants in warfare, and nurses on the battlefield. . . . They also were defiant critics of men, fearlessly outspoken as well as authors of satirical verse aimed at formidable opponents; keepers, in some unclear capacity, of the holy shrine in Mecca; rebels and leaders of rebellions that included men; and individuals who initiated and terminated marriages at

6.4. A *sofreh* held in honor of Abbas ibn Ali (also known popularly as Abul Fadl), one of the youths in the army of Imam Hossain during the battle of Karbala. People believe that honoring Abbas ibn Ali with a *sofreh* wards off danger, misfortune, or sickness. This is one of the most common and often most elaborate *sofrehs*.

will, protested the limits Islam imposed on that freedom, and mingled freely with the men of their society until Islam banned such interaction."[67] Thus the legacy of women engaging in ritual and other healing practices has been passed down through the generations—and has become Islamicized.

Bodies Confined, Spirits Cleansed

Rehana Ghadially states that while Islamic history and all its textual traditions receive considerable scholarly attention, the case is quite different in regard to the ritual forms of Muslim religious life. Various sects within the Islamic traditions differ in their ritual observances—practices shaped not only by textual traditions but also by local sociocultural aspects of each community.[68] Ghadially cites the popular Shi'i communal religious ritual *Hajari nu thai* (a tray with ritual food) that is observed by the Bohra sect of Ismaili Shi'i Islam in South Asia. She demonstrates how this particular ritual serves as an exclusive religious function for women, while also serving as a vehicle for them to mingle socially, exchange ideas, and offer each other support.

Rituals such as Hajari nu thai empower women through shared spiritual experiences. Other ritual expressions, such as those related to performance and music, serve the same purpose. *Bori*—a term that refers to the spirit-possession religion of the Hausa of West Africa—most likely originated among the Maguzawa people, a northern Nigerian tribe. Even after Islam was introduced, Jacqueline Cogdell Djedje writes, bori remained an integral part of the Hausa culture: "Hausa bori rites are generally performed for entertainment at social events such as weddings, naming ceremonies, and festivals, or specifically as a means for treating maladies or ill-fortunes believed to have been caused by spirits."[69] A large number of bori affiliates are female. Djedje posits the following theory about pre-Islamic Hausa culture:

Women were sometimes politically equal to men, for some were rulers and held political offices. They were also often economically independent, owning farms and employing themselves in various economic activities. One of the aftermaths of intensive Islamization was the rapid change in the status of women. . . . [On] becoming Muslims, [women] lost their pre-Islamic political, legal, and economic freedom. They could no longer hold state offices; they became dependent economically and legally on husband or kin. When married, they were secluded inside the compound. Therefore, the reason that women [continue to participate in] bori lies deeper than merely for illness or entertainment. . . .

The bori practice allows Hausa women to maintain significant status socially and politically, a holdover from pre-Islamic times. Alfons Teipen concurs by emphasizing that as far as the historical records are concerned, "pre-Islamic institutions and practices have not only survived with minor modifications, but oftentimes been appropriated by the new religion [Islam]."[70]

In North Africa and Sudan, female healers participate in rituals to cleanse the spirit and heal the body. These *Shaykhat* or *Moghadame* use incense, colorful fabrics, and a genre of music commonly known as Gnawa. Frequently all-night ceremonies (*lila*) are performed, a ritual dating back to the fifteenth century. These women are respected members of their communities, representing a long tradition of mastery in the healing arts.

Margaret Rausch's research points to a number of reasons why Muslim women seek help from female healers. Based on her interviews with Moroccan women, Rausch notes that they suffer from restrictions placed upon them as a result of normative cultural settings and societal gender roles. Obligated to conform to social and religious norms, the women report being overworked, dominated by family, and plagued by feelings of isolation:

Consulting a *shuwwafat* (female healer) therefore allows these women to articulate their personal problems and individual needs, to find emotional relief, support, and practical advice, and to become agents of change by reflecting and acting on their condition.[71]

In short, women turn to women healers, participate in healing rituals, and gather in religious ritual settings in order to assert some degree of autonomy and independence. In these private spaces, women find opportunity to speak, act, and think as they wish without fear of reprisal. Perhaps by participating in empowering rituals, by remaining steadfast in their grassroots activism, and by acknowledging their shared humanity, some Muslim women resist restrictions placed on them by fundamentalist doctrine.

While Muslim cultures are hugely diverse in terms of local traditions and regional distinctiveness, communities of women in each culture have cultivated and preserved time-honored rituals to lend each other support. In response to being excluded from male-dominated environments, women have developed their own ritual spaces and ceremonies to provide psychological comfort, establish and maintain friendships, and spiritually enrich their lives.

Conclusion

Muslims do not all think, act, and believe in the same way. Many Muslims hold fast to the belief that liberty, framed within the context of basic human rights, is and ought to be synonymous with Islam. In his novel *Animal Farm*, George Orwell suggested, "If liberty means anything at all, it is the right to tell people what they do not want to hear." Fifteen centuries after Muhammad, Muslim women are using powerful voices to denounce the use of Islam as a bully pulpit to justify misogyny. It is every woman's right to think, act, and believe according to her own conscience, in response to her own needs, and in alignment with her own intelligence. It is every woman's right to speak her truth—even if the powers that be do not want to hear. Islam has reached the same age at which Christianity experienced its reformation. The face of Islamic reform is slowly coming into focus, as adherents to the velvet jihad challenge the zealotry of an entrenched clerical establishment. This face of reform is primarily the face of women and, as this book demonstrates, they are pushing forward agendas that impact both national and global policy. The process of reform is one of evolution, not revolution. I made this point clearly in the introduction; that is, the velvet jihad is a natural extension, or evolution, of earlier reformist movements.

In her book *The Idea of Women in Fundamentalist Islam*, Lamia R. Shehadeh discusses specific attitudes that lie at the core of Islamic fundamentalism:

Men . . . are physically stronger and, therefore, fit for heavy work of the public sphere; they enjoy a higher mental acuity, making them more suitable for the rational judgments required in decision making positions; and they are providers and protectors of women. . . . [Men's] sex drive must be controlled by removing the source of temptation [women]. This is most efficiently solved by veiling and segregating women. Women, on the other hand, are incapacitated by menstruation, child bearing, and child rearing, making it difficult for them to work in the public sphere, and they are therefore necessarily confined to the home.[1]

Despite the number of Muslim women (approximately 450 million) serving as the favorite topic of Islamic fundamentalist discourse, only a small fraction of those women have actually been able to join in the debate. Velvet jihadists are inspiring others to join forces in global networks, such as Women Living Under Muslim Laws (WLUML). For these women, issues such as veiling are of secondary concern. They are far more interested in the substantive issues of freedom of speech, freedom of expression, and freedom to participate politically.

While writing *Velvet Jihad,* I unexpectedly discovered what a powerful role the Internet, as a global medium of communication, plays in supporting both progressive Muslim thought and fundamentalist ideology. On the one hand, the Internet is used as a site of resistance and mobilizing for Muslim feminists and dissenters. On the other hand, the Internet serves as a site for hate messages as well as surveillance by the authorities. In both cases the Internet provides a common advantage of invisibility.

The Internet as Burqa

One of the most extreme forms of veiling is the burqa, which in Afghanistan may also be referred to as chadri. Covering the entire female body and face, the top part features a lattice work mesh allowing the woman to breathe and see. Anyone wearing a burqa remains invisible and unidentifiable. Likewise, any Web user may effectively "veil" his true identity while reaching an incredibly large audience. Both fundamentalists and those who oppose Islamic fundamentalism are learning how to master online technology. Indeed, the Internet is proving to be the perfect burqa—obscuring identity, credential, location, and even underlying agendas.

With the resurgence of Islamic fervor in the twentieth century, many of the "faithful" have returned to medieval religious guidebooks. I refer to these manuals in chapter 3 ("Even Dolls Must Wear Hijab"), particularly their emphasis on patriarchal cultural traditions meant to control women and their sexuality. These manuals, which for hundreds of years were only available to religious scholars, are now accessible to millions of Muslims with Internet service.

For Islamic fundamentalists, especially those wannabe sheiks, imams, muftis, mulanas, and mullahs, the Internet has proven a dream come true. As mentioned in the introduction, they have created Web sites where fatwas are issued daily for every occasion and against every individual, particularly women, who disagree with their brand of Islam.

No one should take the threat of any fatwa lightly, even if issued by faceless Web-based entities whose religious credentials are questionable. For example, in chapter 5 ("Gender Preference: An Islamic View"), I cite a 2004 online fatwa issued against lesbians by a group of anonymous muftis. This fatwa, which labels lesbianism a crime, does not assign authorship to any individual person. This is an excellent example of how the Internet has been used to target minorities, especially those challenging established cultural norms. As I also pointed out in chapter 5, online technology has been responsible for the arrest and torture of Egyptian gays responding to personal ads placed by police agents. Internet users must therefore exercise caution and discernment, questioning the credibility of online information, to avoid falling prey to deliberate entrapment.

Internet users often assume that fatwas handed down are from the highest religious authorities. According to Ziauddin Sardar, the "Muslim world has gone fatwa-mad," and the most disturbing aspect is that many of these "legal statements" are issued by ignorant and semiliterate mullahs. In fact, Sardar claims that "fatwas are used as weapons against the marginalized. The powerful obtain fatwas to harass the less privileged. Sunnis used fatwas to persecute Shias, minority sects, and Christians; chauvinists use them to oppress women. In most cases, the spurious nature of these fatwas is all too evident."[2]

Even rulings regarding music, dancing, singing, playing musical instruments, and entertaining are posted online, and as I pointed out in chapter 4 ("Arts and Athletics: Stepping over Boundaries"), fatwas pertaining to these issues are blithely peddled on Web sites such as www.Ask-Imam.com.

On the positive side, online technology has made it possible to expose fraudulent and/or criminal practices. For example, in chapter 1 ("Honor and Virginity"), I referred to a tribal practice that sanctions the "marriage" of virgin girls to the Qur'an. No one can say how long this inhumane practice has been taking place, without penalty or intervention. Only when Pakistan's government realized the damage to its global image (via the Internet) was any action taken. Because of the online exposure, Pakistan's government has prepared a legislative bill to abolish these sham marriages.[3]

Not only is the Internet used to expose unjust practices, such as "marrying the Qur'an," but it is also emerging as a virtual venue for human rights campaigns. An excellent example is the One Million Signatures Campaign alluded to in chapter 6 ("Bodies Confined, Spirits Cleansed"). This enormous online project, exposing and challenging the oppressive conditions women face in Iran, could never have achieved the same level of success without the World Wide Web. According to Shirin Ebadi, Iranian lawyer, human rights activist, and winner of the Nobel Peace Prize 2003, this campaign "has no formal leadership, in part to lessen the chances of retaliation."[4] Its online signatories, unlike those jailed activists inside the Islamic Republic of Iran, enjoy immunity from the mullahs' judgment. As such, they stand invisible and united under the chador of the Internet.

A different type of affirmative action campaign, which seems to follow the Iranian model, began in Kenya in May 2007. Also known as the One Million Signatures Campaign, the objectives of this Internet project included expanding parliamentary representation for Kenyan women. This online campaign suggests that successful political strategies put in place by one group of women can be adopted by another group continents away to effect positive change. Although the Kenyan effort is not about Muslim issues per se, it does suggest that the Internet is a powerful tool for educating, uniting, and strengthening the bonds among women as they struggle for gender equality. As Valentine Moghadam acknowledged at the beginning of the twenty-first century:

Today, feminist groups and women's organizations remain rooted in national or local issues, but their vocabulary, strategies, and objectives have much in common with each other and have taken on an increasingly supra-national form. Moreover, some of these groups and organizations . . . have a common agenda across national borders. They engage in information exchange, mutual support, and a combination of lobbying, advocacy, and direct action toward the realization of their goals of equality and empowerment for women and social justice and social democratization.[5]

This movement toward transnationalism is gaining momentum, as women acknowledge that the discriminatory issues they face are shared across national boundaries. Activists such as Wafa Sultan share universal concerns regarding discriminatory policies:

Conclusion

The clash we are witnessing around the world is not a clash of religions or a clash of civilizations. . . . It's a clash between a mentality that belongs to the Middle Ages and another that belongs to the twenty-first century.[6]

According to the *Times of India,* Sultan's statement was viewed in 2007 by more than a million Internet users and was distributed on YouTube by a nonprofit, nonpartisan group, Middle East Media Research (MEMRI). As the Internet age connects Muslim bloggers, writers, and activists, new online communities are emerging. Web groups such as Muslims for Progressive Values are providing vital forums for moderate Muslim voices.

Obstacles to Solidarity

One of the most surprising obstacles to a successful velvet jihad—and perhaps the most disturbing face of radical Islam—is the fundamentalist Muslim woman. In attempting to explain this phenomenon, Dr. Mona Siddiqui makes the following observation:

> Freedom is a scary word for many women who are psychologically, emotionally, and physically tied in structures that at times barely allow them to breathe, but from which the possibility of escaping is even scarier. This has long been an issue, and many parts of the Muslim world are still grappling with the social instability that often accompanies female emancipation. The illusion that such societies have created is that such autonomy is un-Islamic.[7]

When Muslim women, particularly those habituated to fundamentalist ideology, are offered a vestige of independence, their response often reflects a fear of the unknown, an unwillingness to challenge existing authority, and a distrust of their own decision-making capabilities. Even in Kuwait, one of the more liberal Gulf states, tribal patriarchy evidently discourages women's solidarity. For the first time in Kuwait's history, women were given the opportunity to vote in the 2006 Kuwaiti elections. Instead of supporting female candidates, however, "the majority of Kuwaiti women voted for [male] conservatives, helping Islamist MPs to clinch the first place in their constituency. The ascent of the Islamists means the conservative bloc in parliament will continue to try and marginalise women, and stand in their way when it comes to attaining equal status in parliament."[8]

The fact that women voted along the same lines as their tribal leaders, catapulting to power the very same conservatives who would have barred them from voting, carries a disturbing signal. These women, under the influence of patriarchal power, apparently relinquished their right of *ijtihad*, or independent judgment, which Islam accords to all believers.

To understand how religion is manipulated for such ends, it is helpful to examine Erika Friedl's article "Islam and Tribal Women in a Village in Iran." Although Friedl is describing a specific regional tradition, her findings may be extrapolated to the wider patriarchal sphere. She notes how fundamental Islam is purveyed through proverbs that stress the importance of a woman's submissive role: "For men, moral imperatives are outlined in general terms; for women, they are conveyed in specific terms and keyed to submission to male authority."[9]

The resurgence of fundamental Islam in the Middle East, beginning in the 1960s and 1970s and culminating with the proliferation of radical ideology in the twenty-first century, is leading Muslim women to a critical juncture. In the face of staggering odds, some are falling back in alignment with the status quo.

Others, however, are advancing to the front. These women are tearing asunder veils of centuries-old repression and demonstrating a willingness to take extraordinary risks. For many of these women, writes Siddiqui, "this means . . . going against community expectations; for some it can be the biggest jihad of their lives."[10] Inarguably many velvet jihadists are dedicated feminists. However, in *Who Speaks for Islam?* Esposito and Mogahed have noted that not all Muslim women are interested in adopting the Western model of feminism in order to achieve gender equality. Indeed, Muslim women prefer to achieve gender parity on their own terms and within the boundaries of their respective cultures.[11]

A Muslim Is a Muslim Is a Muslim

We are one extended human family, interconnected and interdependent—regardless of national identity, cultural preference, or religious persuasion. Each of us holds the potential to exert positive change. The importance of the individual—and the impact of one person's actions—cannot be underestimated. I hold fast to the belief that the key to peaceful jihad rests in the hands of men and women of conscience everywhere.

In chapter 6, I mentioned a forty-year-old Muslim Indian who, in my opinion, represents the highest possible expression of a velvet jihadist. Her name is Daud Sharifa, and her objective is to build a mosque for women in the town of Pudukkottai, India:

As one reads more about Daud Sharifa, the symbolic project of actually building a women's mosque . . . begins to seem somewhat secondary to what might be her main goal: building a broad-based, national movement to support the rights of Muslim women. Since the government has done little to help (and sometimes much to hurt) the cause, Sharifa and her NGO, STEPS, have gone ahead and created a women-only Jamaat . . . to arbitrate family disputes using a feminist slant on Islamic law.

I also presented the issue of the jamaat in chapter 6—an all-male Islamic council that regularly makes decisions impacting women without the women's input. Sharifa insists:

The male jamaats are unlawful kangaroo courts that play with the lives of women. A mosque-jamaat axis is a power centre that controls the community. When women are refused representation here, we have no choice but to have our own jamaat. And since a jamaat is attached to a mosque, we have to build our own mosque.

Armed with a postgraduate degree in history and a fearlessness that is palpable, Sharifa states that "the Qur'an does not stop women from praying in mosques; only society does." Her NGO reaches out to women in distress from India's southernmost state where the majority of the population is Hindu rather than Muslim. One finds velvet jihadists like Sharifa emerging with passionate vision to better the living conditions of *all* women, proving the immeasurable impact of one individual's actions.[12]

As I have said, Muslims do not all think, act, and believe in the same way. Religious Muslims are not necessarily progressive, and progressive Muslims are not necessarily irreligious. Some velvet jihadists are fervently religious, such as countless young Muslim women pursuing Qur'anic scholarship. Others walk secular paths, such as Bangladeshi writer Taslima Nasreen, steadfast in her commitment to resist extremism, even when faced with death threats and physical attack.[13]

Many are devout Muslim men, reformers such as Dr. Abdulkarim Soroush, who have challenged Ayatollah Khomeini's claim that Iran's mullahs have a God-given right to govern.[14] Even in the most religious sectors of

Islam, one finds support for the velvet jihad. Grand Ayatollah Yusef Saanei particularly deserves acknowledgment. Saanei, a progressive cleric who supports Islamic rule in Iran, is receptive to the idea that the Iranian people may decide to oust the clerics. Judging from his statements, one gathers that Saanei envisions this possibility as a democratic process. Saanei has "openly challenged many of the traditional strictures that have kept women in a second-class position in Iranian society."[15]

Coming Full Circle

I have lived in the United States most of my life, arriving as a college student in 1971. Every trip home to Iran made me increasingly aware of the plight of women, both under the shah and after the 1979 Islamic revolution. I noticed that neither system of government—one with crown, the other with turban—gave equal rights to 50 percent of the population. Under the Islamic Republic, religion and political authority became tightly intertwined. What followed were interpretations of the Qur'an sacrificing its universal humanitarian message in favor of a selective process that honored neither the text nor its historical context. This rigid interpretation, by no means exclusive to the Islamic Republic of Iran, continues to dominate countless Sharia-driven societies. Tariq Ramadan eloquently counters the acceptability of such narrow interpretations:

> Some [individuals] have falsely claimed that because Muslims believe the Koran to be the word of God, interpretation and reform are impossible. This belief is then cited as the reason why a historical and critical approach cannot be applied to the revealed Text. The development of the science of the Koran—the methodological tools fashioned and wielded by the ulema and the history of Koranic commentary—prove such a conclusion baseless.[16]

I have tried throughout each chapter to call attention to the misogyny resulting from a narrow and selective interpretation of the Qur'an and related religious texts. The tension between Islam as religion and Islam as culture has produced enormous challenges for women.

This book questions the assumption that Muslim women, in response to these challenges, view themselves as passive victims, desperate for Western feminists to guide them on the path to emancipation. I wanted to provide women in the West, feminists included, a new and more authentic description of their Muslim counterparts. With great compassion, this book is written for them and for my Muslim sisters.

I have also attempted to address the positive and negative aspects of contemporary Islam, particularly in light of the events of September 11, 2001. In the wake of that tragedy, I observed the Western media—supported by ultraconservative political and religious groups—handily portraying Muslims as "suicide-belt wielding fanatics and head-to-toe burkha-clad women."[17] No thoughtful attempt was made to give the American people historical and cultural contexts or to demonstrate the phenomenal differences among Muslims in terms of political leanings, religious practices, and beliefs. Therefore, very little meaningful discourse ensued. Instead, America, the land of rich resources and unlimited possibilities, reverted to a fear-based, Cliff-notes mentality. What was there to know about Islam, after all? Beyond the turbans, veils, belly dancers, flying carpets, harem girls, and camel caravans, did anything else of substance lie in those desert enclaves? The West embraced a conveniently packaged, xenophobic version of Islam. Distinctions were blurred so effectively that Americans easily succumbed to war with a faceless enemy. The humanity of a billion practicing Muslims was reduced to a single tribe of fanatical bearded men and their victimized veiled women.

In this book, I have attempted to counter stereotypes, while detailing the unorthodox ways Muslim women resist oppressive patriarchal systems. These peaceful warriors, fighting for breathing space and discovering clever pathways to solidarity, are achieving positions of religious, political, and social influence. Their phenomenal effort is perhaps best viewed through the feminist lens of Ziba Mir-Hosseini as a "movement to sever patriarchy from Islamic ideals and sacred texts and to give voice to an ethical and egalitarian vision of Islam [that] can and does empower Muslim women from all walks of life to make dignified choices.[18]

The velvet jihad, then, is a response to the Qur'anic call.

> Let there arise out of you
> A band of people
> Inviting to all that is good,
> Enjoining what is right,
> And forbidding what is wrong.[19]

NOTES

Introduction

1. The "velvet revolution" began on November 17, 1989, when riot police attempted to suppress a peaceful student demonstration in Prague. By November 20 the number of protesters gathering in the streets of Prague had grown to an estimated half million. This expanding peaceful protest against the Communist Party ended in the Communists relinquishing power and Václav Havel ascending to the presidency of Czechoslovakia on December 29, 1989. The first democratic Czech elections (since 1946) were held in June 1990, as a result of this country's first entirely nonviolent velvet revolution.

Martin Beck Matustik was a signatory of Charta 77. He fled his native Czechoslovakia for political reasons in 1977 and settled in the United States, where he is professor of philosophy at Purdue University. Among his books are *Postnational Identity: Critical Theory and Existential Philosophy in Habermas, Kierkegaard, Havel* (Guilford, 1993); *Specters of Liberation: Great Refusals in the New World Order* (SUNY Press, 1998); and *Jürgen Habermas: A Philosophical-Political Profile* (Rowman and Littlefield, 2001).

2. See Ramadan's essay "Reading the Koran."

3. Mir-Hosseini, "Muslim Women's Quest for Equality," 13.

4. Gushee, "Oppressed Women Have Men to Thank."

5. Hiro, *Holy Wars*, 1–2.

6. For more information and a relevant discussion on the interchangeability of the terms *fundamentalist, Islamist, Islamic radicalism,* and *Islamic fundamentalism,* see Lamia Rustum Shehadeh, *The Idea of Women in Fundamentalist Islam,* 6–7.

7. Moallem, *Between Warrior Brother and Veiled Sister,* 9, 10.

8. According to Wikipedia, "The term *Islamism* denotes a set of political ideologies holding that Islam is not only a religion but also a political system, the teachings of which should be preeminent in all facets of society."

9. Jensen and Oster, "The Power of TV," abstract.

10. Engineer, "Why Reform Movements Are Necessary." Asghar Ali Engineer's most recent book is *Rational Approach to Islam* (2000).

11. Cooke, "Women, Religion, and the Postcolonial Arab World."

12. Abu-Lughod, *Veiled Sentiments: Honor and Poetry in a Bedouin Society.*

13. Cooke, "Women, Religion, and the Postcolonial Arab World," 151.

14. Cooke, "Multiple Critique: Islamic Feminist Rhetorical Strategies," 107, 109.

15. See *Class of 2006: Morocco's Female Religious Leaders*, 2006, DVD NRH36343–KS; *Red Lines and Deadlines: Inside Iran's Reformist Media*, 2004, DVD NRH36145–KS; and *Turkey's Tigers: Integrating Islam and Corporate Culture*, 2006, DVD NRH-36345KS.

16. Kaufman, "Transforming Our Interventions for Gender Equality by Addressing and Involving Men and Boys."

17. Ali, "Islam's Coming Renaissance Will Rise in the West."

18. Hessini, "Women Contesting Islamist Movements in the Arab World."

19. El-Akkad, "Muslim Teens Seek Belief in Its Perfect Form."

20. Badran, "Islamic Feminism Revisited."

21. Ahmed, "American Muslims Reimagined."

22. *Sunna* is the Arabic word for tradition or custom. *Ahadith* is the plural form of the Arabic word *hadith*, which means "story." In Islamic tradition, *ahadith* refers to the sayings of the prophet Muhammad.

23. Kassam, "Response in Roundtable Discussion, Feminist Religious History. Margaret R. Miles."

24. Mernissi, *The Veil and the Male Elite*, 75–76.

25. Ibid., 77.

26. Heath, *The Scimitar and the Veil*.

27. Hessini, "Women Contesting Islamists Movements in the Arab World."

28. Quoting van Doorn-Harder's book in "Muslim Women Can Reshape Islam."

29. Van Doorn-Harder, *Women Shaping Islam*, 55.

30. Mohammadi, "Iranian Women Activists: In It to Win It."

31. FAMA International, founded in 1991, is a Sarajevo-based media-publishing house with a network of affiliated partners in Europe, the United States, and Japan. It is a leading advocate for global preservation, integration, and educational application of the collective memory pertaining to the siege of Sarajevo (1992–96). See its Web site: www.famainternational.com/who/who-ff.htm.

32. Ehsan Masood is a writer and journalist based in London. He is the editor of *Dry: Life without Water* (Cambridge: Harvard University Press, 2006) and *How Do You Know: Reading Ziauddin Sardar on Islam, Science, and Cultural Relations* (Ann Arbor: Pluto Press, 2006).

33. For a selected group, see Amina Wadud, *Qur'an and Woman*; Wilcox, *Women and the Holy Qur'an: A Sufi Perspective*; Barlas, *"Believing Women" in Islam*; Barazangi, *Women's Identity and the Qur'an*; Stowasser, *Women in the Qur'an, Traditions, and Interpretation*.

34. Barlas, *"Believing Women" in Islam*, 53.

35. Moallem, *Between Warrior Brother and Veiled Sister*, 3.

36. Yesim Arat, "Combating Restrictions on the Headscarf."

37. The International Covenant on Civil and Political Rights is a United Nations

treaty based on the Universal Declaration of Human Rights, created in 1966, although not enforced until 23 March 1976.

38. The ICESCR is a legally binding treaty that protects a range of economic, social, and cultural rights without discrimination based on creed, political affiliation, gender, or race. For more information, see www.franciscansinternational.org/issues/icescr/icescr.php.

39. Arat, "Combating Restriction on the Headscarf."

40. Shirazi, *The Veil Unveiled*, 80–109.

41. Arat, *The Patriarchal Paradox*. Yesim Arat is a professor of political science and international relations at Bogazici University, Istanbul, Turkey.

42. The women's branch of the Refah Party was established in Turkey in 1989. The party itself was founded in 1983. Both branches were shut down by a Turkish constitutional court decision in 1998. The court maintained that the Refah Party undermined principles of secularism in the Turkish constitution.

43. Arat, *Rethinking Islam and Liberal Democracy*, 115.

44. Ibid., 109.

45. Moghadam, "Patriarchy and the Politics of Gender in Modernising Societies."

46. Shirazi, *The Veil Unveiled*, 94.

47. Tohidi, "Guardians of the Nation: Women, Islam, and the Soviet Legacy of Modenization in Azerbaijan," 137.

48. Quoted in Louis Dris-Aït-Hamadouche's "Women in the Maghreb: Civil Society's Actors or Political Instruments?"

49. Ilkkaracan, *Women and Sexuality in Muslim Societies*. Pinar Ilkkaracan is cofounder of several NGOs, including the Coalition of Sexual and Bodily Rights in Muslim societies, a biregional network of academicians and NGOs working toward sexual rights. She is editor of *Women and Sexuality in Muslim Societies*, translated in both Arabic and Turkish, published by Women Living under Muslim Law. She is coauthor of *The Myth of the Warm Home: Domestic Violence and Sexual Abuse and Human Rights Education for Women: A Training Manual* (Istanbul: Canan Arin Metis Yayinlari, 1996).

50. Joseph, "Gender and Citizenship in Middle Eastern States," 4.

51. Moghadam, *Women, Work, and Economic Reform in the Middle East and North Africa*, 8.

52. Ibid., 10.

53. Moghadam, ed., *From Patriarchy to Empowerment*.

54. Badran, "Islamic Feminism Revisited."

55. Smith, "Women in Islam: Equity, Equality, and the Search for the Natural Order."

56. According to Soraya Altorki's essay "Women and Islam," in *The Oxford Encyclopedia of the Modern Islamic World*, three different categories describe the Islamic worldview: modernist, traditionalist, and scripturalist. Of these, the scripturalists embrace an entirely literal interpretation of the Qu'ran.

57. Nomani, "A Gender Jihad for Islam's Future."

58. Wadud, *Inside the Gender Jihad,* 183.

59. Lite, "Woman Leads Muslims in Prayers."

60. Sayyid Muhammad Rizvi is the imam of the Ja'ffari Islamic Centre, the largest Shi'a center in Toronto. He has an MA in history from Simon Frasier University in Vancouver and is the author of numerous books on Islam, including *Marriage and Morals in Islam* and *Islam: Faith, Practice, and History.* Rizvi is also a trustee on the Council of Shi'a Scholars of North America.

61. Badran, "Islamic Feminism Revisited."

62. Ketabchi, "Iran: Women's Protest Brutally Attacked."

63. Masood, "Islam's Reformers."

64. Tariq Said Ramadan (born August 26, 1962, in Geneva, Switzerland) is a Francophone Swiss Muslim academic and scholar. He advocates that Muslims living in the West should not view themselves as foreigners or temporary residents of their countries, but rather as full citizens with full rights and responsibilities. In some respects, he argues for integration and not alienation from the surrounding society. Indeed, the main theme of his book *To Be a European Muslim* attempts to bridge the gap between being a Muslim and being European. He also advocates that immigrant parents should not confuse culture with religion. Muslims born in western countries should adopt the tastes and cultural norms of their country and not those of their parents' homeland.

Dr. Abdulkarim Soroush (born in Tehran in 1945) is a leading Iranian thinker, philosopher, reformer, and Rumi scholar. Soroush's main contribution to Islamic philosophy is the assertion that one should distinguish between religious ideology as divinely revealed and the interpretation of religion or religious knowledge which is based on socio-historical factors. Soroush is primarily interested in the philosophy of science, philosophy of religion, the philosophical system of Maulana Jalau'd-din Muhammad (Rumi), and comparative philosophy. He is a world expert on Rumi and Persian Sufi poetry. During the 1990s, Soroush gradually became more critical of the political role played by the Iranian clergy. The monthly magazine that he cofounded, *Kiyan,* soon became the most visible forum for religious intellectualism. His most controversial articles on religious pluralism, hermeneutics, tolerance, and clericalism appeared in this magazine. *Kiyan* was shut down in 1998 by direct order of the supreme leader of the Islamic Republic. About 1,000 recorded speeches by Soroush on various social, political, religious, and literary subjects enjoy wide circulation in Iran and across the globe. As the target of ongoing harassment and state censorship, Soroush lost his job. His public lectures at universities in Iran are often disrupted by hardliner Ansar-e-Hizbullah vigilante groups.

65. Kamrava, ed., *The New Voices of Islam: Rethinking Politics and Modernity,* 27.

Chapter 1. Honor and Virginity

1. Weitz, ed., *The Politics of Women's Bodies,* ix.

2. Foucault, *Discipline and Punish.*

3. Shirazi, *The Veil Unveiled*.

4. Weitz, *The Politics of Women's Bodies*, 3.

5. Ibid., 4.

6. Originally, "Chetniks" referred to a resistance movement loyal to the kingdom of Yugoslavia's government in exile during World War II.

7. Mydans, "Sexual Violence as Tool of War."

8. Haeri, "The Politics of Dishonor: Rape and Power in Pakistan."

9. For more information on Hudood Ordinances, see www.pakistani.org /pakistan/legislation/zia_po_1979/ord7_1979.html.

10. Khan, "Jubilation in Jail."

11. Katz, "Honor Killings."

12. Schneider, "Of Vigilance and Virgins: Honor, Shame, and Access to Resources in Mediterranean Societies," 1.

13. Namus: Law: "The sacred law which Muhammad, and before him Musa, received from God through an angel, who is sometimes also called Namus." Found at www.pantheon.org/articles/n/namus.html.

14. Schneider, "Of Vigilance and Virgins," 1.

15. Ibid., 18–19.

16. Wali, "Muslim Refugees, Returnees, and Displaced Women."

17. Al-Khayyat, *Honour and Shame*, 21–22.

18. Sadr, "Women in Iran Deem Rape Laws Unfair."

19. Dareini, "Iran Women Lawmakers Step Up Campaign to Save Woman from Execution."

20. Arman, "Rape Victim Who Killed Her Attacker to Be Released." Afsaneh Norouzi was finally released after spending 2,760 days in detention.

21. Buddell, "Crimes of Passion: Should They Be Distinguished from the Offence of Murder in England and Wales?"

22. Katz, "Honor Killings."

23. Webster, "Women, Sex, and Marriage in Moroccan Proverbs."

24. Jehl, "Arab Honor's Price: A Woman's Blood."

25. Wilson, "What Makes a Terrorist?"; Dworkin, "The Women Suicide Bombers."

26. Jehl, "Arab Honor's Price."

27. *Ab* is water in Persian; *rou* means face. *Aberou*, or "water of the face," is a metaphor for shame because when one's face perspires, it is highly visible and can be seen by others.

28. Abu-Lughod, "Honor and the Sentiments of Loss in a Bedouin Society."

29. Mayell, "Thousands of Women Are Killed for Family 'Honor.'"

30. International Commission of Jurists, 2001, at www.icj.org/news.php3?id_ article=2584&lang=en.

31. Shirkat Gah Women's Resource Center, "Not All the Islamic Countries Practice Honor Killings," *Az-Zaujus Salih*, Winter 2000 (www.shirkatgah.org). Published for Women Living Under Muslim Laws (www.WLUML.org) and posted on Women for Women's Human Rights (www.wwhr.org/?id=777).

32. Mayell, "Thousands of Women Are Killed for Family 'Honor.'"

33. Ibid.

34. Koppel, "The Pakistani Who Fought Back and Won."

35. From a Web site devoted to Mukhtar Mai at http://michaelthompson .org/mai/.

36. "Over 1,700 Honour Killings in Five Years Reported in Pak's Punjab." *Malaysia Sun,* August 12, 2007.

37. Davie, "World Diary: Honor Killings."

38. Kraemer, *An Etymological Dictionary of Classical Mythology.*

39. Choi, "Restoring Virginity: Hymen Repair Surgery Saves Lives at the Expense of Deception"; Paterson-Brown, "Commentary: Education about the Hymen Is Needed."

40. Mernissi, *Women's Rebellion and Islamic Memory;* Weitz, *The Politics of Women's Bodies,* 3–11.

41. Banashek, "The Seat of Intolerance."

42. The Muslim Women's League is a nonprofit American Muslim organization working to implement the values of Islam and thereby reclaim the status of women as free, equal, and vital contributors to society.

43. Weitz, "The Wage of Innocence."

44. Choi, "Restoring Virginity."

45. Gonzalez-Lopez, "De madres a hijas: Gendered Lessons on Virginity across Generations of Mexican Immigrant Women," 230.

46. Ratchanisawat, "The Importance of Being a Virgin."

47. Kandela, "Egypt's Trade in Hymen Repair."

48. The official Web site of Grand Ayatollah Al Rohani is http://www.emamro hani.net/home/. His e-mail address is rohani@istefta.net.

49. Dr. Troy Robbin Hailparn, Laser Vaginal Rejuvenation Institute of San Antonio, at www.cosmeticgyn.net/about.htm.

50. Paternostro, "Please Make Me a Virgin Again."

51. Mernissi, *Women's Rebellion and Islamic Memory.*

52. Kobrin, "Restoring Virginity Becomes Risky Business." Also see Kobrin, "More Women Seek Vaginal Plastic Surgery."

53. Jaffee, "Maidenhead Revisited."

54. Buckley, "A Sex Ploy: 2 Times a Virgin—for Only $199!"

55. Sex Sultan, *Salam Worldwide,* June 15, 2003.

56. Cindoglu, "Virginity Tests and Artificial Virginity in Modern Turkish Medicine," 257.

57. Erdim, "Women Ask Female Minister to Resign."

58. Morris, "Forced Virginity Tests Banned."

59. Lasco, "Virginity Testing in Turkey: A Violation of Women's Human Rights."

60. Imoukhuede, "Virginity Test Case."

61. Obonyo, "AIDS: New Frictions Emerge over Virgin Brides."

62. Girard, "Human Rights and Women's Health: The Light at the End of the Speculum."

63. Khumalo, "Virginity Testing 'Helps Curb AIDS.'"

64. McGreal, "Virgin Tests Make a Comeback."

65. Soros, "Virgins, Potions, and AIDS in Zimbabwe."

66. See www.tibetjustice.org/reports/women/vii.html.

67. Morris, "Afghan Women 'Still Suffer Abuse.'"

68. Dooley, "Houston Woman Joins Ancient Rite as Consecrated Virgin."

69. Waqar, "Pakistan Cracks Down on Anti-Women Tradition."

70. Saeed, "Women Status in Pakistan under Customs and Values and the Controversial Hudood Ordinance 1979." According to Section 295-B of the Pakistan Penal Code, whoever willfully defiles, damages, or desecrates a copy of the Qur'an or an extract or uses it in a derogatory manner or for an unlawful purpose shall be punishable with life imprisonment. The proposed amendment to Section 295-B says: "Defiling, etc. of, and marriage with, the Holy Qur'an: whoever willfully defiles, damages or indirectly allows the Holy Qur'an to be used for the purpose of its marriage with a female or fraudulently or dishonestly induces any person to swear on the Holy Qur'an never to marry anyone in her lifetime or knowingly uses it in any derogatory manner or for any unlawful purpose shall be punishable with imprisonment for life." For additional information on this bill, see Imran, "Bill to Abolish Qur'an Marriages Prepared." For additional information about this, see "Haq Bakhshish: No Right to Wed."

71. Stuever, "Viva Las Virgins!"

72. See www.hh76.com/pro_life_products.asp?group_id=888&site_id=3. Examples of the logo on promotional items—including the FDA-approved tattoos available for "classroom, fairs, groups, kids, adolescents, and adults"—are "Worth Waiting For" and "A Man's Strength Is in His Character."

73. Soros, "Virgins, Potions, and AIDS in Zimbabwe."

74. Bain, "Defining Virginity Part of Validating Relationships."

75. Zakaria, "Honour Killing: Crime & Abetment."

Chapter 2. Sterility, Childbirth, Taboos, and Popular Religious Practices

1. Abu-Lughod. "Islam and the Gendered Discourses of Death," 189.

2. Inhorn, *Infertility and Patriarchy*; Inhorn, *Infertility around the Globe*; Inhorn, *Local Babies, Global Science*; Inhorn, *Quest for Conception*.

3. Masse, *Persian Beliefs and Customs,* 5.

4. Wikan, *Behind the Veil in Arabia,* 185.

5. Khanna, "The Goddess-Woman Equation in Sakta Tantras," 44.

6. Woollett and Pfeffer, "Update to Discovering That You Are Infertile," 396–97.

7. Bhatti, Fikree, and Khan, "The Quest of Infertile Women in Squatter Settlements of Karachi, Pakistan." For other studies on the social and psychological effects on in-

fertile women in general and in other Muslim countries and Middle Eastern regions, see Adams, "Families and Family Study in International Perspective"; Koh and Tan, "Favoritism and the Changing Value of Children"; Azadarmaki, "Families in Iran: The Contemporary Situation"; Al-Naser, "Kuwait's Families."; Andres, Abbey, and Halman, "Stress from Infertility, Marriage Factors, and Subjective Well-Being of Wives and Husbands"; Meyers et al., "An Infertility Primer for Family Therapists: I. Medical, Social, and Psychological Dimensions."

8. Remennick, "Childless in the Land of Imperative Motherhood."

9. Vom-Bruck, "Elusive Bodies."

10. The role of hakim should not be confused with that of the ulama. The hakim is a medicine man with knowledge of herbs, talismans, and other types of remedies—including cure through prayer. Ulama are religious scholars.

11. Tokhy, *Al-Kabrit,* 24.

12. Ibrahim, *Haftad Du Div, Ulume al Ghariba* (Seventy-two demons, the science of magic). The book opens with praise to Allah, the Prophet, and his descendants.

13. Shaykh Baha'i, "Ulume Gharibah, Matn-e-Kamel-e Kashkoul-e-Shaykh Baha'i" (The virtues of the beautiful names of Allah), 192.

14. Ali, *The Holy Qur'an,* 1807.

15. Ibid., 1808.

16. Tokhy, *Al-Kabrit,* 30.

17. Sarbazi, *Shafaul Isteqam wa al Hazan,* 31.

18. Khansari, *Kolsum Naneh,* 44.

19. Ibid, 83. The footnote on 83 states that "āl is an invisible spirit similar to jinn. According to folk tales, if a woman who recently delivered a baby is left alone, āl is able to harm her. It is said that the new mother should not be left alone for the first six days after her delivery. In his book *Neyrangestan,* Sadegh Hedayat (27) writes that "āl looks like a woman with skinny hands and legs, whose face is reddish in tone, with a nose made of clay." However, according to Mohammed Reza Ghanoonparvar, professor of Persian literature and culture in the Department of Middle Eastern Studies at the University of Texas at Austin, in Esfahan, āl is a male figure that appears only at night, is sexually aroused, and is interested mostly in virgins, thus creating sexual anxiety among the populace.

20. Doumato, *Getting God's Ear,* 153–54; *Encyclopaedia of Islam,* 9:484–86; and al-Wahhab, *Kitab at-Tawhid: Essay on the Unicity of Allah,* chap. 8, p. 29 (quoted in Doumato, 262).

21. Doumato, *Getting God's Ear,* 148.

22. Regis, *Fulbe Voices,* 106.

23. Ibid., 90.

24. Dundes, *Interpreting Folklore,* 101.

25. Babanah, "The Story of the Mysterious Pouch and Women's Fear of Ash and Feathers in Mauritania."

26. Abu-Lughod, "Islam and the Gendered Discourses of Death," 190.

27. Noor Kassamali, "Healing Rituals and the Role of Fatima."

28. Ali, *The Holy Qur'an.*
29. Grima, *The Performance of Emotion among Paxtun Women,* 64–65.
30. Sarbazi, *Shafaul Isteqam wa al Hazan,* 25.
31. Khansari, *Kolsum Naneh,* 43.
32. Ibid., 83.
33. Sawalha, "Barriers of Silence."
34. Sharma, "No Girls, Please, We're Indian," 1.
35. Ibid. See also Iyer, "Religion and the Decision to Use Contraception in India."
36. See also Remez, "Prevention of Unwanted Births in India Would Result in Replacement Fertility." This report showed that when women were asked the preferred sex of the next child, the proportion preferring a boy was almost four times that preferring a girl (41 percent vs. 11 percent).
37. Cong, "Criminal Penalties Pondered for Aborting Females."
38. "Is It a Boy or a Girl?"
39. Weiss, "Girl or Boy?" For scholarly information on medical ethics and demographics, see the following site: National Library of Medicine (NCBI), www.ncbi .nlm.nih.gov/entrez/query.fcgi?db=pubmed&cmd=Display&dopt=pubmed_ pubmed&from_uid=12816188.
40. I also found this posting on *www.worldmagblog.com*: Home gender test. A new blood test has hit the market, which will allow pregnant women to find out the sex of their baby as early as five weeks into the pregnancy. For $275, a woman can prick her finger and send a drop of blood to a lab, which can detect fetal DNA floating in the mother's blood. She can now know whether she is carrying a boy or a girl much earlier than with ultrasound pictures and much more safely than with amniocentesis. Ethicists worry that this new technology will be used for sex selection—aborting the child if she is not the gender the parents want (girl babies being nearly always the victims). This concern applies especially to Asian countries. Already in China, where little girls are often killed after they are born, there are only 100 women for every 120 men. In India, for every 1,000 boys birthed in 2004 only 762 girls were born. Surely there is no ethical problem with the test itself, if the results are not misused. Posted by Veith, June 28, 2005.
41. *Fuqaha,* Arabic plural of *Faqih,* translates to "expert in Islamic jurisprudence." Not to be confused with *ulama,* a more generic term for a learned person or scholar.
42. Dawood, *The Qur'an.*
43. In this verse, "We" refers to God.
44. Bowen, "Abortion, Islam, and the 1994 Cairo Population Conference," 164.
45. Ibid., 165.
46. Asman, "Abortion in Islamic Countries—Legal and Religious Aspects."
47. Boonstra, "Islam, Women, and Family Planning," 5.
48. Asman, "Abortion," 88.
49. Bowen, "Abortion."

50. Hoodfar and Assadpour, "The Politics of Population Policy in the Islamic Republic of Iran."

51. Boonstra, "Islam, Women, and Family Planning," 16.

52. "Report on Reproductive and Sexual Health (Strategies, Programs & Measures) in the Islamic Republic of Iran."

53. Muir, "Condoms Help Check Iran Birth Rate."

54. Abbasi et al., "Revolution, War, and Modernization," 25.

55. Ibid.

56. Kogacioglu, "The Tradition Effect: Framing Honor Crimes in Turkey." Kogacioglu is an assistant professor in the Faculty of Arts and Social Sciences at Sabanci University, Istanbul.

57. McBride, "Nawal Saadawi."

58. Casey, "Editor of Feisty Iranian Magazine Faces Prison."

59. "Women Lift the Veil in Kashmir."

60. Dorr, "Azizah Celebrates Muslim American Women."

61. For more information on organizational profile and mission, see www.kit .nl/smartsite.shtml?ch=FAB&id=4356.

62. For example, the following link exists to the Shirkat Gah Web site: www .shirkatgah.org/pubs_women_law&rights.htm. *Great Ancestors: Women Asserting Rights in Muslim Context—Information & Training Kit*, by Farida Shaheed and Aisha L. F. Shaheed, is a two-volume training kit that profiles women who have defied authority to improve women's lives from the eighth to twentieth centuries. Texts also include details and guidelines for adaptation. Vol. A: Training Manual, and Vol. B: The Narratives. Another important example is a book in Urdu, especially targeting illiterate women, *Faujdari Kawaneen Ka Tasweeri Kitabcha*. This illustrated booklet explains a citizen's legal rights vis-à-vis the high-handed tactics of police. *From a Grain to a Pearl: True Stories from the Field*, is available in English and Urdu. "This unique collection of real-life stories, gathered by Shirkat Gah's Women, Law, and Status team, illustrates the strategies women in the community have used to improve their own lives and the lives of those around them. The stories cover a range of issues including consent in marriage, dowry, polygamy, education, decision-making, income-generation, divorce, domestic violence, disability, mobility, and inheritance."

63. Hughes, "New Challenges for Women Campaigners."

64. Federation of Muslim Women at www.fmw.org/english/about.html.

65. "Women Living Under Muslim Laws" at www.wluml.org/english/about .shtml.

66. Muslim Women Lawyers for Human Rights (KARAMAH) at www.karamah .org/home.htm.

67. Baitul Hemayah, Inc., at www.baitulhemayah.org/about.html.

68. WLP works with partner organizations in Afghanistan, Brazil, Cameroon, Egypt, India, Iran, Indonesia, Jordan, Lebanon, Malaysia, Mauritania, Morocco, Nicaragua, Nigeria, Palestine, Turkey, Uzbekistan, and Zimbabwe.

69. Accessed at http://learningpartnership.org/about.

70. Shirazi, "The *Sofreh:* Comfort and Community among Women in Iran," 309.

Chapter 3. Even Dolls Must Wear Hijab

1. Both the title of this second book and the name of its author are rendered in English in myriad ways. I have chosen one spelling for each and will deviate from that spelling only when citing another's work.

2. The spelling of the first title, *Az-Zaujus Salih,* appears this way on the Bilal Books (published in Bombay). However, I believe *Az* should be replaced with *Al,* indicating the article *the* in Arabic.

3. Excerpts cited in this chapter are my own translations.

4. Metcalf, *Perfecting Women,* 1.

5. See www.halalco.com/family&soc.html.

6. Astrolabe.com, for example, offers a Fulla Singing Doll named Yatayba. Yatayba, which is ordinarily spelled Ya Tayba, means "the good, virtuous female." This Web site describes their Fulla Doll as "a major source of connection and comfort for Middle Eastern and European children. Now, American girls can not only learn about a lifestyle a world away, but they can also learn core values and acceptance of other cultures. The best part is girls can learn these virtues while having fun." This is marketing language at its best, feigning the importance of cross-culturalism while playing down their real agenda: turning a profit. For more information, see www.astrolabe.com.

7. See www.hedeyah.com/products.asp?cat=9.

8. Ali, *The Holy Qur'an.* This is the first part of verse 32 in chapter 7, *Araf* (Heights).

9. A Sufi is a member of mystical sect of Islam who believes in a simple lifestyle and the denunciation of worldly things, including material goods and extravagant habits such as overindulgence in eating and drinking. Sufis wear a garment made of thick, coarse, undyed white wool known for its itchiness and lack of comfort.

10. Tehran *Hamshahri,* February 2002.

11. Al-Bukhari, *Sahih al-Bukhari,* 7: 513–14. Bukhari reports that Ibn Abbas narrated that Allah's apostle (the prophet Muhammad) cursed those men who assumed the manners of women and those women who assumed the manners of men.

12. Thanvi, *Behishti Zewar,* 334.

13. A modern-day example of the "intention" principle would be a male technician reading a mammogram. Clearly his intention is not lascivious ogling of a naked woman but rather analyzing an X-ray for medical purposes. Nevertheless, some clinics in Iran post announcements giving female patients the option of having female radiologists read their X-rays.

14. Metcalf, *Perfecting Women,* 4.

15. Mujlisul-Ulama of South Africa, *Al-Mar'atus Salihah* (The pious woman), 1.

16. Ibid.

17. Ibid., 28.

18. Ibid.

19. Ibid., 9. The reader should note that this is a direct quotation from the source manuscript.

20. Ibid., 24–27.

21. Ibid., 25.

22. *Sallallahu Alayhi Wasallam* means "May God forgive him and bestow peace upon him." The phrase is almost always used as a blessing after the mention of the prophet Muhammad, who has many titles, such as Rasulullah (messenger of God) and Nabi-e-Kareem (the kind Prophet).

23. *Al-Mar'atus Salihah,* 9–10.

24. *Aurah'* is a reference to the sexual organs of both genders, which need to be concealed.

25. *Al-Mar'atus Salihah,* 18.

26. Shirazi, "Florida Case Veils Truth about Muslim Ways."

27. Sharmeen Obaid-Chinoy, undercover documentary filmmaker and freelance journalist, infiltrated Hashmi's seminar and documented her statement that the Kashmiri earthquake was God's punishment for "immoral activities" and that Muslim women should permit their husbands to marry more than once so that "other sisters can also benefit."

28. Hasan, "Quake God's Punishment for 'Immoral Activities': Farhat Hashmi."

Chapter 4. Arts and Athletics:
Stepping over Boundaries

1. Al-Faruqi, "Music, Musicians, and Muslim Law," 3, 5.

2. Sabri, "A Topic of Dispute in Islam: Music," *Beyan-ul-Haq* 3, no. 63 (1910). Born in Turkey in 1869, Mustafa Sabri memorized the Holy Qur'an as a child. He completed his education in Istanbul, where he taught Islamic sciences. Elected to the Ottoman Parliament in 1908, he was appointed Sheikh Al-Islam (the highest religious authority) in 1919. He died in Egypt in 1954.

3. Al-Kanadi, "Music and Singing in the Light of the Qur'an and Sunnah." Abu Bilal Mustafa al-Kanadi was born in Italy in 1950. At the age of four, he migrated with his family to British Columbia. In 1972 he graduated from the University of British Columbia, the same year he embraced Islam. Quickly he developed a yearning for Islamic knowledge, and this quest led him to Umm al-Qurra University in Makkah, Saudi Arabia, where he completed the Arabic-language program. He went on to graduate from the College of Shari'ah after which he obtained a master's degree in Qur'anic sciences.

4. Danielson, "Shaping Tradition in Arabic Song," 57–75.

5. Daniels, "Taarab Clubs and Swahili Music Culture."

6. Ibid., 6.

7. Aiello, "Continuity and Change in Zanzibari Taarab."

8. Mitra, "When Caged Women Try to Sing of the Skies."

9. Lengel, "Performing In/Outside Islam," 215.

10. Ibid.

11. Safa-Isfahani, "Female-Centered World Views in Iranian Cultures."

12. Al-Bukhari, *Sahih al-Bukhari*, vol. 7, hadith 773.

13. The *Shahnameh* is also known as *The Epic of Kings*. It took Ferdosi thirty years to complete this masterpiece. One of his main objectives in narrating these ancient tales was to do so using only the Persian language and omitting all Arabic.

14. Habibian quoted from www.jadidonline.com.

15. Rahman, "Kabul Stage."

16. *Moseghiye moftazah* is also understood as a useless type of entertainment.

17. Reuters, June 9, 2007.

18. The Hudood Ordinance is a law in Pakistan that enforces punishments mentioned in the Qur'an and sunnah for crimes such as adultery, rape, and theft. It was enacted in 1979 as part of military ruler Zia-ul-Haq's Islamization process. It is based on Muslim Sharia law. The Hudood Ordinance criminalizes all extramarital sex. Even when the woman claims that she was raped and not involved in adultery, she must have four pious male witnesses to prove rape. If four witnesses are not provided by the woman, but rape is proved by other means (e.g., medical evidence), then the jury can punish the accused according to the Pakistani penal court. For married couples, the punishment for adultery is death by stoning, but this has never been carried out. Unmarried people receive one hundred lashes. This ordinance has been misused against rape victims if they are unable to provide four male witnesses; however, the extent to which this occurs is disputed. In certain situations, the alleged rapist accuses the raped woman of confessing to consensual intercourse. See Wikipedia for "Hudood Ordinance." See also www.pakistani.org/pakistan/legislation/zia_po_1979/ord7_1979.html.

19. In Afghanistan, the Revolutionary Association of the Women of Afghanistan (RAWA) is working to expose crimes of violence. During the Taliban rule, members of RAWA risked their lives to secretly film violence perpetrated against women by the Taliban and disseminated this information to the outside world. RAWA continues to provide shelter, vocational training, and education for homeless women and prostitutes in Herat, Kabul, Mazar-e-Sharif, and Jalalabad.

20. Eva Fenn, "Women and Music Censorship—Past to Present."

21. "Bittersweet Success of Secret Girl Band."

22. Jiménez, "Women Artists, Performers Criticize Muslim Festival Restrictions," globeandmail.com, August 13, 2005.

23. "PMU Denounces Exclusion, Restriction of Muslim Women Performers," www.pmuna.org/archives/pmu_positions_on_current_issues/index.php#000076.

24. Jiménez, "Women Artists, Performers Criticize Muslim Festival Restrictions."

25. Harris, "A Report on the Situation Regarding Teaching Music to Muslims in an Inner-City School," 50.

26. Sistani's Web site was accessed at www.sistani.org.

27. "Sex Change Film Tests Iran Attitudes," *Aljazeera*, July 26, 2006.

28. "A Muslim First," Planetout.com, April 24, 2008.

29. Quoted at www.witness-pioneer.org/vil/Books/Q_IP/ch4s3pre.htm.

30. Ayatollah Behmanesh, *The Second Meeting*, 40

31. Boulmerka, "Defying Prejudice and Oppression."

32. Accessed at www.islamonline.net.

33. "Islam's Stance on Women's Practicing Sport."

34. Taheri, "Muslim Women Play Only an Incidental Part in the Olympics," Gulf News, August 18, 2004. www.benadorassociates.com/article/6651.

35. Amir Taheri, "Censoring the Olympics," *New York Post*, August 16, 2004. http://mrspkr.blogspot.com/2004_08_01_archive.html.

36. "A New Voice for New Pakistan."

37. Beiruty, "Muslim Women in Sports." No doubt Sister Hikmat Beiruty would find a solution to the problem of a woman's natural "perfumed" scent. After all, men are aroused significantly by the smell of women's sweat. What to do, Sister Beiruty?

38. Hughes, "Iran's New Easy Riders Challenge a Taboo."

39. Faezeh Hashemi Rafsanjani (born 1962) is an Iranian politician and the daughter of former president Akbar Hashemi Rafsanjani. She was a Majlis (Iranian Parliament) representative from Tehran in the fifth Islamic Assembly, from 1996 to 2000. She has also pushed for women's rights in Iran and was one of the first women who dared to wear jeans, visible under her chador, and was the founder of the Women Islamic Games. She has also been an advocate of women and sports and, as a result of her pressure, was able to establish female sports teams. The mother of two, she is among the most popular pioneers of the reformist movement, and she has called for women to unveil, ride bicycles, and run for president.

40. Faezeh Hashemi Rafsanjani, *Second Olympic Meeting*, Tehran, Islamic Republic publication, September 21, 2005.

41. Ibid., 10.

42. "Faezeh Hashemi Launched Attack against Ahmadinejad."

43. Margonelli and Shekarloo, "A Place Where It Doesn't Suck to Be a Woman."

44. Hughes, "Soccer: The Delicate Overlap between Sports and Politics."

45. "Iran President Says Let Women into Sports Stadiums," Reuters, April 24, 2006.

46. Moore, "Iran Allows Women to Attend Soccer Matches."

47. "Iran: "Sisters, Don't Give Up," Associated Press, May 23, 2006.

48. Headquartered in Geneva, Switzerland, the UNHCR (established December 14, 1950) protects and supports refugees at the request of a government or the UN and assists in their return or resettlement.

49. Brown, "The Burkini."

50. Zaman, "Islamic-Style Swimsuits Give Women Freedom to Dive In," *Los Angeles Times*, August 21, 2005.

51. Fam, "Muslim Women Seeking Fun in the Sun under Veil of Secrecy on Private Beaches."

52. Murray, "Unveiling Myths: Muslim Women and Sport," January 16, 2002. Sarah J. Murray is the web producer at the Women's Sports Foundation. She oversees the content and architecture of WomensSportsFoundation.org and various other Foundation Web sites and makes sure that female athletes have a constant and true presence in the media.

53. Ali, *Holy Qur'an*, 1759, note 6199.

54. Malti-Douglas, *Woman's Body, Woman's Word.*

55. Mernissi, *The Veil and the Male Elite*, 194.

56. Abbasid refers to the dynasty of the Caliph of Baghdad (750–950 AD). The Abbasid caliphate transferred the capital of the Arab empire from Damascas to Baghdad. The Abbasids took their name from al-'Abbas, paternal uncle of the prophet Muhammad.

57. Mernissi, *The Veil and the Male Elite*, 194–95.

58. Reported by al-Bukhari and al-Muslim.

59. Walseth and Fasting, "Islam's View on Physical Activity and Sport."

Chapter 5. Gender Preference: An Islamic View

1. Kugle, "Sexuality, Diversity, and Ethics in the Agenda of Progressive Muslims."

2. *Hur* has more than one meaning, according to Yusuf Ali's commentary: purity, truth, or beauty, especially of eyes, where the intense white of the eyeballs stands out against the intense black of the pupil, giving the appearance of luster and intense feeling, as opposed to dullness or want of expression. Ali, *Holy Qur'an, Dukhan* (Smoke), 44:54, 1352, note 4729.

3. Ibid., note 4728. "The women as well as the men of this life will attain to this indescribable bliss: 9.72: and objects of beauty, grace, and satisfaction, described symbolically, must apply to both." Ibid., 1352.

4. Ibid., 1759, note 6199.

5. *Encyclopaedia of Islam*, new ed., "Al-Insan Al-Kamil," 3:1240.

6. Ali, "Same-Sex Sexual Activity and Lesbian and Bisexual Women. Special Focus: Islam." The following is Kecia Ali's footnote:

> Reproduced as an appendix in Nuh Ha Mim Keller, trans. and ed., Ahmad ibn Naqib al-Misri, *Reliance of the Traveller: A Classic Manual of Islamic Sacred Law* (Beltsville, Md.: Amana Publications, 1994 [1991]), 986. Keller gives both the English and Arabic versions of the text. My English rendering differs in several aspects from Keller's. Most notably, he translates *ityan . . . al-mara'a al-ajnabiyya fi duburiha* as simply "sodomizing a woman." He brackets off the qualifying term *ajnabiyya* ("unrelated"—meaning a woman over whom a man has no sexual rights, since she is neither his wife nor his

slave-concubine), thus changing the meaning of the text. However, Ibn Hajar does condemn a man having anal intercourse with his wife earlier in the list.

7. Stephen O. Murray and Will Roscoe, *Islamic Homosexualities*, 307.

8. The Arabic terms *liwat* and *lutiyya* come from the story of Lut in the Qur'an. This is a reference to male homosexuality.

9. Mackay, "Culture and Medicine."

10. Lut (Lot), vi: 86, vii: 80–86, xi: 77–83, xv: 57–77, xxi: 74–75, xxvi: 160–175, xxvii: 54–58, xxix: 26, 28–35, xxxvii: 133–138, li: 31–37, liv: 33–39. Lut's wife disobedient, xi: 81, xv: 60, lxvi: 10.

11. Ali, *Qur'an*, 183–84.

12. *Sahih Al-Bukhari*, vol. 7, hadith 773.

13. Accessed at www.brandeis.edu/projects/fse/muslim/mus-essays/mus-ess-homo sex.html. The Feminist Sexual Ethics Project is supported by a grant from the Ford Foundation and Brandeis University. For more information, contact Department of Near Eastern and Judaic Studies, Brandeis University, Mailstop 054, P.O. Box 9110, Waltham, Mass. 02454, or see www.brandeis.edu/projects/fse.

14. Duran, "Homosexuality and Islam." An Internet search reveals that Khalid Duran has created numerous orthodox Muslim enemies due to his liberal support of many issues in addition to homosexuality in Islam. One of the articles called Duran a "new Rushdie," labeling him as one who has turned his back on Islam.

15. Najmabadi, *Women with Mustaches*, 17.

16. Ibid., 19.

17. For more information on this topic, see Ze'evi, *Producing Desire*, 48–76.

18. Wright and Rowson, *Homoeroticism in Classical Arabic Literature*.

19. Kidwai, "Introduction," 113.

20. Ibid., 111.

21. Vanita, preface to *Same-Sex Love in India*, iii.

22. Vanita, "Rekhti Poetry."

23. Sprachman divides Persian literature (which has been censored on moral or religious grounds) into three broad categories: Verbal Aggression and Assault (*hajv* or *heja*), Bawdy (*hazl*), and Satire (*tanz*) (vii). Here I am referring to Bawdy literature.

24. Sprachman, *Suppressed Persian*, viii.

25. AbuKhalil, "Gender Boundaries and Sexual Categories in the Arab World," 103, 107 (notes).

26. Schimmel, *The Mystic Dimensions of Islam*.

27. Accessed at www.brandeis.edu/projects/fse/Pages/femalehomosexuality.html.

28. Hedayat was an Iranian short-story writer, novelist, playwright, and essayist—the most important Persian author of the twentieth century. His short stories combine his deeply pessimistic worldview with a love for his country. His most famous tale is *The Blind Owl* (1937). Hedayat died in Paris in 1951. My copy of

Neyrangestan is an offset copy produced by the library of the Da'rat al-ma'ref-e bozorg-e Eslami in 1983.

29. In Persian *pa* means foot; *sabz* is translated as green. The term *pa sabz* is a metaphor for someone who brings good luck and prosperity. Here the reference is to an intermediary.

30. Choubine, *Kulsom Naneh*, 89–90. Choubine refers to this wax figurine as Chouk or Tschok, meaning a dildo. He further explains that in olden days when commercial adult toys were not available, women would make a wax phallus to use on their female partner.

31. According to Shi'i belief, Qadir-e Khom is a location where the prophet Muhammad raised Ali ibn Abu Talib's hand and nominated him to be his first replacement, or caliph for the Muslim community. In the Shi'i calendar, Eid-e Qadir-e Khom is a joyous holiday and celebrated annually.

32. Khaybar is an oasis about ninety-five miles north of Medina in Saudi Arabia. Whereas Mecca is known for its barrenness, Khaybar is green and lush. Khaybar, inhabited by Jews before the rise of Islam, fell to Muhammad in 628. The king and conqueror of Khaybar is a reference to Muhammad. Thus the woman is swearing by the Prophet's name.

33. Here, Sadegh Hedayat references *Kulsom Naneh,* originally written at the end of the seventeenth century by a famous Mula named Agha Jamal Khansari. See Choubine, *Kulsom Naneh.*

34. Most often, an older married woman from the upper classes would take a younger woman from a less advantaged socioeconomic background. The younger woman was usually unmarried.

35. Choubine, *Kulsom Naneh*, 89.

36. Khansari, *Kolsum Naneh*, 109. Also see Choubine, *Kulsom Naneh*, 60.

37. Najmabadi, *Women with Mustaches*, 64. In this context Najmabadi is describing the visibility of sun (female) and lion (male) motifs in Iranian modern society. These motifs appeared on the Iranian flag until the end of the monarchy in 1978. After the Islamic revolution, these motifs were removed from the flag, although they still serve in a decorative sense throughout the culture.

38. Boellstorff, "The Emergence of Political Homophobia in Indonesia," 467, 469.

39. *HOMAN: A Cultural and Scientific Journal of Homosexual Studies in Persian and English,* nos. 10/11 (June 1996): 7.

40. Ibid., 6.

41. Accessed at http://www.helem.net.

42. Bradley, "Queer Sheik."

43. Nur, "Malaysia."

44. Murray, "Let Them Take Ecstasy," 167, 171, 181.

45. Assfar, "Jordan," 104.

46. Kilic and Uncu, "Turkey," 104.

47. Mansiya, "The Story of the Forgotten."

48. Stack, "Iran Bans Being Gay, but Allows Sex Change." See also Aresu Eqbali, "Iran's Transsexuals Get Islamic Approval, But!" Middle East Online, September 30, 2004; Fathi, "Sex Changes Are Gaining Acceptance in Iran," International Herald Tribune, August 2, 2004.

49. A panel of three psychiatrists must approve the candidates before they begin hormonal therapy and the surgical procedures. The psychiatric team differentiates homosexuality from gender disorder by a series of questions.

50. YouTube.com has featured a clip from the documentary Be Like Others, in which Dr. Bahram Majlali discusses sex-change surgery.

51. Yip, "Queering the Religious Texts," 48.

52. Zaydaan, Al-Muslim Fi Ash Shari'ah al-Islamiyyah. For matters related to women, see vol. 5, Al- Mufassal fi Ahkam al-Mar'a, p. 450.

53. This statement is from www.islamonline.net, quoting Al-Mawsu'ah Al-Fiqhiyyah Al-Muyassarah fi Al-Adyan wal Madhahib Al-Mu'asirah.

54. "Death Fall as Punishment for Homosexuality."

55. This fatwa does not assign authorship to any individual person; instead, the Web site refers to "a group of Ulama" as the origin of the fatwa.

56. See "Punishment for Non-marital Sex in Islam; Examples of Convictions under Sharia Law" at www.religioustolerance.org/isl_adul1.htm.

57. For more information on Ahmadi (Ahmedi) Islam, see www.aaiil.org.

58. Accessed at www.religioustolerance.org/hom_isla2.htm. For more information on Mission Islam, see www.missionislam.com.

59. Al-Fatiha in Arabic means "the opening." Taken from the first chapter in the Qur'an, it is recited in daily Muslim prayer

60. Miwalla, Rosser, Feldman, and Varga, "Identity Experience among Progressive Gay Muslims in North America, 116.

61. "Potentially Bad News," March 18, 2006, posted on www.classicalvalues.com/archives/003440.html.

62. Kalman, "A Muslim Calls for Reform—and She's a Lesbian."

63. Pharr, Homophobia.

64. Yip, "Queering the Religious Texts," 59.

65. Yip, "Uniquely Positioned?" 6.

Chapter 6. Bodies Confined, Spirits Cleansed

1. Cooke, "Multiple Critique: Islamic Feminist Rhetorical Strategies," 93.

2. Ibid., 105.

3. It should be noted that Zoroastrianism, Judaism, and Hinduism also include restrictions regarding purity and pollution during menstruation. This is particularly true for fundamentalist branches of these religions.

4. Mernissi, The Veil and the Male Elite, 72–73, 75.

5. Ali, Holy Qur'an, 87–88.

6. Weitz, ed., *The Politics of Women's Bodies*, 84. See also Göcek and Balaghi, "Reconstructing Gender in the Middle East through Voice and Experience."

7. Al-Muslim, *Sahih Muslim*, 173.

8. Ibid., 173, 174.

9. Ibid., 175.

10. Al-Bukhari, born Abu Abdillah Muhammad Ibn Ismail Ibn Ibrahim Ibn al-Mughirah Ibn Bardizbah al-Bukhari in West Turkistan (810–80), was an eminent imam and hadith collector.

11. The English word *cube* comes from the Arabic word *ka'bah*.

12. Al-Muslim, *Sahih Muslim*. See note 505 as a supplementary material for hadith 587.

13. The Urdu word *purdah*, or *purda*, is from the Persian term *pardeh* meaning "curtain." The term *neshini* is from the Persian verb *neshastan*, to sit down; hence the term *purdah neshini* is a reference to the act of sitting in a purdah (veil, hijab), indicating the person is in seclusion.

14. Sufism, or *tasawwuf*, as it is known in Arabic, is a branch of Islam and may be understood as the mystical or psycho-spiritual dimension of Islam.

15. Shirazi, *The Veil Unveiled*, 180.

16. Ali, *The Holy Qur'an*, 1124.

17. Ibid., 1126–27.

18. Ibid., 1124, note 3756.

19. Mernissi, *The Veil and the Male Elite*, 85–101.

20. Yusuf Ali's commentary on verse 59 sheds light on the fact that when the verse was written, all Muslim women—including those of the Prophet's household—were living in times of insecurity and potential danger. They were asked to cover themselves and stay close to home simply as measures to ensure their safety.

21. Imam Qurtubi, *Tafsir-e-Qurtubi*.

22. Mernissi, *The Veil and the Male Elite*, 91–92.

23. Ahmed, *Women and Gender in Islam*, 2.

24. Mir-Hosseini, "Religious Modernists and the 'Woman Question': Challenges and Complicities."

25. Hanbali is considered to be the most conservative of the four schools of Sunni Islam. The Hanbali School was started by the students of Imam Ahmad, whose name was Ahmad bin Hanbal (d. 855). Hanbali jurisprudence is predominant among Muslims in the Arabian Peninsula.

26. Ibn al-Jawzi, *Kitab ahkam al-nisa*, 201, 202, 205, 209.

27. Abudullah, *A Comparison between Veiling and Unveiling*, 28–29.

28. Imam Khomeini, *Simaye Zan Dar Kalame Imam Khomeini*, 44. The translation from the Persian text to English is mine.

29. Taheri, "Domestic Terror in Iran."

30. "Support Iranian Women: Join the 'One Million Signatures Campaign,'" petition, Women's Learning Partnership for Rights, Development, and Peace, July 6, 2007.

31. Hassan and Hatrash, "Nadia Bakhurji Pledges to Back Women Engineers."

32. Wikipedia.org, Nadia Bakhurji.

33. Burk, "A Crude Awakening for Women."

34. Albone, "Woman MP Is Attacked in a Blow for Democracy."

35. Jones, "Fundamentalism: Is It a Threat to Women's Rights?"

36. Ibid.

37. Anjani, "Miniskirts Clash with Islam as Indonesia Drafts Pornography Law."

38. Stephanie Phang, Bloomberg.com, May 5, 2006.

39. Ibid.

40. Amirpur, "The Changing Approach to the Text: Iranian Scholars and the Qur'an."

41. Wiedemann, "Sisters in Islam in Malaysia: Women Working for Reform."

42. Postgraduate conference held on March 18–19, 2006, at the School of Literature and Language Studies, University of the Witwatersrand, Johannesburg, South Africa.

43. Shamima Sheikh, "Denying Women Access to the Mosque: A Betrayal of the Prophet."

44. Biswas, "Storm over Indian Women's Mosque."

45. Geeta Pandey, "Women Battle On with Mosque Plan."

46. McDonald, "China's 'Lost' Muslims Go Back to the Future."

47. *Ahong* is derived from the Persian word *akhund,* a reference to a cleric, or *imam.* The word *akhund* is from the Persian verb *khundan,* meaning "to read." The term *akhund* designates a literate person and, by extension, one who is capable of reading religious texts. It should be noted that ahongs in China neither deliver sermons to a mixed-gender congregation nor lead prayer in a mixed-gender environment.

48. McDonald, "China's 'Lost' Muslims."

49. "Morocco promotes moderate Islam," April 5, 2006. Accessed at www .news24.com/News24/Africa/News/0,6119,2-11-1447_1926858,00.html.

50. Niah, "Fifty Moroccan Women Preachers to Teach Moderate Islam."

51. "Morocco Gets First Women Preachers."

52. "Mourchidat—Morocco's Female Muslim Clerics."

53. Birch, "Turkey's Women in Forefront of Islamic Reform."

54. According to Sharia terminology, *mahram* refers to a husband or to male kin with whom one would not marry, such as a father, grandfather, brother, son, nephew, etc.

55. Ahmed Nassef, "Amina Wadud Leads Mixed-Gender Friday Prayer in Barcelona."

56. A mufti is a religious authority somewhat akin to a bishop—a scholar of Islamic theology, law, and jurisprudence who is qualified to issue fatwas (religious rulings). Ben Cheikh received his education at Al-Azhar, the premier university in Sunni Islam, and has been the spiritual leader of Marseille for ten years.

57. Taylor, "Leading the Mufti: Progress in the Islamic Tradition."

58. Blair, "Grand Ayatollah Who Would Talk to Satan."

59. Khan, "Bravo! CAIR."

60. Accessed at http://pa.cair.com/files/women_friendly_mosques.pdf.

61. Eltantawi and Zonneveld, "As You Are, You Will Be Led."

62. Sorabji, "Mixed Motives."

63. I refer to those holy women related to the Prophet after the Revelation. This necessarily excludes Muhammad's mother. However, Sorabji includes Muhammad's mother as one of the holy women, perhaps out of respect.

64. Kassamali, "Healing Rituals and the Role of Fatima." See also the Pluralism Project at Harvard University, Center for the Study of World Religions, Harvard Divinity School. Religion, Health, and Healing Initiative, accessed at www.pluralism.org/affiliates/sered/whw.php.

65. Rasmussen, "Only Women Know Trees."

66. Centlivres, Centlivres, and Slobin, "A Muslim Shaman of Afghan Turkestan," 169, 171.

67. Ahmed, *Women and Gender in Islam.*

68. Ghadially, "A Hajari (Meal Tray) for Abbas Alam Dar."

69. Djedje, "Song Type and Performance Style in Hausa and Dagomba Possession (*Bori*) Music," 167.

70. Ibid., 438.

71. Rausch, "Bodies, Boundaries, and Spirit Possession: Revision of Tradition."

Conclusion

1. Shehadeh, *The Idea of Women in Fundamentalist Islam,* 219.

2. Sardar, "A Fatwa for Every Occasion."

3. The proposed amendment to Section 295-B says: "Defiling etc. of, and marriage with, the Holy Qur'an: whoever willfully defiles, damages, or indirectly allows the Holy Qur'an to be used for the purpose of its marriage with a female or fraudulently or dishonestly induces any person to swear on the Holy Qur'an never to marry anyone in her lifetime or knowingly uses it in any derogatory manner or for any unlawful purpose shall be punishable with imprisonment for life." Imran, "Bill to Abolish Qur'an Marriages Prepared."

4. Casey, "Challenging the Mullahs, One Signature at a Time."

5. Moghadam, "Transnational Feminist Networks," 61–62.

6. Ahmad, "Fighting the Fanatics."

7. Siddiqui, "Islam and Feminism: Are They Poles Apart?"

8. Derhally, "Despite Heavy Turnout Women Failed to Pick Up Any Seats after Voting."

9. Friedl, "Islam and Tribal Women in a Village in Iran."

10. Siddiqui, "Islam and Feminism: Are They Poles Apart?"

11. Esposito and Mogahed, *Who Speaks for Islam? What a Billion Muslims Really Think,* 107.

12. "Asra Nomani, Daud Sharifa, and the Women's Mosque."

13. On August 9, 2007, Taslima Nasreen was attacked in Hyderabad at a book release function. The attack began when three Majlis Ittehadul Musilmeen (MIM) legislators stormed the dais and shouted slogans against Nasreen. They beat anyone who tried to shield her. Journalists joined with press photographers and TV crews to physically remove the MIM activists from the building. Later the activists threatened to behead Nasreen if she dared visit Hyderabad again.

14. In 2005, *Time* magazine named Soroush one of the one hundred most influential people in the world.

15. Hirsh, "Tehran Diary: The Question of Qom."

16. Ramadan, "Reading the Koran."

17. Ahmed, "American Muslims Reimagined."

18. Mir-Hosseini, "Muslim Women's Quest for Equality," 17.

19. Ali, *Holy Qur'an*, 149–50.

BIBLIOGRAPHY

While the Internet proved invaluable as a current and up-to-date informational source, unfortunately many of the links will be inactive at the time of this publication. Hopefully, many of these links can be accessed in the archives on individual sites.

Abbasi, Mohammad Jalal, Amir Mehryar, Gavin Jones, and Peter Mcdonald. "Revolution, War, and Modernization: Population Policy and Fertility Change in Iran." *Journal of Population Research* 19 (May 2002): 22–25.

Abdullah, Halah Bint. *A Comparison between Veiling and Unveiling: A Book for the Muslim Woman*. Saudi Arabia: Maktaba Dar-us-Salam, 2000.

AbuKhalil, As'ad. "Gender Boundaries and Sexual Categories in the Arab World." *Feminist Issues* 15, nos. 1/2 (Spring 1997): 91–104.

Abu-Lughod, Lila. "Honor and the Sentiments of Loss in a Bedouin Society." *American Ethnologist* 12, no. 2 (1985): 245–61.

———. *Veiled Sentiments: Honor and Poetry in a Bedouin Society*. Berkeley: University of California Press, 1986.

———. "Islam and the Gendered Discourses of Death." *International Journal of Middle East Studies* 25, no. 2 (May 1993): 189–90.

Adams, Bert N. "Families and Family Study in International Perspective." *Journal of Marriage and Family* 66 (December 2004): 1076–88.

Ahmad, Ashwin. "Fighting the Fanatics." *Times of India*, August 26, 2007.

Ahmed, Leila. *Women and Gender in Islam*. New Haven: Yale University Press, 1992.

Ahmed, Tanzila. "American Muslims Reimagined." *Nation*, July 26, 2007.

Aiello, Flavia. "Continuity and Change in Zanzibari Taarab." *Swahili Forum* 11 (2004): 75–81.

El-Akkad, Omar. "Muslim Teens Seek Belief in Its Perfect Form. On-line Forum and Internet Imams Provide Key Sources of Interpretation." *Globe and Mail*, July 1, 2006.

Albone, Tim. "Woman MP Is Attacked in a Blow for Democracy." *Times*, May 9, 2006.

Ali, A. Yusuf. *The Holy Qur'an: Text, Translation, and Commentary*. Brentwood, Md.: Amana Corporation, 1983.

Ali, Amear. "Islam's Coming Renaissance Will Rise in the West: A Wave of Rationalism Is Spreading from Émigré Muslim Intellectuals." *Australian,* April 30, 2007.

Ali, Kecia. "Same-Sex Sexual Activity and Lesbian and Bisexual Women. Special Focus: Islam." Revised December 10, 2002. Accessed at www.brandeis.edu/projects/fse/Pages/femalehomosexuality.html.

al-Naser, F. "Kuwait's Families." In *Handbook of World Families,* ed. B. N. Adams and J. Trost, chap. 23. Thousand Oaks, Calif.: Sage, 2004.

Altorki, Soraya. "Women and Islam." In *The Oxford Encyclopedia of the Modern Islamic World,* ed. John L. Esposito, 4:322–27. New York: Oxford University Press, 1995.

Amirpur, Katajun. "The Changing Approach to the Text: Iranian Scholars and the Qur'an." *Middle Eastern Studies* 41, no. 3 (2005): 337–50.

Andres, F. M., A. Abbey, and L. J. Halman. "Stress from Infertility, Marriage Factors, and Subjective Well-Being of Wives and Husbands." *Journal of Health Soc. Behavior* 32, no. 3 (1991): 238–53.

Anjani, Karima. "Miniskirts Clash with Islam as Indonesia Drafts Pornography Law." *Bloomberg.com,* May 10, 2006.

Arat, Yesim. *The Patriarchal Paradox: Women Politicians in Turkey.* London and Toronto: Associated University Press, 1989.

———. "Combating Restrictions on the Headscarf." *Human Rights Watch Report.* Formerly available at www.hrw.org/reports/2000/turkey2/Turk009-05.htm.

———. *Rethinking Islam and Liberal Democracy: Islamist Women in Turkish Politics.* Albany: State University of New York Press, 2005.

Arberry, A. J. *The Koran Interpreted.* New York: Simon and Schuster, 1996.

Arman, Leyli. "Rape Victim Who Killed Her Attacker to Be Released." RadioFarda, December 24, 2003.

Asman, Oren. "Abortion in Islamic Countries—Legal and Religious Aspects." *Medicine and Law* 23 (2004): 82–83.

"Asra Nomani, Daud Sharifa, and the Women's Mosque," October 26, 2006, at www.lehigh.edu/~amsp/2006/10/asra-nomani-daud-sharifa-and-womens.html.

Assfar, Akhadar. "Jordan." In *Unspoken Rules: Sexual Orientation and Women's Human Rights,* ed. Rachel Rosenbloom, 104. London: Cassell, 1996.

Azadarmaki, T. "Families in Iran: The Contemporary Situation." In *Handbook of World Families,* ed. B. N. Adams and J. Trost, chap. 21. Thousand Oaks, Calif.: Sage, 2004.

Babanah, Bashir. "The Story of the Mysterious Pouch and Women's Fear of Ash and Feathers in Mauritania." *Sayidaty* 24 (April 2004): 3–9.

Badran, Margo. "Islamic Feminism Revisited." Countercurrents.org, February 10, 2006. Accessed at www.countercurrents.org/gen-badran100206.htm.

Baha'i, Shaykh. "Ulume Gharibah, Matn-e-Kamel-e Kashkoul-e-Shaykh Baha'I" (The virtues of the beautiful names of Allah). Manuscript.

Bain, Kristen. "Defining Virginity Part of Validating Relationships." *Oklahoma Daily,* April 1, 2002.

Banashek, Mary-Ellen. "The Seat of Intolerance." *Psychology Today,* February 1997.

Bibliography

Barazangi, Nimat Hafez. *Women's Identity and the Qur'an: A New Reading.* Gainesville: University Press of Florida, 2004.

Barlas, Asma. *"Believing Women" in Islam: Unreading Patriarchal Interpretations of the Qur'an.* Austin: University of Texas Press, 2002.

Ayatollah Behmanesh. *The Second Meeting.* Tehran: Sazman-e-Chap va Entesharet-e Vezarate-Farhang va Ershad-e Eslami, 2000.

Beiruty, Sister Hikmat. "Muslim Women in Sports." Reprinted from *Nid'ul Islam Magazine.* Available at www.zawaj.com/articles/women_sports.html.

Bhatti, Lubna Ishaq, Fariyal F. Fikree, and Amanullah Khan. "The Quest of Infertile Women in Squatter Settlements of Karachi, Pakistan: A Qualitative Study." *Social Science and Medicine* 49, no. 5 (September 1999): 637–49.

Birch, Nicholas. "Turkey's Women in Forefront of Islamic Reform." *Washington Times,* May 2, 2006.

Biswas, Soutik. "Storm over Indian Women's Mosque." BBC News, January 27, 2004.

"Bittersweet Success of Secret Girl Band." *Freemuse,* October 2005. Available at www.freemuse.org/sw10902.asp.

Blair, David. "Grand Ayatollah Who Would Talk to Satan." *Daily Telegraph,* August 10, 2007. Accessed at www.telegraph.co.uk/news/main.jhtml?xml= /news/2007/08/09/wiran309.xml.

Boellstorff, Tom. "The Emergence of Political Homophobia in Indonesia: Masculinity and National Belonging." *ETHNOS* 69, no. 4 (December 2004): 465–86.

Boonstra, Heather. "Islam, Women, and Family Planning: A Primer." *Guttmacher Report on Public Policy* 4 (December 2001).

Boulmerka, Hassiba. "Defying Prejudice and Oppression." *Women Warriors,* 2000.

Bowen, Donna Lee. "Abortion, Islam, and the 1994 Cairo Population Conference." *International Journal of Middle East Studies* 29, no. 2 (1997): 161–84.

Bradley, John. "Queer Sheik: The Strange Emergence of Gay Culture in Saudi Arabia." *New Republic,* March 15, 2004.

Brown, Stephen. "The Burkini." *FrontPageMag.com,* February 2, 2007. Available at www.frontpagemag.com/Articles/ReadArticle.asp?ID=26731.

Buckley, Cara. "A Sex Ploy: 2 Times a Virgin—for Only $199!" *Miami Herald,* February 22, 2003.

Buddell, Ruth. "Crimes of Passion: Should They Be Distinguished from the Offence of Murder in England and Wales?" Accessed at http://web.ukonline.co.uk/ruth .buddell/dissertation2.htm.

al-Bukhari. *Sahih al-Bukhari.* Al Medina Al Munauwara, Saudi Arabia: Islamic University, n.d.

Burk, Martha. "A Crude Awakening for Women." *Ms.,* Summer 2006.

Casey, Maura J. "Editor of Feisty Iranian Magazine Faces Prison." *Women's eNews,* February 27, 2001. Accessed at www.womensenews.org/article.cfm?aid=462.

———. "Challenging the Mullahs, One Signature at a Time." *New York Times,* February 7, 2007.

Centlivres, Micheline, Pierre Centlivres, and Mark Slobin. "A Muslim Shaman of Afghan Turkestan." *Ethnology* 10, no. 2 (1971): 160–73.

Choi, Sue Yeon. "Restoring Virginity: Hymen Repair Surgery Saves Lives at the Expense of Deception." *Issues: Berkeley Medical Journal,* Fall 1998.

Choubine, Bahram. *Kulsom Naneh.* Koln: Ghassedak, 1999.

Cindoglu, Dilek. "Virginity Tests and Artificial Virginity in Modern Turkish Medicine." *Women's Studies International Forum* 20, no. 2 (1997): 253–61.

Cong, Hu. "Criminal Penalties Pondered for Aborting Females." *China Daily,* February 28, 2005.

Cooke, Miriam. "Multiple Critique: Islamic Feminist Rhetorical Strategies." *Nepantla: Views from South* 1, no. 1 (2000): 91–110.

———. "Women, Religion, and the Postcolonial Arab World." *Cultural Critique* 45 (Spring 2000): 150–84.

Daniels, Douglas Henry. "Taarab Clubs and Swahili Music Culture." *Social Identities* 2, no. 3 (October 1, 1996).

Danielson, Virginia Louise. "Shaping Tradition in Arabic Song: The Career and Repertory of Umm Kulthum." PhD diss., University of Illinois, 1991.

Dareini, Ali Akbar. "Iran Women Lawmakers Step Up Campaign to Save Woman from Execution." Associated Press, October 5, 2003.

Davie, Mick. "World Diary: Honor Killings." *National Geographic Channel.* Aired February 13, 2002.

Dawood, N. J. *The Qur'an.* New York: Penguin Books, 1974.

"Death Fall as Punishment for Homosexuality." *IslamOnline,* July 22, 2003.

Derhally, Massoud A. "Despite Heavy Turnout Women Failed to Pick Up Any Seats after Voting." ITP, July 16, 2006. Accessed at www.arabianbusiness.com/493472?ln=en#continueArticle.

Djedje, Jacqueline Cogdell. "Song Type and Performance Style in Hausa and Dagomba Possession (*Bori*) Music." *Black Perspective in Music* 12, no. 2 (Autumn 1984): 166–82.

Dooley, Tara. "Houston Woman Joins Ancient Rite as Consecrated Virgin." *Houston Chronicle,* May 14, 2004.

Dorr, Rebecca G. "Azizah Celebrates Muslim American Women." *Women's eNews,* April 3, 2006.

Doumato, Eleanor Abdella. *Getting God's Ear: Women, Islam, and Healing in Saudi Arabia and the Gulf.* New York: Columbia University Press, 2000.

Dris-Aït-Hamadouche, Louis. "Women in the Maghreb: Civil Society's Actors or Political Instruments?" *Middle East Policy* 14, no. 4 (Winter 2007): 118.

Dundes, Alan. *Interpreting Folklore.* Bloomington: Indiana University Press, 1980.

Duran, Khalid. "Homosexuality and Islam." In *Homosexuality and World Religions,* ed. Arlene Swidler, 181–97. Valley Forge: Trinity Press International, 1993.

Dworkin, Andrea. "The Women Suicide Bombers." *Feminista!* 5, no. 1 (2002).

Eltantawi, Sarah, and Zuriani Zonneveld. "As You Are, You Will Be Led: Khaled Abou El Fadl Leads a Town Hall Meeting on Woman-Led Prayer in Los Angeles." *Muslim WakeUp!* June 19, 2005.

Encyclopaedia of Islam. New ed. Vol. 3. Leiden: E. J. Brill, 1971.

Encyclopaedia of Islam. Vol. 9. Leiden: E. J. Brill, 1997.

Engineer, Asghar Ali. "Why Reform Movements Are Necessary." *Progressive Dawoodi Bohras*, August 2001.

Eqbali, Aresu. "Iran's Transsexuals Get Islamic Approval, But!" Middle East Online, September 30, 2004.

Erdim, Zeynep. "Women Ask Female Minister to Resign." *Turkish Daily News,* January 7, 1998.

Esposito, John L., and Dalia Mogahed. *Who Speaks for Islam? What a Billion Muslims Really Think.* New York: Gallup Press, 2007.

"Faezeh Hashemi Launched Attack against Ahmadinejad." September 21, 2005. Accessed at www.salamiran.org/Women/Olympic/hashemi.html.

Fam, Mariam. "Muslim Women Seeking Fun in the Sun under Veil of Secrecy on Private Beaches." Associated Press, October 24, 2005.

al-Faruqi, Lois Ibsen. "Music, Musicians, and Muslim Law." *Asian Music* 17, no. 1 (Autumn/Winter 1985): 3.

Fathi, Nazila. "Sex Changes Are Gaining Acceptance in Iran." *International Herald Tribune*, August 2, 2004.

Fenn, Eva. "Women and Music Censorship—Past to Present." *Freemuse,* April 2005. Available at www.freemuse.org/sw8939.asp.

Foucault, Michel. *Discipline and Punish: The Birth of the Prison.* Trans. Alan Sheridan. New York: Vintage, 1979.

Friedl, Erika. "Islam and Tribal Women in a Village in Iran." In *Unspoken Worlds: Women's Religious Lives in Non-Western Cultures,* ed. Nancy A. Falk and Rita M. Gross, 126–33. San Francisco: Harper and Row, 1980.

Ghadially, Rehana. "A Hajari (Meal Tray) for Abbas Alam Dar: Women's Household Ritual in a South Asian Muslim Sect." *Muslim World* 93, no. 2 (April 2003): 309.

Girard, Françoise. "Human Rights and Women's Health: The Light at the End of the Speculum." Presented at "Health, Law, and Human Rights: Exploring the Connections" conference, Philadelphia, September 29–October 1, 2001.

Göcek, Fatma Müge, and Shiva Balaghi. "Reconstructing Gender in the Middle East through Voice and Experience." In *Reconstructing Gender in the Middle East: Tradition, Identity, and Power,* ed. Fatma Müge Göçek and Shiva Balaghi. New York: Columbia University Press, 1994.

Gonzalez-Lopez, Gloria. "De madres a hijas: Gendered Lessons on Virginity across Generations of Mexican Immigrant Women." In *Gender and U.S. Immigration: Contemporary Trends,* ed. Pierrette Hondagneu-Sotelo, 217–39. Berkeley: University of California Press, 2003.

Grima, Benedicte. *The Performance of Emotion among Paxtun Women: "The Misfortunes Which Have Befallen Me."* Austin: University of Texas Press, 1992.

Gushee, Steve. "Oppressed Women Have Men to Thank." *Palm Beach Post.com,* June 15, 2007.

Habib, Samar. *Female Homosexuality in the Middle East: Histories and Representations.* New York: Routledge, 2007.

Haeri, Shahla. "The Politics of Dishonor: Rape and Power in Pakistan." In *Faith and Freedom: Women's Human Rights in the Muslim World,* ed. Mahnaz Afkhami, 161–74. Syracuse: Syracuse University Press, 1995.

"Haq Bakshish: No Right to Wed." IRIN News, March 8, 2007. Accessed at www .irinnews.org/Report.aspx?ReportId=70564.

Harris, Diana. "A Report on the Situation Regarding Teaching Music to Muslims in an Inner-City School." *British Journal of Music Education* 19, no. 1 (2002): 51–62.

Hasan, Khalid. "Quake God's Punishment for 'Immoral Activities': Farhat Hashmi." *Daily Times,* November 1, 2005.

Hassan, Javid, and Hasan Hatrash. "Nadia Bakhurji Pledges to Back Women Engineers." *Arab News,* December 26, 2005.

Heath, Jennifer. *The Scimitar and the Veil: Extraordinary Women of Islam.* Mahwah: Hidden Spring, 2004.

Hedayat, Sadegh. *Neyrangestan.* Tehran: Library of the Da'rat al-ma'ref-e bozorg-e Eslami, 1983.

Hessini, Leila. "Women Contesting Islamist Movements in the Arab World." *Conscience: The News Journal of Catholic Opinion,* Summer 2006, 21.

al-Hilli. *Sharial Islam.* Trans. Abual Qasim Ibn-i-Ahmad Yazdi. 2nd ed. Tehran: Tehran University Press, 1967.

Hiro, Dilip. *Holy Wars: The Rise of Islamic Fundamentalism.* New York: Routledge, 1989.

Hirsh, Michael. "Tehran Diary: The Question of Qom." *Newsweek,* June 23, 2007.

HOMAN: A Cultural and Scientific Journal of Homosexual Studies in Persian and English, nos. 10/11 (June 1996).

Hoodfar, H., and S. Assadpour. "The Politics of Population Policy in the Islamic Republic of Iran." *Studies in Family Planning* 31, no. 1 (March 2000): 19–34.

Hughes, Kirsty. "New Challenges for Women Campaigners." BBC News, Ahmedabad, July 22, 2005.

Hughes, Paul. "Iran's New Easy Riders Challenge a Taboo." Reuters News Agency, October 28, 2002.

Hughes, Rob. "Soccer: The Delicate Overlap between Sports and Politics." *International Herald Tribune,* April 25, 2006.

Ibrahim, Shaykh Hossain ibn. *Haftad Du Div, Ulume al Ghariba* (Seventy-two demons, the science of magic), Asef ben Barkhia. 27th of Shawal, 1250 (1835 of CE). No date of place of publication is found on this handwritten photocopied text.

Ilkkaracan, Pinar, ed. *Women and Sexuality in Muslim Societies.* Istanbul: Women for Women's Human Rights (WWHR)—New Ways, 2000.

Imoukhuede, Nogi. "Virginity Test Case." *Lagos Vanguard,* June 17, 2003. Listed on Women's Rights Watch Nigeria, http://lists.kabissa.org/lists/archives/public/womensrightswatch-nigeria/msg00706.html.

Imran, Mohammad. "Bill to Abolish Qur'an Marriages Prepared." *Daily Times,* January 17, 2006.

Inhorn, Marcia Claire. *Quest for Conception: Gender, Infertility, and Egyptian Medical Traditions.* Philadelphia: University of Pennsylania Press, 1994.

———. *Infertility and Patriarchy: The Cultural Politics of Gender and Family Life in Egypt.* Philadelphia: University of Pennsylvania Press, 1996.

———. *Infertility around the Globe: New Thinking on Childlessness, Gender, and Reproductive Technologies.* Berkeley: University of California Press, 2002.

———. *Local Babies, Global Science: Gender, Religion, and In Vitro Fertilization in Egypt.* New York: Routledge, 2003.

"Iran President Says Let Women into Sports Stadiums." Reuters, April 24, 2006.

"Iran: Sisters, Don't Give Up." Associated Press, May 23, 2006.

"Is It a Boy or a Girl?" Accessed at www.seasonsindia.com/pregnancy/boyorgirl_sea.htm.

"Islam's Stance on Women's Practicing Sport." *Islam OnLine,* February 16, 2004.

Iyer, Sriya. "Religion and the Decision to Use Contraception in India." *Journal of the Scientific Study of Religion* 41, no. 4 (2002): 711–22.

Jaffee, Valerie. "Maidenhead Revisited." *Harper's,* May 2003.

Jahanpour, Farhan. "Iran Awakening?" *Payvand's Iran News,* June 29, 2006. Accessed at www.payvand.com/news/06/jun/1267.html

Jaschok, Maria. "Violation and Resistance: Women, Religion, and Chinese Statehood." *Violence against Women* 9, no. 6 (June 2003): 655–75.

Ibn al-Jawzi. *Kitab ahkam al-nisa* (Book of rules for women). Beirut: al-Maktaba al-'Asriya, 1980.

Jehl, Douglas. "Arab Honor's Price: A Woman's Blood." *New York Times,* June 20, 1999.

Jensen, Robert, and Emily Oster. "The Power of TV: Cable Television and Women's Status in India." Working paper 13305. National Bureau of Economic Research, Cambridge, Mass., August 2007.

Jiménez, Marina. "Women Artists, Performers Criticize Muslim Festival Restrictions." *Globe and Mail,* August 13, 2005.

Jones, Rochelle. "Fundamentalism: Is It a Threat to Women's Rights?" *Independent-Bangaledesh.com,* April 14, 2006.

Joseph, Suad. "Gender and Citizenship in Middle Eastern States." *Middle East Report* 198 (January–March 1996): 4–10.

Kahf, Mohja. "Little Mosque Poems." In *Shattering the Stereotypes: Muslim Women Speak Out,* ed. Fawzia Afzal-Khan, 116–23. North Hampton, Mass.: Olive Branch Press, 2005.

Kalman, Matthew. "A Muslim Calls for Reform—and She's a Lesbian." *San Francisco Chronicle,* January 19, 2004.

Kamrava, Mehran, ed. *The New Voices of Islam: Rethinking Politics and Modernity.* Berkeley: University of California Press, 2006.

al-Kanadi, Abu Bilal Mustafa. "Music and Singing in the Light of the Qur'an and Sunnah." Accessed at http://islamworld.net/docs/music.html.

Kandela, Peter. 1996. "Egypt's Trade in Hymen Repair." *Lancet* 347 (June 8, 1996): 1615.

Karam, Azza M. "Feminisms and Islamisms in Egypt between Globalization and Post-modernism." In *Gender and Global Restructuring Sightings, Sites, and Resistances*, ed. Marianne H. Marchand and Anne Sisson Runyan. London: Routledge, 2000.

al-Kassam, Tazim. "Response in Roundtable Discussion, Feminist Religious History. Margaret R. Miles." *Journal of Feminist Studies in Religion* 22 (Spring 2006): 64.

Kassamali, Noor. "Healing Rituals and the Role of Fatima." Paper presented at Women Healing Women conference, March 22, 2004, Center for the Study of World Religions, Harvard Divinity School.

Katz, Nikki. "Honor Killings—What You Need to Know about Honor Killings." *About Women's Issues,* November 4, 2003. Accessed at http://womensissues.about .com/cs/honorkillings/a/honorkillings.htm.

Kaufman, Michael. "Transforming Our Interventions for Gender Equality by Addressing and Involving Men and Boys: A Framework for Analysis and Action." *Oxfam.* Accessed at www.oxfam.org.uk/what_we_do/resources/downloads/gem -6.pdf.

Ketabchi, Mahmood. "Iran: Women's Protest Brutally Attacked." *Persian Journal,* June 15, 2006.

Khan, Ashraf. "Jubilation in Jail." *Christian Science Monitor,* July 11, 2006.

Khan, M. A. Muqtedar. "Bravo! CAIR: Better Late than Never. CAIR Revises American Muslim Policy on Women in Mosques." *Muqtedar Khan's Column on Islamic Affairs,* June 24, 2005, at www.ijtihad.org.

Khanna, Madhu. "The Goddess-Woman Equation in Sakta Tantras." In *Gendering the Spirit: Women, Religion, and the Post-Colonial Response*, ed. Durre S. Ahmad. London: Zed Books, 2002.

Khansari, Mula Agha Jamal. *Kolsum Nane, Aghayed-e-al Nesa.* Ed. Bahram Chobineh. Cologne: Ghassedak Azadeh Sepehri Verlag, 1999.

al-Khayyat, Sana. *Honour and Shame: Women in Modern Iraq.* London: Saqi Books, 1992.

Imam Khomeini. *Simaye Zan Dar Kalame Imam Khomeini.* Tehran: Vezarat-e farhang va Ershade Eslami, 1989.

Khansari, Agha Jamal. *Kolsum Naneh.* Tehran: Entesharat Morvarid, n.d.

Khumalo, Sipho. "Virginity Testing 'Helps Curb AIDS.'" *Independent Online* (South Africa), August 13, 2001.

Kidwai, Saleem. "Introduction: Medieval Materials in the Perso-Urdu Tradition." In *Same-Sex Love in India: Readings from Literature and History,* ed. Ruth Vanita and Saleem Kidwai. New York: St. Martin's Press, 2000.

Kilic, Deniz, and Gaye Uncu. "Turkey." In *Unspoken Rules: Sexual Orientation and Women's Human Rights,* ed. Rachel Rosenbloom, 104. London: Cassell, 1996.

Kobrin, Sandy. "More Women Seek Vaginal Plastic Surgery." *Women's eNews,* November 14, 2004. Accessed at www.womensenews.org/article.cfm/dyn/aid /2067.

———. "Restoring Virginity Becomes Risky Business." *Women's eNews*, May 22, 2005. Accessed at www.womensenews.org/article.cfm/dyn/aid/2304/context/ar chive .

Kogacioglu, Dicle. "The Tradition Effect: Framing Honor Crimes in Turkey." *Differences: A Journal of Feminist Cultural Studies* 15, no. 2 (2004): 119–51.

Koh, Evelyn, and Jooean Tan. "Favoritism and the Changing Value of Children: A Note on the Chinese Middle Class in Singapore." *Journal of Comparative Family Studies* 31 (2000): 519–28.

Koppel, Andrea. "The Pakistani Who Fought Back and Won." *CNN Report*, November 5, 2005. Accessed at www.cnn.com/2005/US/11/03/btsc.koppel/index .html.

Kraemer, Elizabeth Wallis. *An Etymological Dictionary of Classical Mythology.* Kresge Library, Oakland University, Rochester, Mich., 1998. Accessed at http://library.oakland.edu/information/people/personal/kraemer/edcm/index.html.

Kugle, Scott. "Sexuality, Diversity, and Ethics in the Agenda of Progressive Muslims." In *Progressive Muslims*, ed. Omid Safi. Oxford: Oneworld, 2003.

Lasco, Chanté. "Virginity Testing in Turkey: A Violation of Women's Human Rights." *Human Rights Brief* 9, no. 3 (2002): 10–13.

Lengel, Laura. "Performing In/Outside Islam: Music and Gendered Cultural Politics in the Middle East and North Africa." *Text and Performance Quarterly* 24, nos. 3–4 (July–October 2004): 212–32.

Lim, Louisa. "Chinese Muslims Forge Isolated Path." BBC News, September 15, 2004.

Lite, Jordan. "Woman Leads Muslims in Prayers." *Daily News,* March 19, 2005.

Mack, Beverly B. *Muslim Women Sing: Hausa Popular Song.* Bloomington: Indiana University Press, 2004.

Mackay, Judith. "Culture and Medicine: How Does the United States Compare with the Rest of the World in Human Sexual Behavior?" *Western Journal of Medicine* 174 (June 2001): 429–33.

Mai, Mukhtar. *In the Name of Honor: A Memoir.* Trans. Linda Coverdale. New York: Atria Books, 2006.

Malti-Douglas, Fedwa. *Woman's Body, Woman's Word: Gender and Discourse in Arabo-Islamic Writing.* Princeton: Princeton University Press, 1992.

Mansiya [pseudonym]. "The Story of the Forgotten." Trans. Gila Svirsky. Dossier #19. Women Living Under Muslim Laws, February 1998. Accessed at www.wluml.org/english/pubsfulltxt.shtml?cmd%5B87%5D=I-87-2686.

Margonelli, Lisa, and Mahsa Shekarloo. "A Place Where It Doesn't Suck to Be a Woman." *Jane* 6, no. 2 (March 2002).

Masood, Ehsan. "Islam's Reformers." *Prospect,* July 2006.

Masse, Henri. *Persian Beliefs and Customs.* Trans. Charles A. Messner. New Haven, Conn.: Human Relations Area Files, 1954.

Matustik, Martin Beck. "From 'Velvet Revolution' to 'Velvet Jihad'?" *openDemocracy .net,* November 18, 2004.

Mayell, Hillary. "Thousands of Women Are Killed for Family 'Honor.'" *National Geographic News,* February 12, 2002.

Mcbride, Jennifer. "Nawal Saadawi." Paper written for seminar, "Women's Intellectual Contributions to the Study of Mind and Society," n.d. Accessed at www.webster.edu/~woolflm/saadawi.html.

McDonald, Hamish. "China's 'Lost' Muslims Go Back to the Future." *Age,* February 26, 2005. Accessed at www.theage.com.au/news/World/Chinas-lost-Muslims-go-back-to-the-future/2005/02/25/1109180106966.html.

McGreal. Chris. "Virgin Tests Make a Comeback." *Daily Mail & Guardian* (Johannesburg), September 29, 1999. Accessed at www.hartford-hwp.com/archives/37a/162.html.

Mernissi, Fatima. *The Veil and the Male Elite: A Feminist Interpretation of Women's Rights in Islam.* Trans. Mary Jo Lakeland. Reading, Mass.: Addison-Wesley, 1991.

———. *Women's Rebellion and Islamic Memory.* Atlantic Highlands, N.J.: Zed Books, 1996.

Metcalf, Barbara, ed. and trans. *Perfecting Women: Maulana Ashraf 'Ali Thanawi's Bihishti Zewar, a Partial Translation with Commentary.* Berkeley: University of California Press, 1990.

Meyers, M., R. Diamond, D. Kezur, C. Scharf, M. Weinshel, and D. S. Rait. "An Infertility Primer for Family Therapists." *Family Process* 34, no. 2 (1995): 219–29.

Mir-Hosseini, Ziba. "Religious Modernists and the 'Woman Question': Challenges and Complicities." In *Twenty Years of Islamic Revolution: Political and Social Transition in Iran since 1979,* ed. Eric Hooglund, 95. Syracuse: Syracuse University Press, 2002.

———. "Muslim Women's Quest for Equality: Between Islamic Law and Feminism." *Critical Inquiry* 32, no. 4 (Summer 2006): 629–45.

Mitra, Nabamita. "When Caged Women Try to Sing of the Skies." Calcutta *Telegraph,* July 8, 2007.

Miwalla, Omar, B. R. Simon Rosser, Jamie Feldman, and Christine Varga. "Identity Experience among Progressive Gay Muslims in North America: A Qualitative Study within al-Fatiha." *Culture, Health, and Sexuality* 7, no. 2 (March 2005): 116.

Moallem, Minoo. *Between Warrior Brother and Veiled Sister: Islamic Fundamentalism and the Politics of Patriarchy in Iran.* Berkeley: University of California Press, 2005.

Moghadam, Valentine M. "Patriarchy and the Politics of Gender in Modernising Societies: Iran, Pakistan, and Afghanistan." *International Sociology* 7 (1992): 38.

———. *Women, Work, and Economic Reform in the Middle East and North Africa.* London: Lynne Rienner, 1998.

———. "Transnational Feminist Networks: Collective Action in an Era of Globalization." *International Sociology* 15 (2000).

———, ed. *From Patriarchy to Empowerment: Women's Participation, Movements, and Rights in the Middle East, North Africa, and South Asia.* Syracuse: Syracuse University Press, 2007.

Mohammadi, Majid. "Iranian Women Activists: In It to Win It." March 15, 2007. Accessed at http://newsweek.washingtonpost.com/postglobal/needtoknow/2007 /03/iranian_women_activists_in_it.html.

Moore, Andrea. "Iran Allows Women to Attend Soccer Matches." All Headline News, April 24, 2006.

"More Women Seek Vaginal Plastic Surgery." *Women's eNews,* November 14, 2004. Accessed at www.womensenews.org/article.cfm/dyn/aid/2067.

"Morocco Gets First Women Preachers." Aljazeera, April 28, 2006.

Morris, Chris. "Forced Virginity Tests Banned." BBC News, January 7, 1999.

Morris, Kylie. "Afghan Women 'Still Suffer Abuse.'" BBC News, December 17, 2002.

"Mourchidat—Morocco's Female Muslim Clerics." *Telegraph,* April 26, 2008.

Muhammad ibn abd al-Wahhab. *Kitab at-Tawhid: Essay on the Unicity of Allah; or, What Is Due to His Creatures.* Trans. Ismail Raji al-Faruqi. Damascus: International Islamic Federation of Student Organizations, 1979.

Muir, Jim. "Condoms Help Check Iran Birth Rate." BBC News, April 24, 2002.

Mujlisul-Ulama of South Africa. *Al-Mar'atus Salihah* (The pious woman). Bombay: Bilal Books, 1998.

Murray, Alison J. "Let Them Take Ecstasy: Class and Jakarta Lesbians." *Journal of Homosexuality* 40, nos. 3/4 (2001): 165–84.

Murray, Sarah J. "Unveiling Myths: Muslim Women and Sport." Womenssports foundation.org, January 16, 2002.

Murray, Stephen O., and Will Roscoe, eds. *Islamic Homosexualities: Culture, History, and Literature.* New York: New York University Press, 1997.

al-Muslim. *Sahih Muslim.* Trans. Abdul Hamid Siddiqi. Originally compiled under the title *Al-Jai'-us-Sahih* by Imam Muslim. Lahore: Shaikh Muhammad Ashraf, 1971.

"Muslim Women Can Reshape Islam." *Christian Science Monitor,* March 14, 2007.

Mydans, Seth. "Sexual Violence as Tool of War: Pattern Emerging in East Timor." *New York Times,* March 1, 2001.

Najmabadi, Afsaneh. *Women with Mustaches and Men without Beards: Gender and Sexual Anxieties of Iranian Modernity.* Berkeley: University of California Press, 2005.

Nasrin, Taslima. Interviewed by Ishad in Toronto, October 28, 2002. Accessed at www.muslim-refusenik.com/news/Taslima_Interview.html.

Nassef, Ahmed. "Amina Wadud Leads Mixed-Gender Friday Prayer in Barcelona." *Muslim WakeUp!* October 29, 2005.

"A New Voice for New Pakistan." Pakistan *Daily Times,* September 10, 2005.

Niah, Bachir. "Fifty Moroccan Women Preachers to Teach Moderate Islam." *Morocco Times,* May 5, 2006.

Nomani, Asra Q. "A Gender Jihad for Islam's Future." *Washington Post,* November 6, 2005.

———. *Standing Alone in Mecca: An American Women's Struggle for the Soul of Islam.* New York: HarperCollins, 2005.

"Not All the Islamic Countries Practice Honor Killings." *WIN News,* Winter 2000.

Nur, Rais. "Malaysia." In *Unspoken Rules: Sexual Orientation and Women's Human Rights,* ed. Rachel Rosenbloom, 107–9. London: Cassell, 1996.

Obonyo, Oscar. "AIDS: New Frictions Emerge over Virgin Brides." Originally published on *AllAfrica.com*; posted on *Peace Women,* December 1, 2003. Accessed at www.peacewomen.org/news/Uganda/Dec03/frictions.html.

Orwell, George. *Animal Farm.* New York: New American Library, 1956.

"Over 1,700 Honour Killings in Five Years Reported in Pak's Punjab." *Malaysia Sun,* August 12, 2007.

Pandey, Geeta. "Women Battle On with Mosque Plan." BBC News, August 19, 2005.

Paternostro, Silvana. "Please Make Me a Virgin Again." *Marie Claire,* August 2002, 102–4.

Paterson-Brown, Sara. "Commentary: Education about the Hymen Is Needed." Response to A. Logmans et al., "Who Wants the Procedure and Why?" in "Ethical Dilemma: Should Doctors Reconstruct the Vaginal Introitus of Adolescent Girls to Mimic the Virginal State?" *British Medical Journal* 316 (February 7, 1998): 459–60.

Phang, Stephanie. *Bloomberg.com,* May 5, 2006.

Pharr, Suzanne. *Homophobia: A Weapon of Sexism.* Inverness, Calif.: Chardon Press, 1988.

"PMU Denounces Exclusion, Restriction of Muslim Women Performers." Accessed at www.pmuna.org/archives/pmu_positions_on_current_issues/index.php#000 076.

"Potentially Bad News." March 18, 2006. Accessed at www.classicalvalues.com/archives/003440.html.

Imam Qurtubi. *Tafsir-e-Qurtubi.* Quoted in Mohammed Ismail Memon Madani, *Hijab.* Alexandria: Al-Saadawi Publications, 1995.

Rahman, Maseeh. "Kabul Stage: Actresses Play Roles in Several New Plays." *Christian Science Monitor,* November 26, 2004.

Ramadan, Tariq. "Reading the Koran." *New York Times,* Sunday Book Review, January 6, 2008.

Rasmussen, Susan J. "Only Women Know Trees: Medicine Women and the Role of Herbal Healing in Tuareg Culture." *Journal of Anthropological Research* 54, no. 2 (Summer 1998): 147–71.

Ratchanisawat, Niltava. "The Importance of Being a Virgin." *Nation* (Thailand), February 16, 2002.

Rausch, Margaret. "Bodies, Boundaries, and Spirit Possession: Revision of Tradition." *International Journal of African Historical Studies* 34, no. 1 (2000): 141–43.

Regis, Helen A. *Fulbe Voices: Marriage, Islam, and Medicine in Northern Cameroon.* Boulder: Westview Press, 2003.

Remennick, Larissa. "Childless in the Land of Imperative Motherhood: Stigma and Coping among Infertile Israeli Women." *Springer Science Business Media B.V.* 43, nos. 11/12 (2000): 821–41.

Remez, L. "Prevention of Unwanted Births in India Would Result in Replacement Fertility." *International Family Planning Perspectives* 27, no. 2 (June 2001).

"Report on Reproductive and Sexual Health (Strategies, Programs, and Measures) in the Islamic Republic of Iran." WHO regional consultative meeting on promoting reproductive and sexual health in the eastern Mediterranean region. Beirut, December 8–11, 2003.

Rizvi, Sayyid Muhammad. "Gender Apartheid or Respectable Interaction?" *Arab American News.com,* July 1, 2006. Accessed at www.arabamericannews.com/newsarticle.php?articleid=5666.

Rosenbloom, Rachel, ed. *Unspoken Rules: Sexual Orientation and Women's Human Rights.* London: Cassell, 1996.

Sabri, Mustafa. "A Topic of Dispute in Islam: Music." *Beyan-ul-Haq* 3, no. 63 (1910). Accessed at www.wakeup.org/anadolu/05/4/mustafa_sabri_en.html.

Sadr, Shadi. "Women in Iran Deem Rape Laws Unfair." *Women's eNews,* December 21, 2003. Accessed at www.womensenews.org/article.cfm/dyn/aid/1650/.

Saeed, Rana Riaz. "Women Status in Pakistan under Customs and Values and the Controversial Hudood Ordinance 1979." December 2004. Accessed at http://129.3.20.41/eps/le/papers/0501/0501003.pdf.

Safa-Isfahani, Kaveh. "Female-Centered World Views in Iranian Cultures: Symbolic Representations of Sexuality in Dramatic Games." *Signs: Journal of Women in Culture and Society* 6 (1980): 33–53.

Sarbazi, Mulana Mohammad Omar. *Shafaul Isteqam wa al Hazan.* Pakistan: Jane Mohammad, 1980.

Sardar, Ziauddin. "A Fatwa for Every Occasion." *New Statesman,* August 2, 2007.

Sawalha, L. "Barriers of Silence: Reproductive Rights for Women in Jordan." *Development* 42, no. 1 (March 1999): 41–46.

Schimmel, Annemarie. *The Mystic Dimensions of Islam.* Chapel Hill: University of North Carolina Press, 1988.

Schneider, Jane. "Of Vigilance and Virgins: Honor, Shame, and Access to Resources in Mediterranean Societies." *Ethnology* 10, no. 1 (1971): 1.

"Sex Change Film Tests Iran Attitudes." *Aljazeera,* July 26, 2006.

Sex Sultan. *Salam Worldwide,* June 15, 2003. Accessed at www.salamworldwide.com/sex10th.html.

Sharma, Kalpana. "No Girl, Please, We're Indian." *Hindu,* August 29, 2004.

Shehadeh, Lamia Rustum. *The Idea of Women in Fundamentalist Islam.* Gainesville: University Press of Florida, 2003.

Sheikh, Shamima. "Denying Women Access to the Mosque: A Betrayal of the

Prophet." Presented to the Jamaat Khanna Committee of the University of the Witwatersrand, 1995. Accessed at www.crescentlife.com.

Shirazi, Faegheh. *The Veil Unveiled: Hijab in Modern Culture.* Gainesville: University Press of Florida, 2001, 2003.

———. "Florida Case Veils Truth about Muslim Ways." *Newsday,* July 1, 2003, A26.

———. "The *Sofreh*: Comfort and Community among Women in Iran." *Iranian Studies* 38, no. 2 (June 2005): 293–309.

Siddiqui, Mona. "Islam and Feminism: Are They Poles Apart?" *Sunday Herald,* May 12, 2006.

Smith, Jane I. "Women in Islam: Equity, Equality, and the Search for the Natural Order." *Journal of American Academy of Religion* 47, no. 4 (December 1979): 530.

Sorabji, Cornelia. "Mixed Motives: Islam, Nationalism, and Mevluds in an Unstable Yugoslavia." In *Muslim Women's Choices: Religious Belief and Social Reality,* ed. Camillia Fawzi El-Solh and Judy Mabro, 109–10. Providence, R.I.: Berg, 1994.

Soros, Eugene. "Virgins, Potions, and AIDS in Zimbabwe." *World Press Review Online,* October 22, 2002.

Sprachman, Paul, trans. *Suppressed Persian: An Anthology of Forbidden Literature.* Costa Mesa: Mazda, 1995.

Stack, Megan K. "Iran Bans Being Gay, but Allows Sex Change." *Los Angeles Times,* January 30, 2005.

Stowasser, Barbara Freyer. *Women in the Qur'an, Traditions, and Interpretation.* New York: Oxford University Press, 1994.

Stuever, Hank. "Viva Las Virgins! Elvis Does the Abstinence Convention, but Only from the Waist Up." *Washington Post,* June 29, 2003.

"Support Iranian Women: Join the 'One Million Signatures Campaign.'" Petition, Women's Learning Partnership for Rights, Development, and Peace, July 6, 2007.

Taheri, Amir. "Muslim Women Play Only an Incidental Part in the Olympics." *Gulf News,* August 18, 2004.

———. "Domestic Terror in Iran." *Wall Street Journal,* August 6, 2007.

Taylor, Pamela. "Leading the Mufti: Progress in the Islamic Tradition." *Muslim WakeUp!* March 2, 2006.

Thanvi, Ashraf Ali. *Bahisti Zewar* (Heavenly Ornaments). Karachi, Pakistan: Zam Zam Publishers, 1999.

Tohidi, Nayereh. "Guardians of the Nation: Women, Islam, and the Soviet Legacy of Modernization in Azerbaijan." In *Women in Muslim Societies: Diversity within Unity,* ed. Herbert L. Bodman and Nayereh Tohidi, 137–61. Boulder: Lynne Rienner, 1998.

Al Tokhy, Abd al Fatah Al Said. *Al Kabrit* (To draw out the demons). Cairo, n.d.

USC-MSA Compendium of Muslim Texts, University of Southern California. Sahih al-Bukhari, translated by M. Muhsin Khan. Accessed at www.usc.edu/dept/MSA/fundamentals/hadithsunnah/bukhari/.

Van Doorn-Harder, Pieternella. *Women Shaping Islam: Reading the Qur'an in Indonesia.* Urbana: University of Illinois Press, 2006.

Vanita, Ruth. Preface to *Same-Sex Love in India: Readings from Literature and History*, ed. Ruth Vanita and Saleem Kidwai. New York: St. Martin's Press, 2000.

———. "Rekhti Poetry: Love between Women (Urdu)." In *Same-Sex Love in India*, ed. Ruth Vanita and Saleem Kidwai, 220–28. New York: St. Martin's Press, 2000.

Vom-Bruck, Gabriele. "Elusive Bodies: The Politics of Aesthetics among Yemeni Elite Women." *Signs* 23, no. 1 (Autumn 1997): 175–214.

Wadud, Amina. *Qur'an and Woman: Rereading the Sacred Text from a Woman's Perspective*. 2nd ed. New York: Oxford University Press, 1999.

———. *Inside the Gender Jihad: Women's Reform in Islam*. Oxford: OneWorld Publications, 2006.

Wali, Sima. "Muslim Refugees, Returnees, and Displaced Women: Challenges and Dilemmas." In *Faith and Freedom: Women's Human Rights in the Muslim World*, ed. Mahnaz Afkhami, 175–83. Syracuse: Syracuse University Press, 1995.

Walseth, Kristin, and Kari Fasting. "Islam's View on Physical Activity and Sport: Egyptian Women Interpreting Islam." *International Review for the Sociology of Sport* 38 (2003): 53.

Waqar, Mustafa. "Pakistan Cracks Down on Anti-Women Tradition." July 4, 2005. http://dwelle.de/southasia/pakistan/1.132416.1.html

Webster, Sheila K. "Women, Sex, and Marriage in Moroccan Proverbs." *International Journal of Middle East Studies* 14 (1982): 173–84.

Weiss, Robin Elise. "Girl or Boy? Finding Out in Pregnancy." Formerly available online.

Weitz, Katy. "The Wage of Innocence." *People*, March 3, 2002.

Weitz, Rose, ed. *The Politics of Women's Bodies: Sexuality, Appearance, and Behavior*. 2nd ed. New York: Oxford University Press, 2003.

Wiedemann, Charlotte, "Sisters in Islam in Malaysia: Women Working for Reform." *Qantara.de*, 2003. Translation from German. Accessed at www.qantara.de/web com/show_article.php/_c-307/_nr-20/_p-1/i.html?PHPSESSID=5869.

Wikan, Unni. *Behind the Veil in Arabia: Women in Oman*. Chicago: University of Chicago Press, 1991.

Wilcox, Lynn. *Women and the Holy Qur'an: A Sufi Perspective*. Riverside, Calif.: M.T.O. Shahmaghsoudi, 1998.

Wilson, James Q. "What Makes a Terrorist?" *City Journal* 14, no. 1 (Winter 2004).

"Women Lift the Veil in Kashmir." Reuters, August 3, 2006. Accessed at www.the moscowtimes.com/stories/2006/08/03/254.html.

Woollett, Anne, and Naomi Pfeffer. "Update to Discovering That You Are Infertile: One Woman's Experience." In *Women's Health: Readings on Social, Economic, and Political Issues*, 3rd ed., ed. Nancy Worcester and Marianne H. Whatley. Dubuque: Kendall/Hunt, 2000.

Wright, J. W., Jr., and Everett K. Rowson. *Homoeroticism in Classical Arabic Literature*. New York: Columbia University Press, 1997.

Yip, Andrew K. T. "Queering the Religious Texts: An Exploration of British Nonheterosexual Christians' and Muslims' Strategy of Constructing Sexuality Affirming Hermeneutics." *Sociology* 39, no. 1 (2005): 47–65.

———. "Uniquely Positioned? Lived Experiences of Lesbian, Gay, and Bisexual Asian Muslims in Britain." School of Social Sciences, Nottingham Trent University, 2005.

Zakaria, Rafia. "Honour Killing: Crime & Abetment." *Alt.Muslim,* August 10, 2006. Accessed at www.altmuslim.com/perm.php?id=1760_0_25_0_C.

Zaman, Amberin. "Islamic-Style Swimsuits Give Women Freedom to Dive In." *Los Angeles Times,* August 21, 2005.

Zaydaan, Abd al-Kareem, ed. *Al-Muslim Fi Ash Shari'ah al-Islamiyyah.* 11 vols. Beirut: Mu'assasat Ar Risaalah Lil Tiba'ah Wan Nashr Wat Tawzi', 1995.

Ze'evi, Dror. *Producing Desire: Changing Sexual Discourse in the Ottoman Middle East, 1500–1900.* Berkeley: University of California Press, 2006.

INDEX

Page numbers set in *italic* type indicate illustrations.

al (invisible spirit), 68, 234n19
Abbasid dynasty, 154, 241n56
Abdullah, Halah Bint, 195–96
abortion, 88–91; Iran, 91–92; sex-selective, 85–86; women's input, 91
Abstinence Clearinghouse, 52
Abstinence First program, 53
abstinence products, 53
Abu Nawas (Iraqi LGBT-UK) group, 179
abuse of women, focus on, 57–58
activism: education and, 11–14; films on, 136–37; gays and lesbians, 167–73; Islamic feminists, 9; legacy, 2; Malaysia, 201; transnational, 221–22
adadith: of A'isha, 10–11; rigid interpretations, 194; on same-sex behavior, 159–60; as sources for teachings, 9–10; use of term, 228n22; on virginity, 37–38; on women's apparel, 110
adhan (call to prayer), 20, 21
adoptive sister (*khahar kandegi*), 165–67
adornment, 113–14, 117
adultery: in legal codes, 31–32; lesbianism related, 175; punishment for, 29, 175; Qur'an on, 34, 46, 47; seclusion and, 106–7; witnesses, 47
affirmative action campaigns, 221
Afghanistan: amulets, 73; effects of atrocities, 30; gender discrimination,

198–99; gender preference, 83; healers, 214; honor killings, 34; performing arts, 133–34; refugees in Iran, 91; schools for girls, 100; theater, 131; violence against women, 100; women refugees from, 7; women's human rights, 50
Africa: singers, 128; virginity, 37, 39
agency of women, 58
Ahiida sportswear company, 148
Ahmad, Yasmin, 133
Ahmadi Muslim Jama'at, 177, 178
Ahmadinejad, Mahmoud, 96, 144, 146
ahong women preachers, 203, 246n47
AIDS. *See* HIV/AIDS prevention
A'isha, 10–11, 139, 185–86, 187, 188, 209
Alaei, Arash, 96
al-Bukhari collection, 245n10; A'isha's adadith omitted, 10–11; on apparel, 113, 237n11; on homosexuality, 160; menstrual taboos, 188; on veiling, 191–92; on women in mosques, 195
Al-Fatiha foundation, 178–79
Al-Huda school (Toronto), 119–20
Ali, Abbas ibn (Abul Fadl), 215
Ali, Yusuf, commentary, 191, 245n20
Ali Haydari Kardan vow, 85
al-Jawzi, 'Abd ar-Rahman ibn 'Ali ibn Muhammad Abu al-Farash ibn, 194–95
Al-Kanadi, Abu Bilal Mustafa, 124–26, 238n3
Allah, names of, 64, 122
Allan Centre for Women, 42

chastity vows, 50–51
child pornography, 177
children: exposure to haram ideas, 134–35; "protection poems," 76
child sexual abuse, 177
China, 39, 44; gender preference, 86, 235n40; Hui people, 203–4, 246n47; virginity tests in Tibet, 50
Christianity, infertility cures, 58
clerics, subversion of, on Internet, 8
climate of fear: community acceptance, 181–82; nonheterosexual individuals, 172, 180; oppression theory, 181
clitoridectomies, 37
Coalition of Sexual and Bodily Rights in Muslim Societies, 229n49
Coelho, Shebana, 136–37
coitus interruptus, 89
Cole, Juan, 179–80
condom production and use: 92–93, *93, 94, 95,* 96; Malaysian use, 97
contraception. *See* birth control; condoms
conversations with women, 6–7
Council on American-Islamic Relations (CAIR), 208
co-wives: fertility, 59; songs about, 128
crimes of passion, 31
cross-dressing, 160
Czechoslovakia, former, 1, 227n1

dancing, 128, 135–36
Desai, Ebrahim, 125
diaspora communities, 208
directories, 12
discrimination. *See* gender discrimination
divorce: sterility related, 58–59; tribal customs, 36
Doctors Without Borders, 40
documentary films and videos, 6
dolls, 108, *108, 109,* 110, 111
driver's licenses, 118–19

drivers of vehicles, 117–19
drums, 126
Duran, Khalid, 160, 242n14

early Islam, role of women, 9–11
Ebadi, Shirin, 13–14
economic issues: dependency and discrimination, 199; labor market participation, 18
education: activism and, 11–14; economic roles, 13; Mukhtar Mai on, 36; schools for girls, 100; young girls, 13; young Muslim women, 3
Egypt: abortion laws, 89–90; beach segregation, 152; early feminists, 98; early reformers, 4, 5; feminism, 5; fertility taboo, 78–79; homosexuality, 169; honor, 32; hymen repairs, 40; reform debates, 23; singers, 127–28
El-Akkad, Omar, 9
El ʿAzifet orchestra, 131
El Fadl, Khaled Abou, 208–9
emerging technologies, 3–4
emotional needs, 121
empowerment, 193
empowerment programs, 102
England, 27–28; sexual violence in Ireland, 28; South Asian homosexuals, 182
ethnic cleansing, 28, 35
European Muslims, 32, 230n64
evil-eye belief complex, 76
evil spirits, protection from, *65,* 68–82, *72, 73, 77*
extremist movements, effect on Islam, 4

FAMA International, 12–13, 228n31
family planning. *See* birth control
Fatima al Zahra, 33, 82
fatwas (religious decrees): against lesbians, 174–81; against outspoken women, 98; against women in the arts, 135; on athletic participation,

fatwas (*cont.*)
138, 140; efficacy and credibility of,
8, 93, 174, 176, 220; on homosexual
behavior, 24, 167, 174–80, 220; issued on Internet, 6, 8, 174–81; on
performing arts, 126, 135–36; on sex
change operations, 136, 173
Federation of Muslim Women
(FMW), 101
female births, gender preference,
82–88, 235nn36,40
female bodies: arts and athletics, 122;
cultural taboos, 57; as fundamentalism targets, 193; male power and, 56;
medieval era, 57; obsessive interest
in, 57
female body, social construction of,
26–27
female genital mutilation, 37
female infanticide, 88
feminism: Egypt, 5, 98, 185; Qur'anic
basis, 18; three types, 185; use of
term, 193; Western vis-à-vis Islamic,
5, 116, 193–94
Feminist Sexual Ethics Project, 160,
165, 242n13
Ferdosi, Shanameh, 130, 239n13
fertility: importance of, 58–61; remedies for infertility, 61–68; talismans, 62
film industry, 132–33, 136–37
first wives, 59
folk cures and prescriptions, 67–68, *70*
folk practices, religious content, 104
fornication, Qur'an on, 46
France, 31
Freemuse conference (Berlin), 132
Fulbe society (Cameroon), 74–75
Fullah doll, 108, *109*, 110, 237n6
fundamentalism, concept of, 2
fundamentalism, Islamic: art of
"interpretation" analyzed, 200–201;
barriers to female sports, 153; core

attitudes, 218–19; female bodies as
targets, 193; guidebooks revived,
119–21; meanings of *jihad*, 1; on music and singing, 125–26; politicizing
gender-based issues, 209–10; self-appointed experts, 107; spatial segregation, 193–96; in Turkey, 172; twelfth-
century scholar, 194–95; usefulness of
Internet, 219–20; women at holy sites,
189, 208; women proponents, 119–20,
127, 195–96, 222–23. *See also* fatwas
fundamentalism: as modern discursive
formation, 2–3; other religions, 2;
secularism compared, 180; use of
term, 2; U.S. neoconservatives, 52;
women as culprits, 73
fundamentalist Christians, 43
fuqaha (expert in Islamic law), 235n31

Galen, 27
Ganjavi, Mahasti, 164
gender discrimination, 197–201, 221–22
gender equality: full participation,
19; pre-Islamic Hausa, 216–17; as
Qur'anic notion, 18; Saanei on,
207–8, 225; women political leaders,
19
gender inequality: as core issue, 194;
labor markets related, 18
gender preference, 82–88; home gender
test, 235n40; overview, 56; predic-
tions, 86
geomancy, 62
Gordafarid, 130, 138
grassroots organizations, 99–103
Greece, 40–41
guidebooks for leading a moral life, 104;
major versions, 104–7; online versions, 107–8, 219

Habibian, Fatemeh, 130–31
Haftad Du Div (Seventy-two Demons),
talismans and cures, 63–64, *69*

Index

Index

liberal Muslims, 158
literacy classes, 100

mafumbo, in *tarab* poetry, 128
Maguzawa people, 216
mahram (male kin), 205, 246n54
Mai, Mukhtar (Mukhtaran), 35–36
Majlesi, Baqer, 104, 105, 110–13
Majlis Itthadul Musilmeen (MIM),
     248n13
Makoni, Betty, 49–50
Malaysia, 133; activism, 201; head-
     scarves on policewomen, 200;
     Islamic limits on women, 200; lesbi-
     anism, 170–71
male children, and gender preference,
     82–88
male experience and articulation as
     norm, 20
male role in quiet revolution, 1–2, 23
Mali, 213–14
Manji, Irshad, 180–81
marriage: between female lovers, 166,
     243n34; as economic survival, 39; ef-
     fect on legal status, 27–28; forced, 44,
     172, 182; gay Muslims, 182; Qurʿan
     marriages, 51–52, 55, 220, 233n70,
     247n3; remarriage, 192–93; tempo-
     rary, 41
Marzouk, Samira, 204
Masood, Eshan, 14, 228n32
mass media, on honor killings, 54
Matlock, David, 43–44
Matustik, Martin Beck, 1, 227n1
Mauritania, 77
medicinal writing, 75–76, 75
medicine women (*hakima*), 213–15
medieval period in Islam: homosexual-
     ity, 161–67; male authority during,
     57; public singing, 155
melvud religious rituals, 210
Memory Forum, 12

menstruation, 185–89; association with
     "female weakness," 26–27; as "pollu-
     tion," 187; prohibitions surrounding,
     185, 244n3; Prophet and Aʿisha on,
     185–86
Mexico, 39
microcredit, 100
Middle East Media Research
     (MEMRI), 222
Miklos, John, 44
Mirza, Sania, 140
miscarriages, remedies, 63–64, 77–78
misogyny, 218
Mission Islam, 177, 178
mixed-gender congregations, 19
mixed-gender Friday prayer, 205
modesty in interaction, 21
modesty/shame as virtues, 118
moral leadership, 106
Moroccan Association of Democratic
     Women, 12–13
Morocco: activism, 12, 13; amulets,
     73; hymen repair, 43; proverbs, 32;
     women preachers, 204–5
morshidat (female guides), 204
mosques, 201–9; as centers for educa-
     tion, 96; Chinese inclusion, 203–4;
     elders' rulings (*jamaat*), 202–3; men-
     strual taboos, 188–89; mixed-gender,
     19; prayer at home as alternative,
     202; segregation, 20; women at, 195;
     women preachers, 203–9
mosque for women, 202–3, 224
motherhood role, 60
mourning, 189
mufti: fatwa qualifications, 246n56;
     women deputies, 205
Mujahidin, 199
multiple wives, 59
Murray, Sarah J., 153–54, 241n52
music, 123–35; Burka Band, 133–34;
     censorship, 132; children and haram,

popular religious practices, 62–68; gender preference, 83–84

"pouch" terror, 77–78

preachers, women, 203–9

pregnancy: divorce laws, 59; folk prescriptions, 67; gender of child, 84; sorcery, 77–78

pre-Islamic cultures: effects of earlier beliefs, 56–57; Hausa, 216–17; healers, 214–15; lack of seclusion, 117–18; sports, 137–38; virginity in, 38

premenstrual syndrome (PMS), 26–27

Progressive Muslim Union (PMU), 20, 134

pronatalism, 61, 91

property, women as, 27–29, 39

Prophet: on menstruation, 185; as model for piety, 10; as model for women, 10; on singing, 155; on sports and athletics, 155; wives, 10–11

prostitution, association with, 155

"protection poems," 76

public intellectuals, 5

public sphere: exclusion and segregation, 184, 185; fundamentalists on, 218–19

purdah (seclusion), 116, 118, 189, 245n13

Qadir-e Khom holy day, 166, 243n31

Qatar, 139

Qur'an: abortion, 88–89; on adultery, 34, 46, 47, 159, 175; *al Falaq* (Dawn), 64–66, 65, 76; on athletics, 137; birth control, 91–97; conservative interpretations, 15, 19; education of children, 14; feminist interpreters, 14, 19; on fornication (punishment), 46–47, 159; on homosexuality, 159; on honor killings, 34; on human beauty/perfection, 154, 156–58; on idle talk, 125–26; on lesbian behavior, 175; magical qualities, 78; on magic and sorcery, 64–66, 65; on marital

abuse, 201; on menstruation, 186, 187; on music and singing, 124–25; the "queering" of, 182–83; rigid interpretations, 194; sex changes absent, 173; on veiling, 15, 190–91; women in mosques, 201; women in public places, 208

Qur'an marriages, 51–52, 55, 220, 233n70, 247n3

Qureshi, Salma, 20–21

radical Islam: Internet sites, 8; use of term, 2

Rafsanjani, Faezeh Hashemi, 141–46, *142*, 240n39

Ramadan, Tariq, 2, 23, 225, 230n64

rape: female self-defense, 31; honor killings of victims, 30, 35; institutionalized use of, 28; notion of women as property, 28

reactionary teachings by women, 119–20, 238n27

Refah Party (Turkey), 16, 229n42

reform, 218; basic tenets, 4

Rekhti poetry, 163–64

religion, social role of, 57

religious observances, 216

religious rituals, 216

remarriage, 192–93

reproductive norms, 84

reproductive practices, overview, 24

resistance: in activism, 2; in performing arts, 129–30, 134; through ritual, 209–17

revirginization, 52–53, 55

Revolutionary Association of the Women of Afghanistan (RAWA), 100, 239n19

Rezayee, Shaima, 133

ritual experiences, 210–17

Rizvi, Sayyid Muhammad, 21, 230n60

Robert McDowell's Herbal Treatments, 45

Index

Index

277

A native of Iran, Faegheh Shirazi is an associate professor in the Department of Middle Eastern Studies and Center for Middle Eastern Studies–Islamic Studies program at the University of Texas at Austin. Shirazi specializes in textiles, rituals, and material cultures as they relate to the social and cultural practices of Muslim women in contemporary Islamic societies. She is the author of *The Veil Unveiled: Hijab in Modern Culture* (UPF, 2001). Her paintings have been shown in solo and group exhibitions since 2001 in Austin.